Indigenous and Popular Thinking in América

A book in the series
LATIN AMERICA OTHERWISE
Languages, Empires, Nations

A series edited by
Walter D. Mignolo, Duke University
Irene Silverblatt, Duke University
Sonia Saldívar-Hull, University of Texas, San Antonio

Indigenous and Popular Thinking in América

RODOLFO KUSCH

Introduction by WALTER D. MIGNOLO
Translated by María Lugones and Joshua M. Price

DUKE UNIVERSITY PRESS *Durham & London 2010*

© 2010
Duke University Press All rights reserved
Printed in the United States of America
on acid-free paper ∞

Designed by Jennifer Hill
Typeset in Arno Pro by Keystone Typesetting, Inc.

Library of Congress Cataloging-in-Publication
Data appear on the last printed page of this book.

Latin America Otherwise: Languages, Empires, Nations is a critical series. It aims to explore the emergence and consequences of concepts used to define "Latin America" while at the same time exploring the broad interplay of political, economic, and cultural practices that have shaped Latin American worlds. Latin America, at the crossroads of competing imperial designs and local responses, has been construed as a geocultural and geopolitical entity since the nineteenth century. This series provides a starting point to redefine Latin America as a configuration of political, linguistic, cultural, and economic intersections that demands a continuous reappraisal of the role of the Americas in history, and of the ongoing process of globalization and the relocation of people and cultures that have characterized Latin America's experience. *Latin America Otherwise: Languages, Empires, Nations* is a forum that confronts established geocultural constructions, that rethinks area studies and the disciplinary boundaries, that assesses convictions of the academy and of public policy, and that, correspondingly, demands that the practices through which we produce knowledge and understanding about and from Latin America be subject to rigorous and critical scrutiny.

As Walter Mignolo notes in his introduction to this volume, the work of Rodolfo Kusch (1922–1979) is central to de-colonial thinking. Kusch's distinctive philosophy, in relating mestizo consciousness and border hermeneutics, can now be recognized as deeply illuminating of such notions as Du Bois's "double consciousness" and Anzaldúa's "mestiza consciousness / la conciencia de la mestiza." It has been crucial for the contemporary work of Mignolo, María Lugones, Rengifo Vázquez, Pablo Wright, and Ricardo Salas Astrain, among many others. Originally published in 1970, *Indigenous and Popular Thinking in América* is the first of Kusch's work to be translated into English. It details a philosophical journey that takes him from the western coast of South America into the highlands of Peru and Bolivia, from the Latin American mimesis of European modernity—deeply entrenched in the intellectual classes—to an immersion in the indigenous cosmology of Quechua, Aymara, and Chipaya inhabitants from the highlands. Between the urban middle class and the Indians of Bolivia lies a social strata (*el pueblo*) characterized by "popular thinking," a mode of thinking more akin to that of the Indian than to that of the middle classes. Kusch's goal is to identify and help to activate an indigenous and popular way of thinking which interacts with, but at the same time differs from, derivative ways of thinking entrenched in the urban middle class, be they liberal or Marxist. Thus Kusch offers a critique of Marxism and an understanding of Peronism that are logical consequences of understanding popular ways of thinking rather than of attention only to the instrumentality of social claims made by the working class.

Kusch's parents migrated from Germany to Argentina before he was born. As Mignolo suggests, Kusch's notion of a "mestizo consciousness" derives from the experience of displaced Europeans recognizing their out-of-placeness in a foreign context. Yet it is the modernity that Europeans brought with them to America that Kusch seeks to distinguish from indigenous thinking, a modernity with an ideological predisposition to judge problems from a purportedly scientific point of view, to indiscriminately presuppose democratic ideals, and to expect certain predetermined forms of religiosity.

This book has three primary goals: to uncover basic aspects of indigenous thinking, to weigh the possibilities that thought offers, and to establish how it articulates with elements of European modernity. Kusch identifies a connection between indigenous thought and interiority, affectivity, and attention to emotional experience, as well as a resistance to prioritizing the rational over the affective, the exterior world over the interior of the human being. By so doing Kusch uncovers European philosophy's repressed subjectivity, its drive to situate logic before subjectivity, and its inclination to place the person at the service of the institution, instead of the other way round. Kusch's relentless critiques of the idea of "development," which was very much alive during his lifetime, serve to expand his questioning of the instrumentality of Western principles of knowing and understanding. In light of these tendencies, he examines the meaning of knowledge in an indigenous context—a knowledge, he shows, that focuses not on causality (why), but on modality (how). In exploring the articulation of indigenous with urban thinking, he assesses, for example, the implications of forming cooperatives, noting particularly the failure of cooperatives that outsiders organized in Bolivia in the 1960s, despite a tradition of a communal system of reciprocity, *ayni*, which is several thousand years old. Not to be confused with Lévi-Strauss or with the Castañeda of *The Teachings of Don Juan*, Kusch approaches his investigations not only as a constant process of shifting the geopolitics of knowing and understanding, but in a relentlessly de-colonial manner.

Bringing to his analysis a knowledge of Western philosophy, a deep understanding of the foundation of indigenous thought (Guaman Poma de Ayala, Popol Vuh, Huarochiri manuscript), and a sound understanding of Argentinian history, Kusch identifies "negation" as the underpinning of both popular and indigenous rationality (two distinct ethnic configurations). What one learns from Kusch is to dwell at the intersection of indigenous and European legacies, and to be constantly mindful of "the popular."

CONTENTS

ILLUSTRATIONS

Immigrant Consciousness

WALTER D. MIGNOLO

RODOLFO KUSCH: A SOCIOHISTORICAL PROFILE

Gunter Rodolfo Kusch (1922–1979) was the only child of Ricardo Carlos Kusch and Elsa María Dorotea Tschunke de Kusch, a German couple who moved to Argentina from Germany shortly after the First World War had ended. When Kusch was four years old, his father passed away. His late teen years coincided with an exciting decade in Buenos Aires history: 1940–1950. This is the decade when the Second World War came to an end, the decade of Juan Domingo Perón and Eva Perón, and of an intense intellectual and cultural life. A "native" intelligentsia was taking over, a "mestizo consciousness" that nevertheless had its origins among those of European descent (primarily Spanish, Italian, and German). Kusch explored this mestizo consciousness in his first book (*La seducción de la barbarie*). This consciousness reflected the experiences of a community of displaced Europeans in coexistence with the Indigenous population, a dense and strong presence that Kusch himself encountered in northwest Argentina and in Bolivia. Although the Afro-population had practically vanished from Argentina's imaginary by Kusch's time, Kusch was aware of its presence in América. (Kusch consistently uses "América" in all his writing, only rarely mentioning "Latin America"—a telling practice that is coherent with the philosophical explorations he conducted throughout his life.)

As Argentina emerged from the so called "década infame"

(1930–40), a demographic and sociohistorical shift took place, accompanied by an intense intellectual dialogue, lead by Silvina Ocampo and the journal *Sur*, which she had founded in 1931.[1] *Sur* was notable for its cosmopolitan character, and Ocampo counted Waldo Frank and José Ortega y Gasset among her most enthusiastic supporters, and the Argentine writers Jorge Luis Borges and Adolfo Bioy Casares among her closest collaborators. When Kusch published *La seducción de la barbarie* in 1953, he caught a wave of intellectual and political debates that gave little notice to the influence of *Sur*; these debates emerged in the last years of Perón's presidency and immediately after his fall, moving decidedly away from enchantment with Europe toward interrogation of the troubled colonial and, therefore, racial histories in America. In *América Profunda*, published in 1962, Kusch intensified his philosophical reflections anchored in "another history." He described that "other history"—distinctive in its profile and coexisting with European history in America—with metaphors such as "seducción de la barbarie," "América profunda," as "América vegetal," among many others. Crucial to understanding Kusch's sustained meditations, from *La seducción de la barbarie* to *Geocultural del Hombre Americano* (1976) and *Esbozo de una antropología filosófica Americana* (1978), is the existence of a European history as transplanted since its conquest and colonization into the history of "América profunda," a double history at once. On the one hand, Indian memories throughout the Americas needed to be reinscribed in conflictive dialogue and tension with the presence of people of European descent, as well as with the emergence of social institutions (economics, politics, family) modeled on European social organization. It could no longer be an internal transformation as it had been for Europe. On the other hand, the reinscription that couldn't avoid European interference was, and continues to be, one that *re-produces the difference*. For the Indigenous people who decided, through history, not to assimilate, it was essential to resist the fantasy of a bygone past and instead to maintain the reality of a present in which the reinscription of the difference was crucial for just living. After all, if for any European it would have been difficult to live in the skin of an Indigenous person, there would be reason to assume that an Indigenous person would have difficulty living in the skin of a European. The awareness that the states in South America were colonial (or, at their best, modern-colonial), while those in France, England, and Germany were modern-imperial was a starting point both for the emergence of the "nationalist left" (Juan José Herenández-Arregui) and the de-colonial option (Rodolfo Kusch), both options grounded in the subjective and historical experience of Peronism.

THE EPISTEMIC AND POLITICAL MEANING OF IMMIGRANT CONSCIOUSNESS

I could not have made the preceding statements without having read and re-read the work of Rodolfo Kusch. Furthermore, it is in light of the statements I made before that Kusch's idea of "mestizo consciousness" can and shall be understood. For Kusch, "mestizo" has nothing to do with biology, with mixed bloods, with the color of one's skin or the form of one's nose—it is, instead, a matter of consciousness.

"Mestizo consciousness" is a conceptualization that undoubtedly emerges from a body that experiences *existentia Americana*, similar to what the Jamaican philosopher Lewis Gordon has termed and explored as *existentia Africana*.[2] Indeed, approximately fifty years before Kusch published his first book, W. E. B. Du Bois, a U.S. sociologist of African descent, was sensing a similar cultural discomfort, albeit as a black man, rather than as an immigrant of European descent, a discomfort coming from the experience of a history different from that of Kusch. Du Bois found in the concept of "consciousness" a tool for the articulation of his experience translated into a term familiar in the human and social sciences.[3] But his "consciousness"—that is, the way in which he experienced "consciousness"—was different from that of Kusch; a person of African descent in the Americas experiences life and his own existence differently than does a person of European descent. Both, however, share a common experience, the experience of the displaced in relation to a dominant order of the world to which they do not belong. The consciousness of being-such and the awareness of not-being-such (Kusch, for example, being neither European nor Indian), as well as the sensing of a tension between being-such-and-such (Du Bois, for example, being black and American, when being American was assumed to mean being white), points toward the sphere of experience Gloria Anzaldúa articulated as "the mestiza consciousness/la conciencia de la mestiza."[4] It is worthwhile to underline, however, the grammatical twist in Anzaldúa's phrase. She is talking not about "mestiza consciousness" but about "the consciousness of the mestiza," which is how

I would translate "la conciencia de la mestiza," the title of the last chapter in *Borderlands/La Frontera*. Likewise, we should remember, the title of Rigoberta Menchú's *Me llamo Rigoberta Menchu y así me nació la conciencia* (1982), badly translated into English as *I, Rigoberta Menchú, an Indian Woman from Guatemala*—a translation that preferred exoticism to philosophical and political meaning, and that trumpeted Benjamin Franklin's exaltation of the individual, the "I." Finally, the Afro-Colombian Zapata Olivella, self-identified as mulatto, conceived a "mestizo consciousness" to capture the historical essence of the languages, religions, cultures, ways of life, sensibilities, and subjectivities that transformed Anahuac, Abya Yala, and Tawantinsuyu into what Kusch calls "América." For Olivella, as for Kusch, *mestizo* acquires a meaning that goes beyond the biological, a child born of European and Indian.

In retrospect, and in the more recent spectrum in which consciousness has been articulated de-colonially (Du Bois, Anzaldúa, Menchú), it would be apropos to rephrase Kusch's "mestizo consciousness" as "immigrant consciousness," the consciousness of the European immigrant who arrived in the Americas in the late-nineteenth century and early twentieth, and who, instead of assimilating, reacted critically to the displaced conditions of European immigrants in a country already in the hands of Creoles of Spanish descent and mestizos with mixed blood and a European soul and mentality.

Immigrant consciousness, in other words, is an assumed condition of existence, an existence out of place. This was the consciousness of people of European descent, who inhabited a place whose history was not the history of their ancestors; of the Indigenous peoples or ab-originals, who found themselves out of place when their form of life, institutions, educational systems, and economies were displaced, destroyed, and replaced with ways of life and institutions of migrants from European countries. Africans, coming from several parts of the continent, with their own different languages and beliefs, forms of life and institutions found themselves in a land whose histories did not belong to their ancestors and, in contrast to the Europeans, in a land whose social structures placed them at the very bottom of the social scale. "Immigrant consciousness—double consciousness, mestiza consciousness, mulatto consciousness, intercultural consciousness (as Indigenous people in Ecuador maintain to this day), maroon consciousness (as it has been established among Afro-

Andeans in Ecuador)—contains diverse expressions and experiences of the same condition of existence: the awareness of coloniality of being; the awareness of being out of place with regard to the regulations (i.e., the cosmology) of modernity; the awareness, in short, of the colonial wound. It is interesting to note that "critical" intellectuals formulated the idea of peripheral, alternative modernities; this is a complaisant position that mimics dissent, while in fact reproducing colonial standards, albeit with superficial variations. Immigrant consciousnesses (double, mestiza, indigenous, maroon) are different manifestations of an-other paradigm: the paradigm constituted by forms of de-colonial consciousness whose horizon is a pluri-versal horizon conceived as transmodernity.[5]

When one looks at the basic belief system of modernity from the perspective of critical displaced consciousness marked by coloniality of being, one realizes that the modern subject has been constituted by a monotopic consciousness and shaped both the imperial concept of subject and subjectivity itself.[6] Working toward the de-coloniality of being implies de-linking from the imperial concept of the subject and from any pretense to uni-versality, that is, from modernity itself, which has largely been constructed from the experience of the monotopic consciousness of the modern subject in its diversity, from theology to secularism, from empire to nations, from science to philosophy, from Spain to England, from Catholicism to Protestantism, from liberalism to Marxism.[7] All these variations exist within the monotopic consciousness of the modern and imperial subject. Kusch's reflections, sustained over more than twenty years, have greatly contributed to a form of de-colonial consciousness that can connect with colonial subjects of European descent in other latitudes, like New Zealand, Australia, or South Africa (e.g., J. M. Coetzee). And one realizes that the critical de-colonial consciousness, in its variety, can no longer be conceived as alternative, peripheral, subaltern—or what have you—to modern consciousness, but as a consciousness-other that is specifically de-colonial in character. Kusch not only elaborated the concept of "immigrant consciousness," he inhabited it. He thought within that colonial dwelling in the same way that Descartes or Heidegger thought within an imperial one.

For the modern or postmodern reader who suspects that I am thinking in dichotomies, I will introduce two disclaimers. There are many dichotomies between the imperial monotopic and diverse modernity (the dif-

xviii WALTER D. MIGNOLO

ferent moments and types of historical colonialism around the globe), and the pluri-versality of local histories with which European modernity entered into contact for economic, political, and epistemic control, as well as for control of subjectivity. Coloniality of power earmarks precisely that struggle between the coloniality of power and the de-colonial projects. The monotopism of European diverse modernity is framed in the legacies of Greece and Rome and of the Western Roman Empire from its revival in Spanish and British imperialism. Ottobah Cugoano's *Thoughts and Sentiments on the Evils of Slavery* (1787) makes it clear that for a maroon consciousness there is no difference between imperial Spain, France, Holland, or England in the management of enslaved Africans. Thus, the monotopic diversity of Western modernity is visible from the gaze of de-colonial consciousness and not, in fact, from the consciousness of the modern subject, which, like the great contributions of Las Casas or Marx, remain within the limited horizon of the modern subject (and imperial) consciousness.

A BRIEF HISTORICAL PROFILE FOR AND OF KUSCH'S PHILOSOPHY

The following paragraphs are addressed to the reader unfamiliar with Argentine and Bolivian history. To include such a note on history already implies coloniality of knowledge; most likely it would be unnecessary to include a similar note on the history of Germany if I were to introduce, for example, the work of Martin Heidegger. Coloniality of knowledge works by creating hierarchy in a lineal space and silencing the simultaneity of the geopolitics of knowledge and of being. Being in America and in Argentina, where imperial and colonial power relations are in effect, is different than being in Germany and in Europe. Consequently, the only reason to "begin" in Europe and then see what "can be done" in America—How can we think? How can we be?—is already and always a conscious or unconscious act of self-colonization. Kusch's entire effort, from the beginning to the end of his intellectual career, was a struggle to cut the umbilical cord of the coloniality of knowledge and of being.

Argentina obtained independence from Spain in 1810. A turbulent period of civil war ensued, leading to the "dictatorship" of Juan Manuel de Rosas and the "barbarous" leadership of Juan Facundo Quiroga. Rosas and Quiroga dominated Argentine political life until 1852, the former doing so in Buenos Aires, the latter in the western provinces of La Rioja and San Juan. Justo José de Urquiza was the third "caudillo" and the lord of what is called the Argentine Mesopotamia, in the northeast, between the Paraná and Uruguay Rivers. Like Rosas and Quiroga, Urquiza was a rancher, a statesman, and a military man. After a series of internal conflicts, Urquiza overcame Rosas and served as president of the Argentine Federation from 1854 to 1860. Known as the period that started the "National Organization," that was the moment in which Argentinian leaders turned in the direction that global history was taking under the influence of new (in relation to Spain and Portugal) imperial designs. The emerging imperial powers were no longer monarchies and the Christian Church, but developing nation-states: France, England, and Germany. Furthermore, the United States was already on its way to becoming not only a powerful postcolonial nation, but also a new world leader. Its influence was felt already by the leaders of the national organization, following Domingo Faustino Sarmiento's formula "civilization and barbarism," which he posited in *Facundo* (1845), a pro-civilization manifesto that critiqued Rosas and Quiroga as representatives of barbarism. Sarmiento's formula defined the terms of the historical, political, economic, and existential dilemma in every country, but primarily those of South America and the Spanish-speaking Caribbean.[8]

The history of Argentina from 1860 to 1916 was performed and written by an elite that aligned itself with Europe (and sometimes the United States) and, secondarily, with Canada and Australia. Some (like José Ingenieros) thought that Argentina and Australia were moving toward their imperial destiny, that Rosas and Quiroga were buried in a barbarian past, forever superseded by the march of civilization toward a bright future. The interregnum between 1860 and 1916 coincided with the spread of the Industrial Revolution and the growing demand for natural resources from non-European countries. Starting in the 1860s, British railroads were installed in Argentina. Argentina became "el granero del mundo," and even Louis Ferdinand Celine included an episode of wealthy Argentinians in Paris in his *Voyage au bout de la nuit* (1932). But prosperity created the conditions for the development of unintended and unexpected (for the ruling class) consequences. European immigration intensified in the middle of the nineteenth century, but the immigrants weren't the kind that

Sarmiento had envisioned. They were European, they were from the lower classes and seeking opportunities that Europe did not offer them. Thus, in 1916 the Argentine elite, old families of Spanish descent, were faced with the first president who represented the middle class: Bernardo de Yrigoyen. Kusch's parents arrived in 1920, and Rodolfo was born, two years later, in the heart, so to speak, of the middle class. Thirty years later, Kusch translated his experience of the geohistorical (born and raised in Argentina) and of the body-social class (at a particular moment in the formation of Argentine middle class, which began to vanish after 1970) into a sustained philosophical reflection.[9]

Benefiting from the tragedy of the First World War, Argentina enjoyed a decade of prosperity. But Argentina's Roaring Twenties ended with the financial crisis of 1930, and splendors were fast converted into miseries. It should have been clear, by then, that peripheral economies may benefit from disasters in economic centers when those events create a need for natural resources. But peripheral economies suffer twice the consequences of those financial crises that central economies do. If 1920–30 was the "golden decade," 1930–40 was inscribed in the history of Argentina as the "infamous decade." Responsibility for economic recovery moved to the industrial sector (which had emerged in the Roaring Twenties); this also signaled the decay of the prosperous landed aristocracy that occurred during the second half of the nineteenth century and early decades of the twentieth. Industrialization, however, requires workers, and the available workers were not necessarily immigrants, as they had previously established themselves in the official administration, as small retailers, as teachers and university professors, as professionals of various kinds. Immigrant families generally dreamed of having their sons become "Doctors," which meant either physicians or lawyers, and thus few immigrants were available to join the working class. The working class was drawn from the provinces, but the provincial immigrants were likewise unavailable as workers. Immigrants who arrived in the second half of the nineteenth century and established themselves in the provinces managed to acquire, at the least, small pieces of property, which positioned them as a sort of landed middle class. Less educated than the urban middle class, they were nevertheless unwilling to join the industrial work force.[10]

It was, instead, the *cabecitas negras* (black heads), as they were portrayed in the vocabulary of the elite. Cabecitas negras—who in Kusch's reflections appear next to the Chilean *rotos* and the Peruvian *cholos*—were dark-skinned people from Northwest Argentina (Santiago del Estero, Catamarca, Tucumán, Salta, and Jujuy) and from Bolivia. Coincidentally, this is the region of Collasuyu in Inca cosmological and administrative organization. In framing "el pensamiento Americano," Kusch turned to Waman Puma de Ayala's "Mapa Mundi" (Kusch or the editor of Kusch'complete works described it as "Mapa del Perú"), and a recent pedagogical rendering by the Bolivian historian Teresa Gisbert de Mesa further illuminates the suppressed memory expressed in the map of Argentina.[11] If, for example, the point of reference is Buenos Aires, the capital of Argentina, the workers would have come from Northwest Argentina; but if the point of reference is Cuzco, the center of Tawantinsuyu, they would have come from Collasuyu, that is, from Southeast Bolivia.

The cabecitas negras became the emblem of Peronismo, of Perón's "el pueblo argentino." Juan Domingo Perón was elected president of Argentina in 1946, with 56 percent of the vote, and deposed by a military coup in 1955, when he left the country. Perón returned to Argentina in 1973, and in October of that year he was again elected president. He died the following year, after nine turbulent months of economic difficulties and political violence.

The first edition of the book presented here, *Indigenous and Popular Thinking in América*, was published in Mexico in 1970 as *El pensamiento indígena Americano*. The second edition was published in Argentina in 1973 with the current title, *Pensamiento indígena y pensamiento popular en América*, and a third edition followed in 1977. In the prologue to the second edition Kusch stated, "The motive to which this second edition responds is evident. The year 1973 marks an important stage in the country. Argentina has awoken to the possibility of its own authenticity. Among all the economic and social proposals of every sort that are easily adopted as a solution, arises a clear cultural proposal, sprouting from the deepest roots of the *pueblo*. My wish is that these pages be useful toward an understanding of that proposal, so that it will not be misunderstood one more time."[12] Kusch is referring here to the second presidency of Juan Domingo Perón, a proposal that indeed was embezzled once again. Peronismo carried from the beginning the seed of its own failure: what Kusch foresaw in his philosophical reflections—a state founded on popular thinking, not on the thinking of the elite—had finally arrived. However, popular thinking, as

Kusch understood it, did not move Juan Domingo Perón and Eva Duarte de Perón. One could guess that, today, Evo Morales, in Bolivia, is moved by thinking entrenched in and with Indigenous thinking. Perón may have been a populista (in the sense of moving and obtaining popular support), but he was not a popular thinker in the way Evo Morales could be described as an Indian thinker. Peronismo, in any event, was converted quickly into one more political party whose leaders increasingly detached themselves from popular thought, at least as Kusch defined it. But what is Kusch's understanding of popular thought and of the popular? These may not correspond to what Perón (or George W. Bush or any other American president) refers to as "the American people." In other words, "popular thought" is not necessarily "the people's thought."

The fall of Perón and the rhetoric of La Revolución Libertadora, in 1955, not only incurred political and economic consequences, but also profoundly affected subjectivities. The traditional Left and the extreme Right coincided in their critique of Peronismo, although, as it has been throughout the history of socialism and communism, they did so for reasons that opposed them (the Left and the Right) in content but not in principle. A "new Left" emerged from the debris of Peronismo, a sort of national Marxism, from within which José Hernández Arregui and Jorge Abelardo Ramos surfaced as two of the most clear and articulate voices. Hernández Arregui distinguished the new Left from the "Marxist Left" which had been, since the Russian Revolution, an institution of European immigrants out of touch with Argentinian history and sensibility. The Marxist Left coincided with the liberal Right position of the Argentinian oligarchy in critiquing Perón. In contrast, Hernández Arregui (along with Ramos, Arturo Jauretche, and others) opposed to the "national Left," initiated a theoretical and historical discourse.[13] Kusch was not part of this "spirit" of Buenos Aires, and his references (Indigenous histories and thoughts) were also alien to the radical intellectuals of the national Left. However, Kusch and the national Left coincided in their sympathy for Perón and in their critique of the Marxist Left.

Hernández Arregui and Kusch—of Spanish and of German descent, respectively—were both born and raised in the middle class, and were radically critical of it. They initiated in Argentina two distinct but complementary transformations. Hernández Arregui distanced himself from the Communist Party and the Eurocentric Left in the colonies, and through the framework of Peronism articulated the platform and the argument for a nationalist Left. Hernández Arregui's position evolved through his analysis and interpretation of global forces, of the role of England and the United States in the twentieth century, and of the persistence of *coloniaje* (coloniality) in the Americas. Hernández Arregui was in tune with Carlos Montenegro, the Bolivian founder of the Movimiento Liberación Nacional (MLN). The MLN had led the revolution of 1952, but had fallen in the hands of Gonzálo Sánchez de Losada, just as the Peronist Party had led the revolution of 1945, then fallen in the hands of Carlos Saúl Menem. González de Losada and Saúl Menem cleared the path for neoliberalism in the region, under the guidance of Geoffrey Sach and Domingo Cavallo, respectively. Hernández Arregui, Montenegro, and Alvaro Vieira Pinto (a Brazilian and the author of *Conciencia y realidad nacional* [1960]) followed, directly or indirectly, the path opened in the 1920s by José Carlos Mariátegui of Perú.[14] This formidable tradition of thought was, in the Americas, the equivalent of what Antonio Gramsci was in Europe at the time and of what Ashis Nandy and Ranajit Guha were (in the late 1970s) and are for the history of ideas in British India. These three responses carried the imprint of geopolitics and body-politics of knowledge—knowledge and understanding engendered in response to needs created in the modern-colonial world by imperial (within Europe) and colonial (outside Europe: Spanish and Ibero-America and British India) epistemic and ontological differences.

Kusch followed a parallel, although distinct path. While Montenegro (followed by Zavaleta Mercado), Pinto, and Hernández Arregui rethought and remade Marxism and the Left introduced in the Americas by immigrants of European descent in the late nineteenth century, Kusch engaged himself in de-colonial thinking.[15] There are no traces in Kusch's work of Aimée Césaire or Frantz Fanon, who, at the time, were advancing the de-colonial option. However, parallel philosophical and political paths, while not connected with each other, often share common historical and sociological experiences: in this case, coloniaje was lived and experienced, though differently, by both Césaire and Kusch. While Hernández Arregui responded to coloniality by articulating the national Left, Kusch responded by articulating de-colonial thinking and thus advancing arguments toward the de-colonial option.

Although Kusch was radically critical of the Left and of Marxism, he never singled out individual Marxists for censure, instead more generally identifying Marxism with members of the urban middle class in Buenos Aires and with immigrants of European descent. In retrospect it appears that while Kusch does not mention Hernández Arregui or Ramos, and vice versa, they have more in common than they might have thought. The three of them introduced into Argentinean social, political, and philosophical thought a positive and analytic profile of Peronism that can hardly be ignored by contemporary historians, social scientists, area-studies specialists in the United States, or cultural critics. Henández Arregui, Ramos, and Kusch, each in his own manner, thought deep and hard from the colonial wound infringed by imperial histories. In reading Hernández Arregui's *La formación de la conciencia nacional* and *Imperialismo y cultura* one remembers both the five hundred years of imperial and colonial histories (during which Argentina was a point of arrival and passage toward Tawantinsuyu) and the imperial presence primarily of England, as it simultaneously managed both new colonies (like India) and purportedly independent nation-states that were in fact only rhetorically sovereign.

Kusch followed another route. Colonial legacies are always present, but whereas Hernández Arregui focused on the coloniality of economics and authority, Kusch focused on the coloniality of knowledge and of being. By concentrating on knowledge and being, Kusch shed light on how imperial control of knowledge and the imperial transformation of colonial subjects were as powerful and insidious as control of authority (politics, international relations) and control of economics. Both Hernández Arregui and Kusch were risky and creative thinkers, and both were eclipsed by the growing discourse on development and modernization, which reoriented coloniality in economics and politics, and by several of the consequences of development and modernization: the popularity, in Argentina, of structuralism, poststructuralism, psychoanalysis, and the Althusserian version of Marxism. As the complementary forces of economic development, military control of authority, and new waves of ideas, particularly those coming from France, took hold, thinkers such as Hernández Arregui and Kusch were relegated to the past, to a traditional Argentina, even as Argentina was entering a new period: newness in economics and newness in knowledge (postmodernity, structural anthropology, deconstruction) and being (psychoanalysis).

While Hernández Arregui's analysis brought Argentine history together with global-imperial history, Kusch's analysis was rooted exclusively in the history of Argentina and in the Indigenous histories of Bolivia, Mexico, and Guatemala, particularly the histories and memories contained in the Indigenous languages Aymara, Quechua, Nahuatl, Tzotzil, and Maya-Quiché. From the first, Kusch grounded his analysis in sixteenth-century Indigenous documents (mainly Waman Puma de Ayala's *El primer nueva corónica y buen gobierno*; the Huarochirí Manuscript; the Popol Vuh; and the Aztec codices), drawing as well from direct experiences and interviews with Indigenous persons in Bolivia, which he pursued in his own time. He also construed his own locus of enunciation, assuming a critical stance toward his existence and experience as an intellectual of the Argentine middle class. As such, he was distanced and detached from both the elite that ruled the country and the Indigenous people who inhabited the north of Argentina and America, who were "strange" to him. While people of European descent and of Indigenous or ab-original descent both inhabit America, they inhabit different territories; they live within the same state (Bolivia or Argentina), but they do not belong to the same nation. And, as nations, they have different relations to the state in terms of citizenship, economics, and rights. Kusch understood and felt what it means to belong to a nation comprising people of European descent, with all their privileges, who live in the same state with people who inhabit an-other memory, one that the state, being identified with people of European descent, denies. This dilemma is at the core of the current process of rewriting the Bolivian constitution, under the leadership of Evo Morales. The future of the gains of Evo Morales and the Marcha Hacia el Socialismo (MAS) will very much depend on the resolution of this dilemma, which is also faced by the Bolivian Left. Perhaps reading Waman Puma de Ayala, in addition to Kusch, could contribute to the heated debates taking place in Bolivia today.

The experience of the strangeness of co-living and inhabiting different memories and therefore territories (in the Indigenous sense of territoriality) was one of the engines that ignited Kusch's thought. As Greek thinking was to Heidegger, Indigenous thinking was to Kusch—two distinct histories, languages, and memories, each with an inherent set of philosophical reflections. They coexist linked by the colonial epistemic difference, that is, by the coloniality of knowledge and of being. For example, I was familiar with Heidegger before I registered for my first course in Greek philosophy at the Universidad de Córdoba; about twenty-five years later, however, someone in Tucumán chanced to ask me if I knew of

Rodolfo Kusch, and I had to respond in the negative. I was at the office of the director of the cultural supplement of *La Gaceta*, a well-known newspaper in Tucumán. Why did I, in Argentina, know about Heiddeg-ger's philosophical investigations, deep-seated in the history of Europe and of Germany, and not of Kusch, who was reflecting in (and not on) the colonial history of South America and Argentina? Asking this question is another way to understand Kusch's relentless interrogation of *ser* from within feeling, more than from the perspective, the eye, the object, the visual that Kusch critiques as constitutive of *ser* and of the modern sub-ject(ivity). The answer is the alienation and the blindness of the colo-niality of knowledge and of being disguised by the rhetoric of modernity, of *ser alguien* and the devaluation of *estar* and *estar siendo*: two distinctive orientations to life and to living. As an Argentine philosopher of the middle class, Kusch is torn between *ser*, embraced by the middle class, and *estar*, which characterizes both Indigenous and popular thinking. At this point it becomes obvious that Kusch is being torn between two poles that he himself inhabits.[16]

   "Popular thinking" or "popular thought" is located in a sociohistorical experience that is neither that of the Indian nor of the urban middle class, and certainly not that of the elite. Consequently, *pueblo (populus)*—*popu-lar* refers to a sector of the "Argentine people"—is an ambiguous concept. It refers to the people who inhabit the territory of the nation-state. On the other hand, not all the inhabitants are citizens. In terms of social class, Kusch's "pueblo" is formed by those "de-classed" by the war of indepen-dence and the civil wars that contributed to the formation of Argentina in the first half of the nineteenth century. In Kusch's argument *Martin Fierro* is for Argentina the equivalent of Homer's epics for Plato and Aristotle: these poems are not just narrative, but philosophical reflections on life and society, on politics and destiny. As is well known, the character Martin Fierro is a *gaucho*, a gaucho is a substantial sector of the history of Kusch's pueblo, and the poem in which José Hernández immortalized Martin Fierro is a benchmark of "pensamiento popular." Kusch, however, often refers to persons identified with the *populus* as "criollos." In Argentine's everyday vocabulary of the middle and upper class, *gaucho* and *criollo* are synonymous. The gaucho or criollo is a sociohistorical human type whose habitat is the plains (the Argentine pampas, including regions south of the provinces of Córdoba and Santa Fé); the Argentine "Litoral," Corrientes and Entre Ríos; and the northeast of Uruguay and the south of Brazil, where they are called "gauderios." However, *criollo* is a category more extensive than *gaucho*: if every gaucho fits the description of criollo, not every criollo is a gaucho. In the canonical histories of Argentina, the pueblo is characterized by its folklore, manifested in music, narrative, and poetry.[17] For Kusch, all of this is the surface manifestation of philosophical thinking, *pensamiento popular*.

The identification of gauchos or criollos is tied not so much to ethnicity as it is to social status. Neither proletarian nor lumpen-proletarian, they are alien to the Industrial Revolution. Their emergence as a social configuration is part and parcel of the process of Spanish and Portuguese conquest and colonization of the plains. They are recognized as experts in all activities relative to the plains, being masters of the horse and wise in reading the signs of nature, which helps them avoid getting lost in the immense Pampas, where the references for the way are bound to the knowledge of the grass, the tracks, the plants, and the stars. Ethnically, gauchos could have been criollos; mestizos (offspring of Spanish or Portuguese and Indians); Indians who abandoned their communities of origin to join the coming community; criollos of African descent; mulattoes (first- or second-generation children of Europeans and Africans); or Zambos (offspring of Afros and Indians). But not all of Kusch's pueblo and pensamiento popular are located in the history and legacies of the gauchos, for criollos could be, in Kusch's conceptualization, the transformation of gauchos into a social group identified as criollos once the gaucho had vanished as a social type.[18] Criollos are, according to Kusch, not just people of Spanish descent from the provinces of Argentina. The provinces in question will be not only those that gauchos inhabited, but also the northwestern regions of Collasuyu that became the provinces of Santiago del Estero to Jujuy (see map of Perú) in the construction of Argentine nation-state, a region of dry land and Andean landscape that prompted a lifestyle quite different from that of the gauchos. Kusch's pueblo points toward a vast population of Argentine provinces: from the Pampas and the ancient Collasuyu to the outskirts of Buenos Aires, where migrants from the provinces stop and dwell. Kusch devoted an entire book, *De la mala vida porteña* (1966), to pensamiento popular in the city. Pensamiento popular here is expressed in *lunfardo*, the Buenos Aires version of a common "deviation" of the official language of the nation, in this case, Spanish.

One scholarly version attributes the formation of lunfardo to the wave of European immigration starting at the end of the nineteenth century. This is the Eurocentered version of lunfardo. Since the population who migrated to Buenos Aires were also people with speech, they carried with them a vocabulary that was formed in the provinces, not only among gauchos and criollos, but also among Afros and Indians. Lunfardo, as vocabulary and expression (not so much as grammar, which maintains basically the Castilian grammar), is a language that integrates expressions of de-classed people, be they criollos, people of Indian and Afro descent, and even the late-immigrating Spaniards and Italians. But what is key in Kusch's reflection is not so much the sociohistorical and ethnic formation of lunfardo, but the philosophy that is imbedded in it: that is "el pensamiento popular" as conceived and manifested in lunfardo. Kusch's observes in the prologue to *De la mala vida porteña*:

When someone says to us "rajá de ahí" ("get out of here"), we assume that we are being informed to leave.[19] We are sure of that. But to say that an expression is only useful to convey information is too superficial. . . . The one uttering that phrase is not only informing us to leave, he is also, as we say, "nos borra del mapa" ("erasing us from the map"). That is because language is useful to modify reality magically, in this case by suppressing what is bothersome. . . . In sum, words inform first, but then they serve us as a magic fluid, and finally they denounce our true and secret thinking about life and the world.[20]

Here we have Kusch's philosophical method. From anecdotes and verbal expressions (*dichos y decires populares*), from Aymara (mainly) and other languages' vocabularies, Kusch derives, infers, interprets the philosophically unsaid in the expression or the anecdote. One of the anecdotes is found in chapter 2 of *Pensamiento indígena y pensamiento popular en América*, a chapter, significantly enough, that is titled *Conocimiento* (Knowledge).[21] In chapter 12 Kusch moves from pensamiento indígena to pensamiento popular, and in this case he grounds his reflection not in lunfardo and "Buenos Aires bad life," but in the conversation of two criollos (from the provinces). One of them is a folklorist from Jujuy—that is, from the Inca Collasuyu coexisting with Argentina's Jujuy—and one is a farmer from Entre Ríos. That is, one is from the Andes, near Bolivia, and the other is from the northeastern lowlands, bordering with Uruguay, near the south of Brazil.

Thus, pensamiento popular is to be found geographically in a region that goes, metaphorically, from the frontier of the urban middle class (of Buenos Aires) to the frontier of the Aymaras and Quechuas Indians in Bolivia. Historically, this ethnically mixed population emerged and evolved at the margins of the colonial conquistadores; and at the margins of *unitarios* and *federales* (the two factions of the Argentine elite that took over the organization of Argentina after expelling the Spaniards) and that expanded—transformed by demographic and socioeconomic conditions —with peronismo.

As Kusch clearly stated in the second edition, his hopes emerged not as a sociopolitical *analysis* (study of the social science of Gino Germani, which Kusch relentlessly critiques), but as a dialogic scenario in which pensamiento popular and pensamiento culto (e.g., his own philosophical discourse) join forces. And both ways of thinking join forces in what Kusch identifies as the "method" of pensamiento popular: negation (*la negación*). The book Kusch published after *Pensamiento indígena y pensamiento popular en América* is titled *La negación en el pensamiento popular* (1975).

NEGATION AND POPULAR THOUGHT

Kusch's early philosophical reflections on *estar* and *estar siendo* led him, right after finishing *Pensamiento indígena y pensamiento popular en América*, to a long exploration of "negation" as a distinctive principle of popular thought. "Negation" doesn't yet occupy a prominent place in this book, but it is simmering in the last four chapters.

It is telling that the first chapter of *Pensamiento indígena y pensamiento popular en América* is titled "El pensamiento americano," while the first chapter of *La negación en el pensamiento popular* is titled "El pensamiento popular." While the second edition of *Pensamiento indígena y pensamiento popular en América* was published the year that Juan Domingo Perón returned, *La negación en el pensamiento popular* was published one year after Perón's death. Thus, the first sentence of the prologue: "Vivimos en Argentina una crisis cultural y política, que no es de ahora, sino que recién se manifiesta. . . . Irrumpe una nueva, o mejor, una muy antigua verdad."[22]

The prologue is devoted to drive out the confusion between *doxa* and *pensamiento popular* and to reserve episteme to *pensamiento culto*, when that cultivated thought is practiced in the ex-colonial periphery (and it

was a periphery precisely because imperial geopolitics of knowledge operated on colonial epistemic differences that devalued its own epistemic
traditions). *La negación en el pensamiento popular* is an epistemology that
starts by negating imperial epistemic supremacy and affirming an-other
way of thinking and of living, affirming, in other ways, the epistemic rights
violated by imperial epistemology. From imperial perspectives there is no
pensamiento propio in America as there is in France or Germany. Kusch's
task is nothing else than challenging common naturalizations of an imperial geopolitics of knowlege by asserting that living is thinking and that
thinking takes place there where I am (in Europe or in America, in France
or in Argentina and Bolivia). There is no reason therefore—it follows from
Kusch's arguments—to be afraid of being who we are. Fear is a way of
surrendering to imperial knowledge.

For that reason, in the urban and ex-colonial periphery cultivated
thought is derived or applied. Although "el miedo a pensar lo nuestro"
(fear to think ourselves) is announced since *La seducción de la barbarie*
(1953), it becomes a topic and subject of a sophisticated exploration in
*Geocultura del hombre americano: análisis herético de un continente mes-
tizo.*[23] The first section of *Geocultura del hombre americano* is titled "El
miedo de ser nosotros mismos" (The Fear to Be Ourselves), and the first
chapter is titled "El miedo a pensar lo nuestro" (The Fear to Think on Our
Own). In spite of Kusch's critique of modern epistemology and Eurocentrism, there is something that he has explicitly recognized in European
continental philosophy: that they were not afraid of thinking, of being
themselves. And if there is something we should learn from continental
philosophy, it is not their thought itself, but their not being afraid of
thinking, of being where they thought, which Descartes expressed boldly
as "I think, therefore I am," and their asserting themselves as the universal
model. Shifting the geography of reason, Kusch allows us to uncover that it
is by thinking where he was that Descartes was able to affirm that he
thought that because he thought he existed.

Kusch followed these reflections in his last two books. In addition to *La
negación en el pensamiento popular* is *Esbozo de una antropología filosófica
Americana* (1978), wherein Kusch takes to the limits the consequences of
this epistemic and existential schism, which reveals the dependency of
philosophical thinking—and colonial subjectivities—in America; that is, in
the colonies of the South, whether direct or indirect colonies. The very

concept of "geoculture" moves toward a geopolitics of knowledge and understanding and toward asserting the paradigm of coexistence (the paradigm of *estar* and *estar siendo*) in confrontation with the paradigm of linearity of thought and dependency of thinking.

Negation is the negation of what? In short: of modernization and of the modern idea of ser alguien, of being "successful" in the corporate sense of the word. It is the affirmation of someone who doesn't want to be some one, but who prefers *estar nomás*. That is, it is a negation of imperial and colonial designs of modernity to transform the world into "being some one," being successful, being developed, being civilized as the only way to conceive life and to live life. The idea of "success," of "progress and development" are all ideological constructs by subjects for whom life is guided by the will to power and control. One can surmise that there is a huge portion of the six billion human beings in the world whose lives are not necessarily guided by success, progress, and development—which does not mean that they are lazy, that they do not care, that they are barbarians, or the like. It simply means that there are different ways to conceive life and to live it. The ideals of European modernity and Western capitalism (now expanded globally) manage to impose the ideals of success, progress, and development (linked to modernization and the economic interests of the State and the corporations) as the only way to live. "Negation" in Kusch is the negation of the variety of colonial subjects who do not believe in the ideals of modernity and capitalist economy, and who want instead a philosophy in which *el buen vivir*, and not *el vivir mejor*, is the horizon, as Evo Morales constantly reminds us.

The negation is the negation by "them" wanting "us to be" as they want. Affirmation is imperial (development, success, progress); that is, it affirms what imperial designs want colonial subjects to become. That is precisely what "coloniality of knowledge" and "coloniality of being" mean. Negation is, on the contrary, the affirmation of what we, the people of popular thought and Indigenous thinking, want to be, even if we do not yet know exactly what that is. *Estar nomás* is the first moment of negation from where an-other being and an-other knowledge began to emerge; briefly, negation is the first moment in the unfolding of the de-colonial option. Kusch's critique of "development" (which was in full force during the year of his writing) and the opening scene of chapter 2 are good introductory examples. There are two arguments that I would like to quote to make the importance of the concept of negation clearer. One comes from the prologue of *La negación en el pensamiento popular* and the other from Kusch's most recent book, *Esbozo de una antropología filosófica* (1978). One argument is in regard to "negation as disengaging," which he uncovers from popular thought and recasts in his own philosophical thinking and his critique of academic (Eurocentric and self-colonized) philosophy. To understand popular thought and how central negation is to it requires, for Kusch, disengaging or epistemic delinking from the categories of Western thought, which are both cast as categories of European philosophy as reproduced in the (former) colonies. To answer the Kantian question "What is Man?" assumes humanity in the existential diversity mapped by colonial difference, both epistemic and ontologically. That is to say, for a colonial subject, as Frantz Fanon stated, that question cannot be answered philo- or ontogenetically. It has to be responded to sociogenetically. When looking at Fanon in the street, a child grabbed her mother's hand and said, "Look, Mama, a Negro."[24] "What is Man" and "what is Humanity" are pending in that space in which the presence of a black body produces surprise in a white child. For Kusch, based on his own experience of the colonial difference, the point is

Ultimately, as I have said in other works of mine, what is assumed is the search for a new way of thinking or a new logic, maybe a logic of negation, one that implies a giving man a new dimension. . . .

   To philosophy, in the end, corresponds only the task of detecting the foundational or essential axis around which a margin of rationality tends. Because if it limits itself completely to what can be rationalized, it does not comprehend the phenomenon as a whole. The latter always takes place within an academic philosophy, which, because colonial, cannot comprehend a philosophizing that is one's own and which must move from what deforms to the absolute.[25]

   Colonial difference is pervasive. Fanon felt it in the black body, Kusch in the white body of an immigrant in the colonial histories of America.

IMMIGRANT CONSCIOUSNESS AND BORDER THINKING

Kusch's distinctive philosophy—and not only in the context of philosophy in South America, but among continental philosophers as well—is the co-relation between mestizo consciousness and border thinking (or border epistemology or border hermeneutics).[26]

I am using "thinking from" and "thinking a partir de" to capture the experience that nurtures a sustained process or system of thought. The original prologue to *Pensamiento indígena y pensamiento popular en América* is revealing of Kusch's way of thinking (e.g., method): "La búsqueda de un pensamiento indígena no se debe sólo al deseo de exhumarlo científicamente, *sino a la necesidad de rescatar un estilo de pensar* que, según creo, se da en el fondo de América y que mantiene cierta vigencia en las poblaciones criollas" (see page lxxv; my emph.). First a note on Kusch's vocabulary: "creoles population" refers in his language to something closer to what he will describe as "pueblo" in his characterization of "popular thought or popular thinking." *Creoles*, therefore, is not referring as it usually does to the Creole elites of Spanish descent, whose memories goes back to colonial times. In Kusch *creole* (and *Martin Fierro* is a prototypical *criollo*) is—in Argentina—also synonymous with *gaucho*. My interest is Kusch's project of "rescuing a style of thinking." One could debate whether *rescue* is the proper verb here, but this is not crucial to his project. I translate his rejection of a scientific approach to Indigenous thinking from a disciplinary perspective that is not Indigenous but European. And to calm the postmodern impulses of jumping to what appears to be a dichotomy, I will add that his rejection is not Indigenous (in the sense the word has in America), nor is it Arabo-Islamic, or Mandarin and Confucian, or Hindi. That is, "scientific exhumation" is a description of disciplinary thinking (in this case, anthropological and archaeological) that has been formed in Europe, simultaneously with imperial expansion. As such, "scientific exhumation" presupposes the distinction between the known and the knower, the knowing subject and the object. Kusch opts to erase that equation, to de-colonize assumptions that naturalize ideas such as "scientific exhumation" as the only and correct option. Kusch's work instead shifts the attention from the (un)known to the knower: the observer and the enunciation are always the center of attention; the act of saying never vanishes under the spell of what is said, the truth, the event, history, what happened, and so on. As such, "American thought" becomes the name of a locus of enunciation equivalent to "European thought." Both are interrelated in a differential structure of epistemic power. While European thought names the imperial epistemic frame, American thought names the presence of European epistemology, but analyzed from the perspective of the immigrant consciousness taking on Andean (mainly Aymara) episte-

xxxiv   WALTER D. MIGNOLO

mology. In this sense, immigrant consciousness as defined by Kusch is a particular expression of border epistemology.

Thus, Kusch is not interested in *studying* an Indian way of thinking, but in *rescuing* it; that I understand as "thinking from" Indian philosophy instead of "thinking from" Greek philosophy. Today I would prefer *re-inscribe* to *rescue* and would read reinscription of subaltern knowledge in contemporary debate as an act toward de-colonizing being and knowledge, which is how Kusch should (could) be read today. What Kusch proposes is to "rescue" (reinscribe) an Indian way of thinking in a vein parallel and similar to Martin Heidegger's rescuing (reinscribing) of Greek thought in his own philosophy, or to Emmanuel Levinas's rescuing of Hebrew thought, or to the Christian rescue of Rome as the institutional foundation of Christianity. There are two remarkable differences, however, between Kusch's project and those of the other three (Heidegger, Levinas, and Christianity). And both have to do with the coloniality of knowledge and of being. The first difference is that Indian ways of thinking have been "authorized" by Western epistemology as something to be studied (by anthropologists), but not as a source, an energy, and a way of thinking. That is, Indian ways of thinking have been delegitimized by the colonial difference, particularly by the coloniality of knowledge (e.g., Indian knowledge is nonsustainable for the progress of an ideal of civilization that was put in place during the European Renaissance and the first colonial expansion of the modern world). Indian ways of thinking have also been delegitimized by the coloniality of being: Indians are not rational beings to be taken seriously in their way of thinking and in their thoughts.

The second difference (and a consequence of the coloniality of knowledge and of being) is that thinking from Greece and the Greek language, from Jerusalem and the Hebrew language, or from Rome and the Latin language, *is not the same* as thinking from Tawantinsuyu and the Aymara and Quechua languages. Thus, Kusch dwells from the start in a power differential (e.g., coloniality of knowledge and of being) that has been set up by the hegemony of post-Renaissance European ways of thinking in which Christianity, Heidegger, and Levinas have (intentionally or not, it doesn't matter) contributed. He dwells in the epistemic and ontological differences.[27] Kusch is not attempting to *represent* the Indians any more than Heidegger, for example, is *representing* the Greeks. In both cases,

Indians and Greeks offer to both, Kusch and Heidegger, a grounding to their own thinking and, therefore, of their own being in the world. In other words, Western and continental philosophy and Christian theology (of liberation or of institutional salvation through the Church) can unfold their thoughts without paying any attention to Indian ways of thinking. Indians, however, cannot, and neither can Kusch in his project of "rescuing Indigenous way of thinking." Because of this impossibility, an impossibility set up by the coloniality of knowledge and of being, the epistemic mestizo consciousness arises. With this consciousness also arises border thinking. Or, if you wish, border thinking is mestizo consciousness and mestizo consciousness is border thinking. And both, mestizo consciousness and border thinking, are a consequence of the colonial difference: the relocation of thinking, geo- and corpo-politically, in order to be epistemically disobedient and to claim epistemic self-determination. Kusch—as much as Du Bois and Fanon, Anzaldúa and Fausto Reinaga, Vine Deloria Jr. and Ottobah Cugoano, Waman Puma de Ayala, Mahatma Gandhi, the Zapatistas, and so on—is part of a silence and of an unrecognized genealogy of de-colonial options that announces the possible futures, delinking from the imperial nightmare of the modern and colonial (Western and capitalist) world.

I can anticipate a critical reader who will object to the distinction between different ways of thinking and who will assert instead that thinking is thinking and that framing such activities around geopolitical and corpo-political distinctions makes no sense. Still others would reply by saying, "Yes, of course, this was already said by Donna Haraway—it is situated knowledge." Yes, indeed, but how is it situated politically in regions and bodies that have been racialized, epistemically and ontologically, through imperial and colonial differences? The argument can be developed further and suggest that the notion that thinking has its foundation in Greek and Latin (and not in, say, Aymara, Mandarin, Hindi, or Arabic) is simply a question of the natural unfolding of history with its winners and losers. This is, of course, a common and uni-versal argument. Kusch's investigations and thoughts moved in a different direction. That is, he opted for a de-colonial project. Although he never used the word *de-colonial*, the philosophical consequences of coloniality did not escape his reasoning. Therefore, how could one describe a sustained and uncompromising investigation that over approximately twenty-seven years unveiled common

sense and unquestioned principles of the pursuit of knowledge, understanding, and, in the last analysis, liberation? Although contemporary with
philosophy and theology of liberation, Kusch could have not joined the
argument, since his own was a radical questioning not of philosophy or
theology of liberation per se, but of their basic philosophical and ethical
foundations. Kusch was attentive, however, to the metaphysics of *salvation*,
not as a program to *save* someone, but as an insightful analysis of how
salvation is pursued, willingly or not, by persons in different social classes
or different cosmological spectrums, for example, Indians, the urban middle class, or "the people," the latter being a category which is both economic (lower class) and cultural-cosmological (between the culture and
cosmology of the urban middle class and of the Indians from the Andean
region that stretches from Buenos Aires to La Paz).

From the very beginning of his work, represented by *La seducción de la
barbarie*, published in 1952, Kusch grounded his thoughts not in Greece
and Greek, not in Rome and Latin, but in Tawantinsuyu and, for the most
part, Aymara, but also Quechua. Trained in philosophy in Buenos Aires,
he knew Greek and Latin, but he opted to shift to Aymara and Quechua.
This was not opting, however, for an oppositional dichotomy because,
since 1532, Quechua and Aymara had been forced to coexist with Latin and
Greek, through the imperial presence of Spanish. He did not ignore,
either, Anáhuac and Nahuatl; nor did he overlook Maya civilization or
languages with Maya roots, as he frequently made reference to the *Popol
Vuh* in his thoughts and arguments. By shifting the geography of knowing
and knowledge, Kusch engaged in border epistemology and established
the foundation for de-colonial thinking and immigrant (de-colonial) consciousness.

Thus, if Heidegger thinks from or *a partir de* his particular experience
of the modern subject dwelling in European history, which he translated
into something we can call *existentia Euro-Germana*; and if Foucault in a
similar vain thinks from or *a partir de* his particular experience of European history, which he translated into something that could be called
existentia Euro-Franco-Latina (but always dwelling in modern and imperial history); then Kusch shifted to thinking from or *a partir de* imperial
experiences and subjectivies (even if dissenting) to the experience of the
colonial subject. Thinking from or *a partir de* places the accent on the
enunciation and moves away from the tyranny of the *énoncé* that pervades

Western philosophy from Plato's denotation to Bertrand Russell's discussion of meaning and reference to Orientalism, the social sciences, and area studies. One of the consequences of the silence (and the discomfort) of unveiling the locus of enunciation—the act of thinking from or *a partir de*—is that epistemic privileges endowed to Western categories of thought can no longer be sustained in their privileges without recognizing their imperial force. I have heard some discomfort among postmodern philosophers in South America (women and men) who ironically talk about "thinking toward" or "thinking *hacia*" to avoid "thinking from." Furthermore, if one "thinks toward," one ends up in a version, and bad consciousness, of "thinking about"—that is, of blocking and silencing the enunciation in favor of the splendor of an *énoncé* controlled by Eurocentrism, by the principles of knowledge and understanding that find their sacred book in Greek and Latin, and in the six modern European and imperial languages (euphemistically called "vernacular languages").

SEMINAL ECONOMY

As Kusch suggests at the beginning of his chapter "Seminal Economy," it would seem that in America there is, on the one hand, an urban economy and, on the other, an Indigenous economy. The first would be thought out and practiced according to a denotative and causal logic, while the other would favor a seminal logic. Well, this sounds dichotomous, doesn't it? In all likelihood Kusch was aware of the dichotomy, because he spent the latter portions of the chapter dismantling the dichotomy, maintaining, at the same time, the distinction of economic logics. Kusch's arguments amount to the suspicions that economy is not just one type, what political economy has been from Adam Smith to Milton Friedman, and to an invitation to remember what economy and economical thinking was before the seventeenth century, when political economy justifying capitalist accumulation of wealth took center stage, became hegemonic.

Once again, it is not the dichotomy Europe versus America at stake here. What Kusch describes as seminal economy could be found in Europe, too, at the time. But it was not a seminal economy that was implanted by Europeans in the New World (neither in the domain of extraction—gold, silver—nor in the domain of production—coffee, sugar, etc.). Furthermore, seminal economies existed in other part of the world as well.

What is at stake is the emergence of a type of economy, which today we call capitalist, that emerged in the Atlantic in the sixteenth century. Karen Armstrong puts it well in her short history of Islam, when she describes "the arrival of the West." Although she dates that arrival in 1750 (basically because she is looking at England), there are good reasons to date the arrival back to the sixteenth century. In her words, and in relation to the existing Muslim sultanates of the time (Ottoman, Safavid, Mughal) and, we can add, the Chinese and the African kingdoms, "The new society of Europe and its American colonies had a different economic basis. Instead of relying upon a surplus of agricultural produce, it was founded on a technology and investment of capital that enabled the West to reproduce its resources indefinitely, so that Western society was no longer subject to the same constraints as an agrarian culture. This major revolution . . . demanded a revolution of the established mores on several fronts at the same time: political, social and intellectual."[28]

If we go back to canonical histories of how and when political economy came into being, we can see the world behind the simple and apparent dichotomy between urban and causal economy, on the one hand, and Andean and seminal economy, on the other. Let us go back in imagination to the end of the fifteenth century and the beginning of the sixteenth. There was no discourse or conceptualization of political economy. The dominant discourse was theology, and theology was suspicious of merchant morals; in the meantime, the merchants were gaining ground and emancipating themselves from the feudal lords and the Church, the two institutions that regulated Western Christendom (later to become Europe) during the so-called Middle Ages. But, of course, Western Christendom was not the world. It was a minute and marginal corner of the world in relation to the splendors of China. Manuals and introductions to Western economic thought also described Mediterranean commerce (they will recognize the Arabs!) and the commerce in the north of Christendom in the Baltic Sea. They also explain that by the fifteenth century Venice and Florence were thriving financial and commercial centers. And so was Genoa. The reason for this was that the strong commercial circuits at the time were not that of the Baltic Sea or those of the "European" part of the Mediterranean, but those from Venice, Florence, and Genoa to Fess, Timbuktu, and Cairo, from Baghdad to Samarkand.[29] The silk road extended from Damascus and Antioch, in the extreme east of the Mediterranean (what is today the Middle East), to the Chinese Empire. Venice, Florence, and Genoa enjoyed their geographical location in a couple of trade circuits that included them at the extreme (marginal and peripheral) western end. The center, of course, was China, which is why Columbus wanted to go there and why the Chinese, as far as we know, were not particularly interested in traveling to the lands of Western Christians.

One could surmise that until the fifteenth century the connected part of the planet (from the Mediterranean to the Yellow Sea) was operating under the principles of seminal economy. And so were the economies of Anahuac and Tawantinsuyu. I am using *economy*, given the naturalization of Greek terminology. It is common knowledge that *economics*, in the common broad definition, is the study of the allocation of scarce resources. The word *economics* is from the Greek word οἶκος (*oikos*), meaning "family, household, estate," and νόμος (*nomos*), meaning "custom, law"; hence, *economics* literally means "household management" or "management of the state." One could equally use *ayllu*, which in Aymara meant and still means "family," "household management," and also "management of the state" (meaning by *state* a social organization beyond the family and not necessarily the modern State). One could imagine that every culture or civilization *coexisting* in the fifteenth century had a word to designate something equivalent to household management and a word to express the management of a larger unit, or a single word that referred to both. At that point in time, what today is understood as "economy"—based on three hundred years, from the Physiocrats and Adam Smith to Karl Marx and Milton Friedman—could not have been anything except seminal: extraction of the fruits of Mother Earth, Gaia, or *Pachamama* and art-craft and production of commodities that were not extracted were part of the larger unit, household, or state. Because economy was not a salient component of social and human life, there was no conceptual apparatus and philosophical discourse complementing it until the middle of the eighteenth century. And why not, one may ask? The emerging capitalist market economy was based on extraction (gold, silver) before production (sugar and coffee plantations, for example). But both, extraction and production, displaced the existing economies based on regeneration of the living world. It is telling that Waman Puma de Ayala ends his *Nueva crónica y buen gobierno* (finished circa 1616) with a lengthy description of "labor and the days," that is, labor and the cyclical change of the seasons.

When Kusch observes that in America two types of economy coexist (the urban, causal economy and the Indigenous, seminal one), he is putting forward the colonial history of capitalist economy that is missing in most historical accounts of economic thought and of the formation and transformation of capitalism and two lifestyles: the urban style, where the ideas of progress, development, and modernization prevail; and the Indigenous, where these same ideas are kept at bay and looked at with suspicion. Kusch is not affirming that the modern citizen is, essentially, a person inhabited by the values of capitalist economy, while the Indian is a person essentially inhabited by seminal economy. He is clear that the concepts of "modern subject" and "Indigenous subject" are abstractions, and that these two abstractions shall be understood in their particular unfolding in the modern and imperial history of Europe and in the modern and colonial history of America.

This is how I understand Kusch's argument as it unfolds in the final chapters of the book (chapters 13 to 18). In Europe is the growing dimension of the market economy and the growing social influence of merchants who helped the emergence of waged labor and the crisis of the manorial system. The manorial system in Medieval Europe was quite different from the *ayllu* system in the Andes, for example, or the *altepetl* in Anáhuac. Each manor constituted a self-sufficient economic, social, and political unit that functioned according to the orders of the lord who held the most exalted position by virtue of his ownership of the land and everything in it. His position was reinforced by tradition, and in reciprocity for his power he was pledged to protect the lives of the serfs and freemen of his domain, who, in turn, had the obligation to serve in his army. Growing markets in Western Christendom (e.g., the precise space and time of the Middle Ages) and the commercial circuits in the north of Africa (what is today the Middle East, China, and India) made possible for workers to specialize in particular products and to gain skills as artisans. The role of money increased relative to the transformation of the manor system and the growing role of the merchants, who had their own way of accumulating capital. Capital here is not yet capitalism.

In the Tawantinsuyu and Anáhuac things were different. Money was not used in either place. And while the manor system grew over the ruins of imperial Rome, Tawantinsuyu and Anáhuac were, at the time of the conquest, well-structured organizations. If the Inca empire was a macro-*ayllu* (as the Aztec empire was a macro-*altepetl*), communities beyond Cuzco and México-Tenochtitlan (the centers of the Incanate and the Tlatoanate, to build parallels with the designation of "empire" as linked to the Roman emperor, the sovereign) were also organized as *ayllu* and *altepetls*, respectively. Instead, the imperial economy was based on extracting taxes in the form of labor. The local community was the basic unit on which taxes were levied, and obligations were distributed among households by the *kuraka*, or principal, and his *segunda persona* down hierarchical lines. Labor taxation required accurate inventorying of people, resources, and conditions. When Tahuantinsuyu incorporated a new province into its realm, people were counted according to sex, age, and "marital" status, along with their livestock, fields, and pastures. Topographic models of the region were made, and the corpus of data was sent to Cuzco to be acted on. Through this type of organization, three types of levies were extracted, which can be called agricultural taxation, *mit'a* service, and textile taxation.

Thus, by the sixteenth century, when Spaniards arrived in Anahuác and the Andes, they were coming from a Western Christendom that was undergoing economic transformation, in which the manor system and the Church had been the two pillars of the period between the fall of the Western Roman Empire (375–476) and the Renaissance. On the other hand, the fall of the Eastern Roman Empire (395–1453) with the seizure of Constantinople by the Ottoman Turks (which corresponded with a high moment of the Ottoman Sultanate that originated around 1299) turned into an economic and political history significantly different from the model followed by Western Christians, with both the consolidation of the Castilian Empire (expulsion of the Moors in 1492), and the reign of Charles V (Holy Roman Emperor, 1519–58). The Ottoman Sultanate was closer to the Incanate in the Andes and the Tlatoanate in Anáhuac than it was to the Roman Empire. Religious tolerance, which was not an issue in the Incanate and the Tlatoanate, and integration of conquered communities were distinctive features of the Ottoman Sultanate. Western economic historians who studied the Ottoman Empire's economy distinguish two periods: the classic era, from the beginning to the seventeenth century, and the modern or Westernizing era, from the end of the seventeenth century on. During the classic era, they curiously insist, the Ottoman had difficulties in regularizing the money system, and the economy was basically feudal. As it is well known, Western Christian (e.g., European) feudalism was controlled economically by the manor system in the hands of the lords and the absence of a centralized Roman Empire. While the Ottoman organization was centralized in the hands of the sultan it was a sultanate, not a manor system.

I am telling these stories for two important reasons. One is to avoid a narrow understanding of Kusch's thesis on seminal economy and seminal thinking, thus reducing it to postmodern fears of modern dichotomies. Kusch's thought was already an effort of epistemic delinking (of epistemic disobedience), although it was not conceptualized as such at the time by him or by any one else I know of.[30] And the other is to delink from the repetition and reproduction of world history as if it were the history of Western Christendom and of Europe, grounded in Greece and Rome.

Thus, when Kusch observes in passing (chapter 14, "Seminal Economy") that "This is all implicit in the sentiment of the Américan pueblo, not to mention of people anywhere in the world. No doubt any rationalization, translated exclusively into a science as understood today, would be inefficient,"[31] he is writing with an awareness, which appears throughout *Pensamiento indígena y pensamiento popular en América* and in his entire work, of the colonial structure of power implied in that "American thought" that he pursued throughout his life.

There are three basic historical moments (that is, historical nodes, rather than periods) assumed in Kusch's work. The first is the disruption that the Spanish invasion caused in the socioeconomic organization and the subjectivity of the people in Tawantinsuyu and Anáhuac. That is the crucial, radical, foundational moment of what Kusch articulates as "being in America" and of his pursuit of "American thought." This historical moment is crucial in Kusch's thinking because he assumes the coexistence, since then, of the urban centers (basically the transplantation of the Euro-American ways of life, expectations, ideas, and political and economic philosophies) and the Indigenous centers, where the Indian ways of life, expectations, ideas, and political and economic philosophies prevail, although in constant struggle and conflicting dialogue, for five hundred years, with the dominance and hegemony of the political and economic theories and expectations of the urban centers. Why is this important? Because the histories of the "discovery and conquest" have been written under the Christian (sacred) and Hegelian (secular) idea of the universal (or, perhaps, "the global"), that is to say, under the supposition that history is a linear succession of events as performed and narrated from the perspective of those agents who control knowledge. If Christian history, neither as event (e.g., the creation of the world) nor as narrative (e.g., the Bible), *began* in the sixteenth century, the "discovery and conquest of America" was construed as a moment in which "Indian history" (the existence of which Spaniards doubted) ended, as it was superseded by the historical advance of the Christian mission. The invention of "Indians"— in all Christian accounts—relegated Tawantinsuyu and Anáhuac to the past. Their inhabitants were conceived as Indians and Indians as barbarians. Thus a double epistemic managerial move took place here: Indians, as barbarians, were relegated to the *exteriority*. That is, when people in the Incanate and the Tlatoanate were translated as Indians, they were construed as *exteriority from the perspective of Christian imperial history*. But, at the same time, the Incanate and the Tlatoanate began to be conceived— by Christian missionaries and men of letters—as *anteriority*.[32] As time passed, and the Western version of universal history became "uni-versal," as secularized by Hegel, exteriority and anteriority began to be taken as ontological moments of history, and not as imperial historiographic narratives. To understand the extent of this imperial move and the extent of Kusch's sustained and relentless de-colonial effort, one must grasp how exteriority and anteriority played in the Christian and Hegelian versions of non-Christian and European civilizations, as well as in the very history of Europe itself. Sub-Saharan Africans (that is, the "Black") had occupied the lower echelon in Christian classification from a much earlier time. By the time of Saint Agustine (354–430), it was already accepted among Christians that Africans where the descendant of Noah's "bad" son, Ham.

Muslims and Jews were construed also, by Christian intellectuals, as *exteriority* because of their wrong religious beliefs. Muslims where "pushed" beyond the territory of the Christians. Most of the Jews expelled from Castile remained, however, in the territory of Western Christianity, later on Europe. But here, the complementary anteriority-exteriority played in different ways. Muslims were construed as exteriority at first (say, in the discourse of sixteenth century and the seventeenth), but with the advent of Orientalism, Muslims were relocated simultaneously as exteriority and anteriority. Jews, however, were construed differently, not in their anteriority (and that is why the expression Judeo-Christian became an acceptable oxymoron), but in their particular kind of exteriority: the exteriority of those who are inside. Jews, in other words, demanded that in Europe itself *internal colonialism* was not named but articulated. For both reasons—that Jews were not denied coevalness and that they were construed as the *internal difference* (e.g., internal colonialism) that they became, in Europe— Jews were supported in the creation of their own state, Israel, in 1948, while Palestinians were not.

Thus, the "foundational" moment in Kusch's search for "un pensamiento Americano" is not just a dichotomy between Europeans and Indians, but a particular moment that had its equivalent in Spain with the expulsion of the Moors and the Jews. The foundational moment I am referring to was told in the history of the West (Christian and secular Hegelian) as a one-sided history superseding all differences, relegating the Moors and the Jews to the West's exteriority and anteriority. Kusch reversed this trend by assuming, first, the coexistence of separate histories (that of the arriving Europeans and that of the Tawantinsuyan and Anahuacan); second, the coexistence of Tawantinsuyan, Anahuacan, African, and European *in* America; and, third, the coexistence of this dense history in what became America *and* the history of Europe itself. All of these local histories were at once and at the same time *inter-related by imperial/colonial relations of power*. Kusch's works and philosophical reflections assume the coexistence, in America (Kusch refers mainly to South America and the Caribbean), of Indigenous, European, and African (which he does not analyze, but does signal); and also the coexistence of the complex colonial history of America and the imperial histories of Europe and the United States.

The second historical moment was the process of independence and the civilizing mission (here Kusch relies very much on Argentine history) advanced by elite Americans of European descent. Kusch's first book, *La seducción de la barbarie* (1953), is an indictment of such a project and, at the same time, the blueprint of more than a quarter-century of philosophical reflections. And the third moment, after the Second World War, was characterized by the hegemony of the United States, the Cold War (thus, Kusch's recurrent polemic on Marxism), and Kusch's relentless critique of the idea of "development." These three historical moments do not succeed each other chronologically—the new one superseding and leaving behind the previous one—but are accumulated in a dense present. It would be appropriate here to introduce the concept of "heterogeneous structural-history" and describe each moment as a complex node, both synchronically and diachronically constituted.

Consequently, rather than representing a dichotomy, urban (that is, European-oriented and philosophically based) economy and Indigenous (seminal) economy become two signposts that point to the unfolding of a heterogeneous structural-history that demands a mestizo philosophical consciousness as it cannot be understood nor escape the monotopic philosophical consciousness and homogeneous and unilinear history.[33] What Kusch does with his work is to assert coexisting paradigms, to deny the denial of coevalness, while not losing track for a moment that coexistence is regulated by power and that power is what after Aníbal Quijano has been described as the "coloniality of power." Coloniality of power is grounded both in a racial and patriarchal construction from the perspective of Christian, white, European males. That is, coloniality of power (authority and economy), coloniality of knowledge, and coloniality of being are all grounded and supported by patriarchal racialization. What do I mean by that? I mean that racialization consisted in a hierarchical classification of the world population (the enunciated) from the perspective of Renaissance men of letters and theologians and, later, by Enlightenment philosophers and scientists (the enunciation). And patriarchy consisted in the affirmation of a normative regulation of gender and sexuality (the enunciated) from the perspective of a heterosexual and Christian male. Although most of Kusch's philosophical reflections are based on ethno-racial (Indians, blacks, people of European descent), class (middle class, popular, or lower class), and geopolitical distinctions (America: the Atlantic coast, the cities, the Andes, the Pampas, the "natural" space, Europe, U.S.), there are also insights that foreground the gendering and sexualization of history and society. One of these instances appears in chapter 16, "Thinking the 'Así'").

SER, ESTAR, AND ESTAR SIENDO

"Pensar el 'Así'" follows up, at the level of philosophical thought, what Kusch had developed before in terms of urban (e.g., market, objects) and seminal economy. But remember that the first is doubled, as is the colonial urban economy in America (that is South America and the Caribbean), reflecting, mimicking, and serving the imperial urban economy in Europe and the United States. Furthermore, the seminal and Indigenous economy is no longer an economy on its own, as it was before the conquest, but an economy that has to coexist with the dominant urban one, connected to the imperial institutions (banks, investors, imperial states). One can witness the complexity of these imperial and colonial power relations in the government of Evo Morales.

To uncover the coexistence, complexity, and imperial and colonial power relations, Kusch has to move away from the position of the "analytical observer" (the philosopher and the anthropologist) who alienates him- or herself by adopting the categories of thought (theological and ego-logical of the disembodied Cartesian philosopher) that made and were made in the process of structuring the imperial and colonial (racist and patriarchal) world. Kusch's original move was to throw himself in the water and think while swimming for survival. That is, his entire work is a constant struggle to detach himself from a theological and ego-logical philosophical foundation and instead to think in and from the subjectivities constructed in colonial histories. Or, if you wish, his reflections are a constant detachment and removal from the modern subject (theological and ego-logically secular), so as to embrace the constitution of a (de-) colonial subject, geopolitically (colonial and imperial locations) and body-politically (racialized and gendered or sexualized bodies). It is from that turbulent and dense history that "la conciencia mestiza" or "la conciencia del mestizo" emerges in a double bind: in a dominant position with regard to Indigenous and Afros (and, when male, in relation to women; and, when heterosexual, in relation to homosexuality), yet in a subaltern position in relation to European imperial legacies. Being an Argentine of German descent is not the same as being German: the triple HHH (Hegel, Husserl, Heidegger) does not have the same meaning and import in Argentina (and in America, Kusch's América) as it does in Germany (and in Europe). At the same time, being in America is to coexist with Indigenous people and people of African descent. Thus, if one is of European descent in America (Kusch's América), one has two options: the imperial one, following European ideas, subjectivities, and global designs; or the de-colonial one. But the de-colonial option is not just joining Indians and Afro descendents in their claims and protest. It is to embrace their epistemology, thinking through their categories as others can think through Greek and Latin categories of thought. Except that, being in America, one could think from both. And that was Kusch's option, the de-colonial one.

Kusch took advantage of the distinction between *ser* and *estar*, in Castilian, the official language of Spain and its former colonies in America. *Ser* and *estar* run parallel to the distinction between urban, market economy and Indigenous, seminal economy. As in the previous distinction, *ser* (like market economy) has a double edge. One edge is the market economy and the concept and feeling of "being" in Europe, as in Heidegger's on- tological rendering—thus hiding his own geopolitics of knowledge and assuming the uni-versality of the philosophical ego—that links being with Germany and with Europe.[34] The other is the market economy and the concept of being in América, that is, in the former colonies. We see, therefore, the double edge of *ser* in Europe and in the population of European descent in America. *Estar* brings another dimension, which could be dramatically summarized as follows:

- Temporality and urban economy, the logic of the market, belong to the same universe in which Martin Heidegger links "time" with "being" (*ser*). The concepts of "being" in philosophy and "the market" in capitalist economy link continental European philosophy with continental and insular philosophy in América (Kusch's América), with the difference that "being" in Europe carries the weight of imperiality, while in America it carries the weight of coloniality.
- Spatiality and seminal economy seem to co-relate, belonging to the same universe in which Kusch links "space" with *estar*. However, in Kusch's analysis "space" and *estar* go beyond the original seminal economy, before the arrival of Europeans, and, as linked, they infiltrate an array of the population that is as marginal to the colonial and peripheral urban individual as it is marginal to the colonized Indigenous individual. That is the geohistorical space of the *pueblo* (which Kusch renders in the Argentine concept of *criollo*, as exempli- fied in *Martin Fierro*) that Kusch had explored in more detail in a short article that was later expanded into a book: *La negación en el pensamiento popular*. Thus, the title of the book: *Indigenous and Popular Thinking in América*.

Estar becomes pivotal in Kusch's philosophical reflections as it uncovers the wounds of the colonial subject. The colonial wound engendered rage in Indian history, a rage that expressed itself in the myriad revolts and uprisings that have occurred in the history of South America; it includes the rage of such intellectuals as Fausto Reynaga, in Bolivia, and Vine Deloria Jr., in the United States. But in the Argentine middle class, it engendered resentment. Kusch's reflections on "resentment" and "nega- tion" establish a link between what one can call, following Kusch's nomenclature, "philosophy and middle-class thought." Kusch locates philosophy as a professional practice of the middle class, although he makes a sharp and sustained distinction between philosophy as an institutional, bookish, and academic practice at the university, and philosophy as thinking *from* (and not just *about*) the living, sociohistorical condition in which each of us (in China or Greece, in Bolivia or Buenos Aires, in the city or in the mountains) have been and are subjected. In America the main condition of subjectivity and being subjected is colonialism, which not only exerts economic and political colonial control, but also shapes subjectivity. This is the other side of the coin: in order to be able to control politically and economically, a devaluation of the controlled is required. No one will control and manipulate someone who is considered equal or superior.

Kusch's distinction between "cultivated (*culto*) thinking" and "popular thinking"—which are also construed as "two vectors of thinking," one being, say, intellectual and the other affective, one privileging the mind (as in Descartes) and the other privileging the heart (as in Nahuatl philosophy) *La negación en el pensamiento popular* (5)—is mediated by the requirement of a *technology* (that is, the *method*). The lines where difference is felt are expressed in several contexts. In chapter 1 of *Pensamiento indígena y pensamiento popular en América,* "El pensamiento Americano," Kusch writes, "In América we treat philosophy in one of two ways, an official way and a 'private' way. From the university we learn of a European problematic translated philosophically. The other is an implicit way of thinking lived every day in the street or in the countryside."[35] Kusch goes on to clarify that, in América, the affirmation of a philosophy that is related to a lifestyle implies a negation of European philosophy, which, according to Wilhelm Dilthey, was always related to a lifestyle.[36] What Kusch rejects is to practice philosophy, in America, based on a European lifestyle or lifestyles.

When method as mediation is considered, the apparent dichotomy between cultivated and popular thinking dissolves. However, the politics of difference remains: cultivated thinking (in the former colonies) emphasizes technology and hides the eruption of the subject and the living conditions that call for thinking. Philosophy (in the general sense of "thinking with a critical orientation and from existential conditions") comprises both the *how* and the *what,*

the problem inherent in this activity is not merely technical, a *how* question, but also a *that*—something which is itself constituted. Here it is fitting to ask: to what extent within popular thinking, for example, is the *that* constituted before the *how*? It is also fitting to ask: what is constituted? And here maybe we have the first answer. Before anything else, popular thinking constitutes an optic situation crystalized as an ethical affirmation. It is to this that the *that* of which we were speaking points. Thus, the semantic predominates the technical, the how to do. (*El miedo a pensar lo nuestro*, 10)

Kusch's position has been criticized, as expected, by the defenders, endorsers, and practitioners of technical philosophy, that is, philosophy as a discipline, rather than as an existential reflection (e.g., the ontic situation expressed in an ethical affirmation). The classic Argentine narrative poem *Martin Fierro* is for Kusch's philosophy what Homer was to Aristotle's *Poetics*. Not only does *Martin Fierro* enact the ontic situation translated into an ethical affirmation, but it does so beyond the dichotomy civilization-barbarism: *Martin Fierro* becomes, in Kusch's reading, a philosophical reflection from the condition of existence that civilizing discourse classified and denied as barbarism. It is, in other words, a paradigmatic example of border thinking, that is, dwelling in *estar* and from that dwelling reflecting on the condition of *estar* due to the violent imperial and colonial imposition of *ser*, which is endorsed and lived by the economically empowered, the political elite, and a middle class that lives between the envy and the hopes of *wanting to be* and the fear of the *estar*: wanting to be (*querer ser alguien*) as the object of imperial desire and allowing oneself to just be (*dejarse estar*).

What Kusch calls colonialism, and what today one would describe as coloniality (the logic of oppression and exploitation hidden under the rhetoric of modernity, the rhetoric of salvation, progress, civilization, development, etc.), is precisely the triumphal and persuasive rhetoric of *being*: being as success, being someone, being on top of another (e.g., Benjamin Franklin's celebration of competition as an improvement for all). It is precisely this sense of *ser alguien* (being someone) as fulfillment that Kusch contrasts with *estar* as negation of being. *Estar* is, in a sense, a decision of *not wanting to be*, because to be is the imperial way of life imposed in the colonies as the superior destiny of humanity: being, in this sense, is being civilized, is embracing civilization and markets. That is, it was the dream of an entire generation in Argentina (the "generación del 1880," which Kusch certainly knew very well), that dreamed about Argentina (compared with Australia) becoming an imperial country like France,

England, and Germany. That tradition, the tradition of Domingo Faustino Sarmiento's *civilization*, is what Kusch has contested since his first book, *La seducción de la barbarie*. However, his contestation was not a blanket endorsement of "barbarism" (or of Juan Manuel de Rosas and Facundo Quiroga, the prototypes of barbarism in Sarmiento's account), but an acknowledgment of the fact that both coexist and that they coexist in a differential power relation: the power relation behind *the coloniality of being* (the colonial version of being) and the *de-coloniality of estar* (the Indian rage and middle-class resentment) in the face of the imperial imposition. Consequently, Kusch articulates the *seduction of barbarism* as an antidote to the seduction of civilization, of wanting to be (someone). While the seduction of civilization is predicated on the superseding of barbarism, the seduction of barbarism is an affirmation of *estar* as a way of life and a mode of thinking, a philosophical barbarism from the perspective of the academic and bookish practice of philosophy at the university.

In this manner, one finds oneself in the middle of Kusch's reflection on popular thinking: rejecting the academic version of philosophy, he inaugurates, really, a philosophical reflection that nourishes itself from Indigenous and popular thinking, that uncovers the colonial condition of *estar*, both in the resentment of the middle class and the negation in popular thinking, and in the distanced rage of Indigenous thoughts. America (that is South America) is for Kusch the coexistence of the diverse manifestations of the civilizing missions in the hands and pens of the local colonial agents (e.g., the elite and a fearful middle class that wants or pretends to be like the elite) and, on the other hand, a dissenting and numerical minority, middle class like himself, that turns its back toward *ser* and embraces the *estar* manifested, although differently, in Indigenous and popular thinking. One is also in the middle of a current political and ethical conundrum. The increasing dominance (I will not say hegemony) of what during Kusch's years was still the remains of the British civilizing mission and the beginning (in the 1950s) and end (1970) of modernization and developmental dreams (e.g., if people in the Third World act wisely, they will become like the first—an illusion that reappeared in Argentina in 1990 with the unlikely duetto Carlos Menem and Domingo Cavallo) and the increasing presence of Indigenous political and philosophical ideals as well as a governing middle class (like Hugo Chávez and Rafael Correa), who are leaning more toward the "pensamiento popular" than to a middle class supportive of neoliberal local agents both in Ecuador and in Venezuela.

POPULAR THOUGHT AND THINKING
AND POPULIST REASON

Given my discussion of Kusch's "popular thought," I have often been asked about Ernesto Laclau's "populist reason."[37] The question is not surprising. It recalls the logic of bringing up Michel Foucault's biopolitics when I talk about body-politics.[38] Let's start with the second case. In Foucault's brilliant analysis, *biopolitics* refers to State managerial strategies to control (and manage) the lives of the population. It is a top-down analysis. Body-politics refers to the variety of de-colonial ways of thinking of the population that confront and disengage from State biopolitical strategies, which are grounded on the ego-political conception of knowledge on which Foucault's own way of thinking is also grounded. Like Las Casas and Marx, Foucault offers a crucial and sharp internal critique of modern rationality and its political strategies. The body-politics of knowledge (cfr., Fanon listening to a child telling his mother, "Look, Mom, a Negro!") announces and enacts an-other game: the de-colonial game being played by the sorts of de-colonial consciousness I described above.

Laclau's populist reason is located in the same epistemic sphere as Foucault's: that is, in the domain of the ego-politics of knowledge, which is the secular and enlightenment version of the theo-politics of knowledge in which the European Renaissance, and its darker side, was historically founded. Consider, for instance, the three paradigmatic examples of populist reason offered by Laclau: the Omaha Platform and the electoral defeat of the People's Party in 1896; the modernization of the Turkish State by Attaturk after the collapse of the Ottoman Empire (1919–38); and the return of Juan Domingo Perón to Argentina, in 1973. Laclau analyzes, across the board, a situation in which the United States, after the defeat of Spain in 1898, was one step from moving the nation toward imperial designs; the emergence of a nation-state, Turkey, after the collapse of the Muslim Ottoman Empire (1453–1922, although its prehistory is dated back to 1299); and the return of Perón to a popular consciousness that he had helped to create in the early 1940s, but that had been co-opted as a political party and was out of his hands when he reappeared in 1973.[39] In spite of the different historical situations and subjectivities between the history of a collapsing Muslim empire, an emerging imperial Anglo-Saxon nation-state, and a formerly Spanish colonial history entangled with nation-building during the nineteenth century and the twentieth, Laclau captures the common thread of the populist reason in a model that could be worked out for computer software, analyzing the pros and cons of populist reasoning, and the moves that can be made for future, more efficient functioning.

While popular reason is conceived from an analytic top-down (that of Laclau); from a managerial situation also top-down (that of the modern nation-state); popular thought is conceived as an-other thinking in confrontation with the thought of the middle class or that of, say, the department of philosophy at the University of Buenos Aires. It is in this sense that the sector of the population that constitutes "el pueblo" is different from the middle class, the elite, but also from the Indigenous, or the Afro. However, it is common to find among "el pueblo" Indigenous and Afros, as well as mestizos, mulattoes, immigrants who have arrived since the end of the nineteenth century, and even creoles and mestizos whose families can be traced back to the colonial times in eighteenth-century Argentina. While this is the context and the history in which Kusch conceptualizes popular thought and popular thinking, one could engage in the same analysis for the defeat of the People's Party in the United States and for the emergent nation-state of Turkey in the 1920s.

Negation, as the source of energy for popular thinking and popular thought, could be understood as "resistance." This is not wrong, but it is limited for two reasons. First, dominant thinking or thought is also resistant. If subaltern resistance opposes the national and global designs of dominant thinking, dominant thinking also resists the resistance advanced by negation and popular thought. Hegemony, instead, displaces both resistances, because hegemony implies that there is a consensual sphere among those who rule and those who are ruled. Second, to conceive negation only as resistance is to hide the fact that negation in popular thought is also re-existence.[40] Or, as Kusch will put it, it is a negation that opens up to a world different to the one it negates.

Thus, while populist reason registers the strategies of the elite to manage the subaltern or the governed (*el pueblo*), populist thinking is the thought and action that reject and search to delink from the managerial operations of the state, the corporations, the elite. It is when that conflict and struggle is marked by the logic of coloniality that one talks about coloniality of power, the site in which elite thinking and global designs, on the one hand, and popular (or Indigenous, or Afro, or feminist, or queer) thinking collide: coloniality of power is the struggle between the imperial process of colonizing power, knowledge, and being and the process, anchored in "the de-colonial negation," of de-colonizing being, knowledge, and power.

I am not arguing that Kusch is right and Laclau is wrong. Nor will I engage in a debate in which the opposite would be defended. My point is that popular thought and thinking and popular reasons are expressions that belong to two different worlds. They are not necessarily incommensurable or untranslatable, but they are radically irreducible: the irreducible difference between progressive or critical projects within modern epistemology (Laclau) and progressive or critical de-colonial projects (Kusch). This is, in brief, the irreducible difference between the array of the "Marxist Left" and the "de-colonial Left."

Interestingly enough, Kusch and Laclau were born and educated in Argentina. They are one generation apart. When Kusch was in the mature stage of this thinking (as represented by *Pensamiento indígenas y pensamiento popular en América* and *La negación en el pensamiento popular*), Laclau was entering the public debate with his first publication. In retrospect, Kusch would cast Laclau as one of the intellectuals of the middle class dwelling in the imperial and colonial "being," while Laclau would look at Kusch as a traditional thinker, still believing in the authenticity of something called "American thought." The bottom line is that both enact different facets of what modernity and coloniality mean.

CODA

For about four centuries the modern, colonial world was structured in two types of spaces linked by the imperial managerial presence, both in the metropolis and in the presence of imperial subjects and imperial and colonial institutions in the colonies and in the emerging nation-states after de-colonization—which means, the re-articulation of coloniality. One space or domain was the construction of modern and imperial European history, from the Renaissance through the Enlightenment. The other was the conflictive process of modern Europe and its colonies—that is, modernity and coloniality. The domain of Europe was the exemplary point of arrival of universal history (from the Bible to its secular version in Hegel). The other domains (the Americas and the Caribbean, India, North and Sub-Saharan Africa) were and are the spaces of modernity and coloniality, where populations and mentalities of European descent coexist (in the case of the Americas) with natives or enslaved Africans who built their life in the New World.

Kusch and Laclau are in two different fields of the modern, colonial space. But, of course, this is only a dichotomy among those of European descent and ways of thinking. Beyond that, is the rich diversity of Indigenous populations and mentalities, from Mapuches to the First Nations in Canada; and beyond that are the several millions of people of African descent and mentalities.[41]

Kusch's awareness of immigrant consciousness, a critical de-colonial step, joins the colonial wound and the anguish of dwelling in the colonial difference of Indigenous and Afro–South American projects emerging from the brutal and humiliating imperial colonial legacies, from Spain and Portugal, to France, England, and Holland, to the United States.

MARÍA LUGONES AND JOSHUA M. PRICE

There is a cluster of central words in *Indigenous and Popular Thinking in América*. Their meaning is organically embedded in an indigenous cosmology that Kusch sees as a powerful undercurrent in Américan popular thinking and daily living. What words themselves do is to be understood in relation to this cosmology. *Estar, utcatha, habitat, así, uma, nayra, pacha, guauque, kuty* are some of these words. Kusch himself often did not translate words from Aymara and Quechua. He left them to be understood in their centrality to the cosmology. Instead of translating these words, we also will seek in this introduction to situate them within the cosmology and in relation to each other, in a network. This performs an intervention in the English language that we hope will be useful, particularly in expressing the possibility of liberation in América.

This introduction does not seek to explain Kusch's text. Rather, the question it addresses is one of translation. As translators, we have come to understand that to translate the central cluster of words would reduce, deform, and even colonize Kusch's meaning. So how do we avoid backhanded ways of performing the reduction, such as providing a glossary? We introduce the relevant words through a movement: we move from using them to embedding them in their network, coming back to them, each time deepening their place in the Kuschian text, and finally, extending their use outside of Kusch's particular experience, but not outside his reach, keeping the network in mind. The pivotal word in the cluster is *estar*.

Kusch's own intervention takes the form of a journey from an urban, educated, Western-centered thinking to a popular Américan thinking, deeply tied to indigenous thinking. This is a journey from scientific rationality to an affective sensing of the world in its instability, a journey from *ser* to *estar*, from individualism and enterprise to an *estar bien* in community. The journey is not an individual personal one. Kusch performs it from within a social sense that itself becomes transformed as he enters indigenous cosmology.

Estar siendo indicates passivity—not paralysis, not reduction to object, not inactivity, but the absence of a particular form of activity: enterprise. It indicates the absence of an approach to the world in which one takes the world instrumentally, objectifying it, controlling it as something outside oneself, thus producing an external, separate reality.[1] *Estar siendo* enacts a rejection of that separation. Thus, it does not externalize solutions, as is evident in an incident Kusch describes, wherein a grandfather turns away from Kusch and his colleagues and their suggestion to use a water pump to respond to a drought.[2]

Kusch contrasts *estar* and *ser* (to be). He connects *ser* with what is Western and urban. *Ser* marks a relation between subject and objects understood as definable, fixed, having an essence, ordered in relations of cause and effect. Objects are manipulated instrumentally with an efficacious intention, the subject using technology and science. There is a quality of fiction about this Western *ser* when considered from the *estar*: *estar haciendo, estar sentado, estar bien*, or *estar nomás*. *To be* and *to have* stand with respect to *estar* as irreconcilable ways of situating oneself in the world. The enterprising attitude objectifies the world, creates objects as separate, essentially unchanging. Objects are a construction of the Western imagination that makes possible the project of possession and control. *Estar* instead situates one within the world, where one senses its volatility, its mutability, its instability, its bearing fruit. Thus, the logic of *estar siendo* is incompatible with essentializing things and relations. The logical movement of *estar siendo* is connected to seminal activity and to the logic of seminality, life sources, growth.

In light of the contemporary internal critique of essentialism within the

European tradition, it is interesting that in the logic of *estar*, *essence* lacks meaning. But this way of inhabiting the world is very different from the one issuing from the postmodern rejection of essences precisely because the *estar* way of inhabiting the world is germinative, that is, germination is one of its affective moments and movements. Its economy is seminal.

Estar bien is a peopled way of being with respect to a world that is constantly unstable and where the possibility of a *vuelco*, a *kuty*, is always present. The community holds together and constitutes a habitat in equilibrium. It balances the instability, but it does not make it disappear. Aymara and Quechua cosmologies, in Kusch's understanding, exhibit an inseparability between subject and world, and between subject and community. The relation between *estar* and *utcatha* is key in this extension to peopled space. If the subject is to *estar bien*, the subject must be embedded practically in, be of, a habitat, community, *plaza*, dwelling, *nayra*, *amu*, or place of equilibrium in an unstable world. The alienation of the urban dweller lies precisely in this lack of a community that constitutes a habitat structured so that one can contribute toward an equilibrium in the unstable cosmos. The urban dweller seeks to remedy this lack, this alienation, through the home of the nuclear family or the abstraction of the nation. But their very constitution fails as a communal habitat.

The indigenous cosmos is an organism, an "organic totality" in a state of instability, fluctuating toward the two extremes of growth and disintegration. This duality, a tearing, is fundamental or original to the cosmos. The subject who takes the cosmos, the world, non-inferentially, in its immediacy, in its *así*, senses this movement affectively. Since there is no separation between world and subject, the relation can be approximated by thinking that the world in its instability invades or permeates the subject who is of it. The subject takes the world in contemplatively, passively, in his lack of separation.[3] Thus the subject does not understand (*conocer*) the world in the sense of positing an external reality which is explained rationally and modified instrumentally. Rather, the subject knows (*saber*) the world through contemplation of its *así*. The subject takes the world as "pure succession of events and not as a stage populated by things" (41). The subject senses the affective favorable or unfavorable tonality of this succession, of this movement. Man's interiority, *uk'u*, is an opening to affectivity, the inward direction that enables one to seek solutions to the instability of one's reality without positing external solutions.

Because there is always instability and the inauspicious possibility of a rending or tearing, fear is always present, and it is an important affective state in the face of a possible unfavorable turn. Sickness, the loss of one's job, drought, the loss of one's land are the result of a *kuty*, "an inversion from the auspicious to the inauspicious" (44). Earthquakes, wars, cataclysms are also turns to the inauspicious. A turn, *vuelco*, *kuty* is a renovation of time, a revolution in time, a metamorphosis in the-reality-in-which-I-live tending to turn. Such a revolution in time in a cosmos that is torn is a source of life, the auspicious and inauspicious inseparably constituting the original tear in the cosmos.

Estar points to the unstable relation among the elements of the cosmos and the search for stability. Thus *kuty* and the seminal spring which is also the center of equilibrium are expressed through *estar*. Good and bad possibilities are not realized through technological manipulation but are instead inhabited, the subject interacting in the unstable situation with a contemplative attitude that moves the affective tone of the circumstances and is central to the seminal economy.

As one lives daily in this unstable reality, one senses the favorable and unfavorable possibilities, one *está*.[4] Though the cosmos is unstable, being pulled towards extremes, the possibility of its internal equilibrium is both a communal affair and central to *estar bien*. While the internal balance depends on each person, each person is in relation to a habitat, a center, a community, without which one is disoriented, sensing the *así*, but without the complex communal centering that gives the world its possibilities of flowering. This communal center is thus a seed, a seminal source. The attempt to inhabit the intersubjective pull toward this center of equilibrium guided the construction of Cuzco in accordance with a theological architecture. From the center radiated lines (*ceques*) which were oriented to the four directions and in the care of different *ayllus* (communities). In each *ceque* were the shrines (*guacas*). There were over three hundred shrines in Cuzco, attesting to the important symbiosis of peopled community, ritual, and spatiality. They constituted a habitat in which the collectivity's intersubjective balancing of the instability of the cosmos was highly structured. The sense of community in this cosmology is not one of an inferred community, an abstraction, but rather the concrete, peopled, past-before-us sense of the world given to us with all its instability, its movement and fluctuation, its danger. The community steadies us. It is this organic habitat that does not take itself as something to be consumed, controlled. It is a structured, peopled spatiality, peopled both by human beings and by nameable and unnameable beings, able to grow the pressing necessities.

The one that *está*, *está* within circumstances that are always unstable, within the constant turning that includes the overturn, the *vuelco*, the *kuty*. Given the instability constitutive of the cosmos, neither object nor subject are definable or static. Nothing in the cosmos has an essence, no matter at what level of concreteness—neither at the level of the tactile, visible, nameable, the *guauque*, nor at the level of the unnameable—for all levels are inseparable from each other. Because nothing is fixed, static, essentially constructed, words point rather than connote. Words name, and to name is to point rather than define. To say that the *pachayachachic* or the *guanacauri* are unnameable is to say that one cannot point to them.

Only through ritual can the tear in the cosmos be pulled toward germination. In the exercise of ritual knowledge, the subject enters within himself, inhabiting and contemplating the *así* of the world, with its possibility of a turn in time that may spring germinative possibilities. Knowing (*saber*) is related to ritual, and it grows in the person's interiority (*uk'u*) so that the person "does not go around empty." This knowledge is not in relation to abstraction. The one who knows is able to transcend beyond the visible, the nameable, the "here and now of existence" (*pacha*), to an understanding of the structure of the cosmos, its rhythm, and the unnameable extremes. This transcendence is not a question of abstraction. The tearing which is fundamental to the cosmos is structured rhythmically at different levels. Kusch gives us a cosmology articulated not in terms of abstraction but in terms of different levels of concreteness. The contrast is not between concreteness and abstraction, but between *dimensions* of the concrete which are in productive tension or contradiction with each other and which result in a next level. One way to think about dimensions is in terms of beings within and beyond the limits of what is nameable. The logic here has something of the dialectical, but the third term is not a synthesis of the other two. The third term, the visible, nameable, of the here and now (the *pacha*) is a *guauque*, a visible presence of the divine, the tactile, physical plane of the sacred object.

One *está* in the immediacy of the here and now in the physical, nameable, visible plane, the level of the *guauque*. Inward access to the planes that would enable one to go towards a seminal center—and thus also the intersubjective creation of a seminal habitat at the level of the visible—is possible through this knowledge for living that accesses the level of the unnameable, the structure of the cosmos, the tearing that is the seed and source of life. This is the knowledge of ritual. So this knowing is important to the arranging of the habitat (*pacha*) that will give the community its possibility of pulling toward germination, life, metamorphosis. Another facet of the intersubjective quality of ritual inscribed in the habitat is that each subject who is empty can become full, through ritual, through this knowledge for living. Ritual balances the cosmos and maintains the habitat. Balance of the cosmos is constantly created through ritual repetition. It is a daily enactment that touches every aspect of life. The community or habitat is constantly re-created through this balancing of the cosmos.

It is precisely this re-creation of community, of habitat, in the here and now of producing life that we can rethink with Kusch's rendition of Andean cosmology. Kusch reads the terror in the daily living of urban people who are also "pueblo" as a lack of habitat, community, plaza, dwelling, womb, *nayra, uma*. Each of these words is threaded affectively for those who have them and for those who lack them, who have a negative affective sense of the instability of the world. We can bring with us into liberatory, nonreformist, de-colonial, intercultural, grassroots moving Kusch's understanding of the infantile seminality of the urban inhabitant who *está*, but does not *está bien*. As we attempt engagement in insurgent, resistant, liberatory, collective movement, we can come to understand the extent to which we have been adversely affected by the tools that alter intersubjective inwardness, which have been impersonally imposed by colonial and imperial power. We can come to feel affectively the absence of community, and feel it as a sense of disorientation and a fear of being trapped in a reality built to disaggregate us from each other and from nature. As we seek liberatory, nonreformist, de-colonial, intercultural, from the grassroots moving among each other, Kusch uncovers for us the possibility of *estar bien*, of community, of solidarity, and of our coming to sense it as our possibility, instead of being inspired by charismatic leaders or abstract understandings of collectivity. We can come to feel the poverty in subjects isolated from others, which creates an abstract, ideology-bound sense of group or organization or even "movement." And we understand the process of an abstract, ideology-bound way of building collectivity as guided by a logic of control. That process obscures our affective disengagement. A more organic, what Kusch calls "seminal" logic is needed for the sense of community integral to the indigenous cosmology he relates to us. *Pueblo* points not to "the people" as an abstraction, but to the concrete, disoriented human manyness that contains the possibility of community.

In the history of identity politics in the United States, "identifying" has meant not just becoming conscious of the mark of oppressions on oneself. It has, most importantly, meant the formation of a person's sense of relation to insurgent collectivities. These collectivities forged ways, practices, histories, perceptions, knowledges that constituted them in a tense relation to their oppressors. Critiques of "the politics of identity" have been both inward, within the collectivities, and external, not always clearly positioned in relations to structures and practices of oppression. One such critique, which has taken both inward and external forms, has critiqued the homogeneity and fixity of insurgent identities. The most external of critiques has appealed to the problem of essences. The most internal of critiques has rejected the tendency to reduce collectivities of resistance and their creative potentials to copies of oppressive patriarchal and heterosexual understandings of the insurgent social. It has also rejected the unity of reality. Both critiques reject a modern Western understanding of reality, though the rejection takes them to different lived positions. The external critique leaves the critical subject outside any collectivity. The inward critique moves toward a remaking of the insurgent social in a complex vein that affirms a more open, in creation, multiple understanding of the relations among all elements of reality.

The language of *estar siendo* fits this remaking. The logic of *estar siendo* involves one in a concrete re-creation of community and habitat in the here and now of producing life. Consider Cherríe Moraga's play, *The Hungry Woman*.

An ethnic civil war has "balkanized" about half of the United States into several smaller nations of people. These include: Africa-America located in the southern states of the U.S. (excluding Florida); the Mechicano Nation of Aztlán which includes parts of the Southwest and the border states of what was once Northern Mexico; the Union of Indian Nations which shares, in an uneasy alliance with its Chicano neighbors, much of the Southwest and also occupies the Great Plains and Rocky Mountain regions; the Hawaii Nations; and the confederacy of First Nations Peoples in the former state of Alaska. The revolutionaries that founded these independent nations seceded from the United States in order to put a halt to its relentless political and economic expansion, as well as the Euro-American cultural domination of all societal matters including language, religion, family and tribal structures, ethics, art-making, and more. The revolution established economic and political sovereignty for seceding nations with the ultimate goal of defending aboriginal rights throughout the globe. Rebels scorned the ballot box and made alliance with any man or woman of any race or sexuality that would lift arms in their defense. When the Civil War was over, anyone, regardless of blood quantum, who shared political affinities with these independent nations was permitted to reside within their territories; however, the right to hold title to land was determined differently within each nation. Several years after the revolution, a counterrevolution followed in most of the newly-independent nations. Hierarchies were established between male and female; and queer folk were unilaterally sent into exile.

The play's main character, who served as a leader in the Chicano Revolt and was exiled from Aztlán, along with her son and her lesbian lover, now

> resides in what remains of Phoenix, Arizona, located in a kind of metaphysical border region between Gringolandia (U.S.A.) and Aztlán (Mechicano country). Phoenix is now a city-in-ruin, the dumping site of every kind of poison and person unwanted by its neighbors. . . . Phoenix is represented by the ceaseless racket of a city out of control.[5]

Moraga's play expresses the internal critique both starkly and spatially. The spatiality, not of Phoenix, but the intersubjective spatiality of the revolt, which produces the metaphysical border region where the unwanted live, is distinctly at odds with the logic of *estar-utcatha*. The sense of identity that moves the rebellion fractures the social with the logic of abstraction and control. The Chicanismo that places both women into exile fixes and simplifies identity.

The logic of *estar siendo Chicana/o* concretizes identity as inseparable from community and is always in the making. It is not just in the making, but is also always unfixed, unstable, capable of metamorphosis or transformations: a danger as well as a promise, not a fixed, univocal identity. *Estar siendo Chicana/o* points to a subject inhabiting the instability of the cosmos and the social instability, affectively tuned into its possibilities, intersubjectively making a stabilizing, peopled, germinative habitat (*estar-utcatha*). The subject that *esta siendo* is not a separate, distancing subject that has an inferential or causal approach to reality, but rather it takes in the *así* of the world non-inferentially; it is invaded by it; it presses itself on the affectively open subject without separation. The one that *esta siendo Chicana* does not develop a sense of her community as external to herself. *Estar siendo Chicana* is political because it is life affirming in the face of destruction and oppression. It makes a future facing the past, remembering. It re-inhabits its place and its space, invoking, reconceiving, reviving collectivity through a seminal, fertile renovation. Peopled spaces, venues, pathways are the texture of a praxical, life-affirming knowing: a *senti-pensamiento*.[6] Cognition cannot be separate from spatial moving with and in the daily production of life's necessities, in ways that do not destroy the intersubjective habitat.

Kusch's understanding of *estar siendo* thus provides us with a liberatory sense of identity, one lived not in an imaginary spatiality, but in concrete terms, enacted concretely, one that senses the spatiality of life as intersubjectively maintained. Identity politics fractures space by eschewing the complexities of the lived social. Instead, *estar siendo* is a moving-together that captures the density of living our lives that peopled-space presents as a challenge in our lives. The challenge lies in the urgency of the question of community, of from-below solidarity, of the how to of generating communal space, collective space. If the grammar of identity can be a grammar of generating solidarity, how do we understand this grammar in a way that does not ignore the question of habitat and seminal interknowing? *Estar siendo* becomes political, intercultural, intersubjective living. *Estar siendo* gives us a not-definable, on the move, body-to-body collective activity that pulls the cosmos toward a renovation of life understanding of identity. The political question becomes: what are the elements of our lived spatiality that constantly revive balance, which is never permanent but constantly in need of being maintained?[7] How does the inward liberatory collectivity gather changing practices into traditions that we carry into the future?

METHODOLOGICAL REFLECTION: A SENSE OF DISPOSSESSION

In setting the stage for an opposition that structures the entire work, the first lines of Kusch's book pose a methodological contrast between a scientific investigation and a search to recuperate a thinking rooted in América. Kusch's own motivation lies closer to the latter. In seeking to understand Kusch's exploration, the reader is invited in, to join Kusch. In that sense, Kusch's text could be more fruitfully read not as a representation of indigenous thinking, not as ethnography, not as a diagram or explanation, nor as philosophical treatise; it could be taken as a passageway, a crossing, an entrance.

A woman from a working-class suburb of Buenos Aires, whose father was dying from an undiagnosed ailment, wrote to one of us. She was exasperated by doctors who ran ever more tests on her father. The doctors seem to have faith in the tests, she noted with bitter irony. They turn to them when they do not know what is wrong with him or what to do.

This turn to medical tests, an almost metaphysical faith in them and the truths they seem to provide, betrayed for her a desire to solve the problem through technology, a psychological necessity for clarity, for empirical truth. The doctors want, need, try to establish a chimerical order and illusive stability through medicine and science.

Instead, Kusch might argue, one can dwell in that moment of uncertainty, confront the reality of the dying father, that is, one can labor to stabilize one's world, to stop things from falling apart through confronting that brute reality with all of the emotional tonalities intact, even as one sees the possibility of one's entire universe becoming undone. This latter stance approaches what is for Kusch more like "understanding" from the indigenous point of view. This dwelling is evaded by people from the city, the bourgeoisie, and Westernized people generally. They fill their world with activities, seek to find the cause, require external solutions. Indigenous people face down fear and engage in ritual activity to stave off the overturn, or *pachacuty*.

Kusch sees this as a binary that cuts through América: between indigenous modalities and an impulse to try and elude the instability of a shifting, turning universe through appeal to technology and Western reason. The binary was created by colonization; European colonizers imposed their way of knowing. Everything associated with the colonized, with the indigenous, including indigenous thinking, is condemned, suppressed, erased, and devalued by the West.

Nevertheless, an indigenous rhythm of thinking, as Kusch puts it, continues to beat at the base of América and has endured since before Columbus. Repressed by colonization, it manifests itself only in fractured form. This rhythmic thinking eschews the colonizer's split between reason and emotion, mind and body. Consequently, indigenous thinking cannot be forced into the categories of Western thinking without the utmost distortion. Kusch looks at Western philosophy as a philosophy of control, of domination. Causal thinking, the emphasis on the individual, on voluntarism, on enterprise, Western rationality, on essences and definition are aspects of that domination. The problems posed and lived from within indigenous thinking intervene in showing "civilizing," "modern" thinking as resisted at the depth of Amércan life. As Walter Mignolo has remarked, the problems press for a restitution of indigenous knowledge.

Caught in this historical bind of colonization, the Latin American middle class—and Kusch includes people from across the political spectrum, including leftist activists, folklorists, urban professionals, intellectuals, and so on—skirt the crucial questions, cover the disquiet or lack they feel by trying to compensate with externalities that may partly mollify or defer, but will not ultimately resolve, their inner conflict. The conflict is in part an uncertainty built into the cosmos, the *kuty*, but it is also a social condition, a psychic restiveness, based on their own unresolved ambivalent relationship to living in América and situating themselves there.

For Kusch, this split structures social practices, ways of thinking and acting, hopes, fears, investments, and desires. Through daily interactions, fragments of conversation, interviews, interpretation of historical texts, monuments, myths, beliefs, and his own observations, he reads how people maneuver this split.

In a key episode in an early chapter, Kusch and a group of his students ask an *abuelo*, a grandfather, an older indigenous man, why he does not acquire a hydraulic pump from the agricultural extension office to help him irrigate. Kusch notes that at that point the grandfather withdraws a bit into himself, growing taciturn and distant. Later, after they leave, one of Kusch's group calls the grandfather "ignorant." Kusch reflects on the exchange.

Evidently the grandfather does not complete all the stages of understanding. The problem of understanding, according to our Western point of view, seems to have four stages. First, a reality that is given outside of us. Second, an understanding of that reality. Third, a knowledge or science that is the outcome of the administration of understandings, and fourth, an action that returns to reality in order to modify it.

For Kusch, indigenous thinking has an affective content and does not posit an external reality as Western thinking does. According to him, the indigenous approach, with its reliance on magical ritual and its seeming passivity, is generally treated with contempt by the middle class, the city-dweller, the Westernized intellectual. "We wield ignorance like a metric stick which measures what those of us in the middle class have and what the peasant lacks, but which does not reveal what really is the case with the latter. This is because the peasant's personality, just like his cultural world, rotates around a different axis." Kusch reads the contempt of the urban middle class in psychological terms. He suggests that Westernized Latin Americans feel vulnerable when faced with bald rejection of their way of reasoning. Feeling dispossessed, they develop a tendency to condemn the indigenous people as ignorant, instead of reflecting on their sense of dispossession.

Kusch, too, feels dispossessed of his own techniques of understanding, but he does not deprecate the indigenous people. Rather, he begins to think about knowledge and understanding as such, and the interaction or opposition between the way a city dweller copes and how an indigenous person confronts a problem posed by reality. For Kusch, the Western technique of making an appeal to an external reality does not fare well in the comparison. In this way, the interaction between the *abuelo* and Kusch's students indicates not merely the differences in understanding the world and the way in which the indigenous practices are dismissed. Ultimately, Kusch frames the interaction within a broader picture of a dilemma facing the entire continent: "Here one can adumbrate the crisis, not of the Indian, but our own." Drawing this larger conclusion is of a piece with his method. Kusch sees the continent as marked by a basic cognitive split that anticipates a certain crisis, a crossroads. This moment can be evaded, or it can be embraced. Kusch does not appeal to facile techniques to reject or reduce indigenous people. Instead he takes his own sense of dispossession as the occasion for dwelling on that moment and for trying to get inside the indigenous framework of understanding and interacting with the world, and to see it in terms of a larger divide.

It is important to note that on his journey, Kusch does not attempt to translate indigenous culture or to try to make it transparent to the Western reader. This is one way in which he is not engaged in the conventional anthropological task of rendering the foreign in familiar terms. As he retells myths, explains symbols, and interprets customs, they retain some of their opacity. In this sense, his descriptions are not so much an ethnographic inventory as an insertion without translating himself to the familiar. He is not offering us an ethnographic, archaeological, or otherwise social-science description of Andean life. He is not attempting to offer an understanding of the Andean cosmos in terms that fulfill the requirements of Western rationality. Rather, he inhabits the Andean culture and cosmos and indigenous life in its density, and seeks to dwell on the questions, paths, possibilities that do not yield easily to Western philosophy and its requirements. He is rejecting in part the rationality of a Western cosmology preoccupied with causes and explanations. What he gives us instead is a record of his attempt to work into another world and worldview. This world is not entirely other, since Kusch is Latin American. His access to its wellsprings, however, is clogged and blocked by his training as an intellectual.

The consequent methodology he fashions as part of this journey contains elements that resemble the conventional notion of the "field" in ethnographic work. In fact, he does fieldwork by going to speak with and observe indigenous people, witches, and mestizos in Peru, Bolivia, and Argentina. He questions them about their agricultural practices, their economic decisions; he observes rituals; he asks women in the market the meaning of indigenous talismans; he interviews shamans; he describes the spatial arrangement and the contents of shrines, altars, and temples; and he reproduces diagrams of archaeological sites, which he then interprets at length. Yet the fieldwork does not treat all of these things as objects for ethnographic explanation. The part of his research that appears to be ethnographic inquiry is a manner of probing and entering an indigenous way of working. The result is not a text that retains the aim of representing a "them" to a putative "us." It is not a representation.

Nor does he paint his work as indigenous philosophy: Kusch points out that his questions are not what indigenous people might ask, nor is the knowledge he generates indigenous knowledge; rather, it is *of* indigenous knowledge. Drawing on that knowledge, he challenges the organization of the social, of the subject, the externalization of life. By a difficult and tortured path, he comes to challenge his own intellectual inheritance as an intellectual of German descent from Buenos Aires.

From that position, outside of conventional disciplinary knowledge, he poses questions of Western understanding. Thus, Kusch offers his description not as an enhancement, supplement, or adjunct to Western philoso-

phy, nor as an analogous or homologous system of "indigenous philosophy" in counterpart to European or Western systems. Instead, he discusses
indigenous thinking as a way of living that spans many domains that are
usually separate within the West: metaphysics, religion, epistemology,
everyday practices, the realm of the emotions, the body, ontology, technology, physics (causality, matter), time (the past, the future), the subjective
and the objective, the relation to the natural world (earth, animals, natural
history, and so on). Indigenous life is not conceived in terms of separate
domains in this sense. As Kusch understands them, some of the practices,
conventions, and tendencies associated with Western social science and
philosophy are irrelevant within indigenous thinking, such as the formulation of hypotheses; striving to universal claims; the very practice of making abstract claims; defining, verifying, and so on. In this sense, Kusch's
intervention is transdisciplinary. It challenges the terms by which "philosophy," "anthropology," "psychology," and other disciplines operate and are
constituted. Kusch disrupts the policing of knowledge-borders that define
the disciplines.

Yet his work is also, crucially, not just an intervention in the realm of
abstract knowledge. Because many of the Western practices speak to
another, external reality, they block a way of knowing and living that takes
in the cosmos in its terrible and fecund possibilities. Indigenous thinking
is a way of living in which people govern their lives in an affectively rich,
often tense engagement with the material world around them by performing rituals, through which they seek to hold off the overturn. It is a
practical knowledge that determines activities of the everyday.

Kusch's approach to that knowledge marks the inroad to a different way
of thinking and being that precisely does not follow the rules, logics, and
reasons of Western social science and philosophy. He enters alternative
logics, ways of being and thinking, through the concrete, the specific, the
detail, and, significantly, through what he learns from exchanges with the
indigenous peoples he highlights, including deracinated rural people living in the capital. He explores his own initial ambivalence, and the psychologically convoluted justifications the middle class has to vindicate the
idea of progress.

Our translation, correspondingly, seeks to resist the impulse to "translate" Kusch by making him into either an ethnographer or a philosopher in
the Western disciplinary sense. To give in to the tendency to read Kusch as

an ethnographer is to translate his work into something that is in great tension with his own sense of the project.

AMÉRICA

Why retain the accent in *América*? When Kusch describes "América," he depicts a repressed reality, a form of thinking that furnishes and connotes the authentic but suppressed experience of millions of people in their everyday lives. We have kept *América* because the accent marks a difference from what would be known and familiar to the English-language reader. It provides a certain textual resistance to the reader, a defamiliarization with the continent as she or he knows it. The accent makes the word, and its referent, harder to assimilate to a pre-existing understanding of this continent. Like a fish bone, the accent may make the text a bit harder to digest, which is our intention, just as the thinking itself cannot be absorbed by a body that wants to enrich itself through the obliteration of all traces of this other thinking.[8]

América for Kusch houses a metaphysic, a form of life that moves according to its own rhythm. In keeping with his desire to uncover, we would like to expand the conceptual possibilities in English for this *other* América without incorporating it within a dominant understanding of the continent. Some of the alternatives for translating the term *América* bear this out. Despite Los Tigres del Norte's biting admonition that "somos todos americanos," *America* in English too often connotes the United States, and *Americans* is usually taken to mean people from the United States, often in contrast to people from other parts of the continent, as in, "We're not Mexicans, we're Americans." Since Kusch emphasizes his own criticism of and departure from North American philosophy and theory, this rendering would deceive.

Although *Latin America* would seem to capture Kusch's attempt to seat his text primarily within Latin America, the term has clear problems. For example, Kusch approvingly cites Whorf on the Hopi, a group indigenous to what is now North America, yet the Hopi are clearly included in Kusch's *América*. Furthermore, Kusch contrasts indigenous thinking to the urban, middle class of Lima or Buenos Aires, but these groups are obviously Latin Americans; the contrast between the urban and the indigenous, the founding and fundamental distinction in *Indigenous and Popular Thinking in*

América, would be compromised if we rendered *América* as *Latin America*. Finally, non-indigenous North Americans have an ambiguous status in Kusch's text. Though Kusch argues that North American thinking, like European thinking, is an imposition, it is not entirely clear whether or how North Americans themselves fit in. Rendering *América* as "Latin America" would dissipate this ambiguity and exclude North Americans.

We also contemplated translating *América* as "the Americas." Presumably, this would have included the entire continent. However, *the Americas* is embedded in a European optic of the continent, and perhaps preserves the antiquated tone which suggests European "discovery" of new lands. *América*, on the other hand, keeps the reader within another optic, an alternative set of perceptions and understandings that the English reader must grope for, because *América* is not so readily within one's grasp.

Rodolfo Kusch with the monolith in Tiahuanaco, Bolivia.

PROLOGUE TO THE THIRD EDITION

This book was edited at different times, each to an extent significant, as expressed by the dates: Mexico, 1970; Buenos Aires, 1973; and now the present edition, which also issues from Buenos Aires.[1] These have all been moments of internal tension. Today, in a way, we are again facing the same thing. Since then, leftist, right-wing, and centrist models have followed each other. One of them even has its own date. Someone called it the 80s model.

This merits reflection. We Argentinians seem to be model pariahs. Instead of being the creators of models, we search for them with an eagerness to inhabit them. The geocultural structure of the country, dominated from Buenos Aires, permits the installation of a fair of models. An adequate model for the country is always known from the Rio de la Plata, the operating assumption being that the country is empty. It is possible that this book's attempt is to sketch one more model. But it is nothing more and nothing else than the one suggested by a millenarian América that sends us from the Bolivian people, within the center of South América, to Buenos Aires. It is the model of the peasant pueblo of the Argentinian Northwest; the one of the East or of the marginal people of Buenos Aires, and it is also the one carried throughout our history, without ever succeeding in becoming explicit. It may not be a model completely. Maybe it is a lot more: maybe it is our root or our foundation.

It is also possible that this question of a foundation is no more than an archetype. The concept of root or foundation, so much used in philosophy, always incarnates the darkness or the shadow that follows us and that seems to dominate our daily world. But even if it belongs within the domain of the hypothetical, it allows giving a structure to thinking.

But even if the popular and the Américan constitute an archetype, and no more than a simple model at that, it has to be for Argentinians really a foundation. At least that would correct the rhetorical excess, the pompous brilliance of acquired ideas, the evasive modelism of so many leaders, the imported pseudo-efficiency of so many others, all motivated by an unjustified feeling that the country is empty. It could lead us to embark, in the end, on a rigorous examination of our true roots.

Because without question, we must have roots, even as a hypothetical. Because if we do not have roots, and the book that follows is a lie, the mere act of examining them would lead us to recover our own countenance. We would avoid the easy masks and we would create an authentic country.

If this is all that the analysis of popular thinking could accomplish, it would already be a great deal, even for those who believe that everything popular deserves contemptuous pity.

But the fact is that the pueblo exists. It is not my fault. And it is not my fault either that its thinking continues relentlessly to fill the country until we really become a nation.

PROLOGUE TO THE FIRST EDITION

The search for an indigenous way of thinking is motivated not only by the desire to uncover it scientifically, but by the need to rescue a style of thinking which, as I see it, is found in the very depth of América and that maintains a certain potency among people born and rooted here.[1]

This responds to an old preoccupation. Already in *América Profunda* I analyzed pre-Columbian religious ideas; in *De la mala vida porteña* I tried to explore the survival of this style of thinking in large cities like Buenos Aires; and now I try to clarify indigenous thinking itself, particularly given my research during my last trip to the Andean Highlands, in the second half of 1967, when I was able to gather significant material.

The recuperation of an indigenous way of thinking is important because it opens up the understanding of this América populated of late by disparate ideologies: to judge our problems from the supposedly scientific point of view, like that of the sociologists, economists, or of those overly limited branches of Marxism; to presuppose democratic ideals where it is not appropriate; or simply to assume predetermined forms of religiosity. All of that lacks meaning because it never tells the truth. In reality, these are the channels through which Américans funnel their opinions without noticing that the orientation they give to their thinking constitutes the main barrier to under-

standing the real way of life to which they belong. Questionnaires, dialectical Marxism, public education, universal suffrage, or spiritual values are the
slogans of an active América, but at base they are nothing but the thinking
of an enterprising middle class, situated in the coastal cities of the continent. Opposed to them stand a relatively inert and hostile pueblo, or
segregated indigenous people, who seem to resist that active posture.[2]
Besides, the ideals mentioned above are different aspects of the thinking of
a bourgeoisie in crisis, in which I gladly include the most extreme of
utopian revolutionaries as well as the most enterprising of progressives.
The one and the other are segregated—and history shows this—from and
by something that breathes within the continent itself.

That is why, when a peasant does not want to know anything about
Marxism or development, it is not because of ignorance or underdevelopment. We wield ignorance like a metric stick which measures what those of
us in the middle class have and what the peasant lacks, but which does not
reveal what really is the case with the latter. This is because the peasant's
personality, just like his cultural world, rotates around a different axis.[3]

In the present work I did not want to take into account the latest
contributions of anthropology and psychology. These, whether Levi-
Strauss's structuralism, or Jung's archetypes, to cite two examples, are not
totally convincing. They are useful only after observation justifies their
use. I say this because the former responds to the rather intellectualist
vision of French culture that prefers to see the clear and distinct results of
structures instead of following the laborious and epic dynamism that
promotes them. The intellectualization of French culture goes hand-in-
hand with a total lack of vital ideals. In addition, Jung brandishes archetypes only to revitalize an exhausted European bourgeoisie. Both of them
end up being parlor games, in a certain way useless, because neither
restores faith in the face of the crisis of vitality, particularly our own. To
entertain oneself with structuralism or with deep psychology, or with their
successors, like Mircea Eliade and so many others, is at this time in
Argentina one of the most efficacious of entertainments, maybe because of
the belief that one is playing with the ultimate explanation of the world.

Much more important than the foreign instrument is the work of the
Mexican León Portilla on Náhuatl philosophy. I think this author offers us
a very clear method—although I have tried to widen it with fieldwork. I
have done so not only because of the absence of Quechua and Aymara

texts, but also to verify the observations made as a result of the analysis of the few Quechua hymns that have been preserved.

But I could not limit this work to exhuming indigenous thinking. I think this thinking opens our understanding of the problems of América; thus, the second part of the book is devoted to weighing the possibilities this thinking offers. That is why I insist on the opposition between the urban and the indigenous styles of thinking, to the point of distinguishing between a seminal thinking and a causal one, a distinction not difficult to confirm even within modern philosophical Western thinking.

What could not be absent in this work is a sketch of an Américan thinking that turns on the concept of *estar*. I believe this term succeeds in concretizing the true way of life of our América, including white and brown people alike, and that offers an unexpected richness from a phenomenological point of view. Implicit in this term is that Américan peculiarity which could ground our reaching our true place, rather than that burdensome universality to which we all pointlessly aspire.

INDIGENOUS AND POPULAR THINKING IN AMÉRICA

In América we treat philosophy in one of two ways, an official way and a private way. From the university we learn of a European problematic translated philosophically. The other is an implicit way of thinking lived every day in the street or in the countryside. Félix Schwartzmann had already hoped to resolve this problem in his book *El sentimiento de lo humano en América*, where he notes that a philosophy typical of América at this point exists only in poetry and in the novel, as he demonstrates in his analysis of Pablo Neruda's work and of the Brazilian novel.[1]

Clearly, the issue is not to negate Western philosophy, but to look for a formulation closer to our own lives. When Kant enunciates his theory of knowledge, he does so because it was necessary at that moment. The same is true of Hegel, who expresses the intimate feeling of the German bourgeoisie of his time. Descartes had thought his *cogito ergo sum* because the century of Richelieu, with its reason of state, demanded it. European thinking, as Dilthey has so ably demonstrated, always linked itself to a way of life. In this sense philosophy has the same degree of receptivity as art and religion.

It is also true that Nicolai Hartmann was not in agreement with this approach. But his defense of a philosophical "science" is nothing but the ideal of every philosophy professor. It is true that a harmonious and coherent doctrine fits the nature of teaching. Yet every generation demands, in spite of what Hartmann may think, the philosophical conceptualization of its particular sense of life.

But this is what is so weighty. In order to carry out such a conceptualization, it is necessary not just to know philosophy, but above all—and this is very important—to face reality abiding a degree of distortion few can sustain. To investigate daily life in order to translate it into thinking is a dangerous venture, since it is necessary, particularly here in América, to make the grave mistake of contradicting the frameworks to which we are attached.

Colloquia on indigenous thinking in some Andean universities evidence this tendency. It is not possible to begin the rescue of Inca thinking with, for example, a philosophical attitude still entangled in a Comtean system of a hundred years ago, or with a phenomenology studied only so as to be repeated in the university classroom. All that would result from this practice is a version of Inca thinking entangled in the researchers' fear of overcoming their own philosophical prejudices.

And if we ourselves still cleave to this perception; if we are used to invoking a comfortable and worn positivism—and to this we add contemporary North American neopositivism—the work of translating our life into philosophy becomes doubly unrewarding.

And let me add one more thing. A uniform way of life does not exist in América. The ways of life of the Indian and the well-off city dweller are impermeable to each other. On the one hand, the Indian retains the structure of an ancient form of thinking, a thousand years old, and on the other, the city dweller renews his way of thinking every ten years.

If Europe has succeeded in solidifying a philosophy, it has been because since the end of the Middle Ages it established a relatively homogeneous social body, in spite of Tönnies's theory of the transition from community to society.[2] Evidently, an elite has promoted that specific manner of thinking and was able to make it official without further ado. We should not forget here the "School of Wisdom" in which the principal German thinkers of the first half of the twentieth century participated.

What to do, then, in América? I have never before seen with such clarity the radical contrast that runs through everything Américan as when I examined the curious map of Perú drawn by the chronicler Guaman Poma.[3] It is oval shaped, and in its center one finds four couples ruling the

1   Map of Perú, according to Guaman Poma.

four cardinal points, with a sun and a moon presiding over the picture and a series of monsters disseminated throughout its contours (figure 1). Such a map is today discarded as something "subjective," and considered incommensurate with a modern map of Perú, scientifically in sync with reality.

What Guaman Poma drew does not accord with reality, but it does encapsulate all of its Indian and Inca inheritance; and whether one likes it or not, it is *his* map—the real habitat of his community, we are tempted to say. In this sense his four ruling couples, presiding over the four zones of the old Tahuantinsuyu, symbolize the maternal protection within which the ancient Indian found himself sheltered. In the final analysis, the Perú Guaman Poma traversed must have been the one reflected in his map and not the one plotted by contemporary science. If we take this into consideration, can we reject without further ado the "subjectivity" contained in his drawing? Furthermore, a map of Perú made with modern instruments will be real, but it will have nothing to do with what Peruvians think of their country. It is an impersonal map, produced by the anonymity of science, and statistically accepted by the majority, but it is not *my* country, the one each person lives daily.

Geographically, it is possible to plot a map from the *scientific* angle while living in another country. Such cannot be done in philosophy. That is because philosophy manifests itself as a translation of a subjectivity—such as Guaman Poma's—to a conceptual level, according to a jargon minted by the academy and upheld even when it contradicts the rigidity of scientific formulations. I think América oscillates to a great extent between two things: a candid subjectivity that affects all of us and that follows a downward path to the simple formulation "it seems to me" and the scientific attitude whose rigidity is used precisely to mask in each of us a subjectivity we do not succeed in channeling. Let us think about the pressure exerted on our interiority by an imported culture, and the importance of that interiority in the elaboration of a culture that is our own.

That same pressure in Argentina does nothing more than perpetuate and legitimate a way of thinking which has been meticulously imported, perhaps due to the absence of a *pueblo* who would challenge it with its own formulations. But is it different in the rest of América? Can the resounding opposition between indigenous people and the bourgeoisie give rise to an autochthonous way of thinking?

The real distance between an indigenous way of thinking and a way of thinking consistent with traditional philosophy is the same as that between the Aymara term *utcatha* and the German term *Da-sein*. Heidegger takes up this word from ordinary German speech, first because *Sein* signifies *being* (*ser*)—which allowed him to take up again the themes of traditional ontology—and second because *Da*—which means "there"—signaled the *circumstance* into which being had fallen. Heidegger's problematic is centered on an awareness of a diminished being, a *thrown* being. His merit lies in having taken up in the twentieth century the theme of being with an exactitude that befitted the lives of the German middle class. This class had always felt the fall of being as its own, with all of the anguish that implies. If we add to it the concepts of time and authenticity, we notice that a thematic so threaded is not so far from the thinking of a European bourgeoisie which feels the crisis of the individual and tries to remedy it.

It is different among the Aymara. An equivalent to *Da-sein* might be *cancaña*. According to Bertonio, *cancaña* means "barbecue spit, being, or essence"; it is also linked to "flow of events."[4] But the term *utcatha* is much closer to the indigenous sensibility. Bertonio translates *utcatha* as "estar."[5] Moreover, it appears to carry in the first syllable a contraction of the term *uta*, or dwelling, which would link it to the concept *domo*—that is *domicile* or *being-in-the-house* (*estar en casa*)—so vilified by Heidegger and Gusdorf. It also means "to be sitting down," which paradoxically takes us to *sedere* which is the source of the Spanish word *being* (*ser*). Finally, Bertonio mentions the form *utcaña*, "the seat or chair and also the mother or womb where woman conceives."[6] In short, the meanings of *utcatha* reflect the concept of a mere givenness or, even better, of a mere *estar*, but linked to the concept of shelter and germination.

The depth of feeling of an Indian when he is on Buenos Aires Street in La Paz and decides to take a bus to his *ayllu* must be understood in terms of *utcatha* and not *Da-sein*. That is, he will inhabit his mere *estar* and under no conditions will feel the fall of any being (*ser*). Why? Because it appears that in that mere *estar* of *utcatha*, another element is present, which Bertonio points to when he transcribes a related term, namely, *ut.ttaatha*, "to exhibit or take things out to sell . . . in the *plaza*."[7] Here the concept of *plaza* has an evident archetypal sense from the point of view of deep psychology since it is a symbol of the center of a world plotted in a magic plan—*my* world—the same one that Guaman Poma plots when he draws the map of Perú with the four couples that govern it. It is the existential and vital world of Guaman Poma and of the Indian in general that consequently has little or nothing to do with the *real* world detected by science, but rather with the *reality* lived daily by each person. And now the question can be posed: is this preference for the real which comes from a full feeling of *estar no más* [mere *estar*]—is this not perhaps profoundly Américan—something in which both Indians and whites participate?

It is evident that a way of thinking sparked by a term like *utcatha* will not lead to a philosophy in the sense in which we understand that term today, but rather to a strict "love of wisdom." That is why it will not give rise to a theory of knowledge, but rather to a doctrine of contemplation.[8] Terms such as *sasitha*, which Bertonio translates as "fasting in the manner of gentiles,"[9] or *amuchatha*, "to remember,"[10] whose first part, *amu*, or flower, also has a deep meaning in the psychology of the unconscious, seem to corroborate that the contemplative attitude toward the world predominates in indigenous thinking.[11]

2   The indigenous
philosopher,
according to
Guaman Poma.

Now, if all of this were true, it would be fitting to pose the following question: if our role as middle class intellectuals is to lead the thinking of a nation, do we really have the freedom to adopt any philosophy? In sum, what is our mission? Will it consist in representing and sifting through the depth of the sensibility of our people, or does it consist simply in lodging ourselves in its periphery, retaining specializations our people do not require? Evidently, this is the paradox that the philosophical task poses when it is taken in its depth.

But it is not a question of advocating a rabid philosophical folklorism, because if we did that we would be exposing a great weakness. It is instead a question of understanding freely our South Américan truth, which to our excessively schematic mind as middle-class intellectuals turns out to be surprising and unexpected from every point of view. Comprehending the "meaning" of South Américan life requires overcoming the barriers we have placed in its way. It is necessary to think at the margins of the categories of economics, of civilization, or of culture, and to recover, in sum, that wonderful ingenuousness of a Guaman Poma when he describes his philosopher (figure 2): "Indian astrologer-poet who knows the flight of the Sun and the Moon, and the clip (eclipse) and the stars and comets— day Sunday month and year and of the four winds of the gold world to sow foodstuffs since antiquity. Indians, the Indian philosophers / astrologers who know the hours and the Sundays and days and months year to plant and harvest each year's food."[12] Of course it will not be a knowledge of the "eclipse" nor of the "flight of the Sun and the Moon," but it will be— and this is completely equivalent—the recovery of a consciousness of unity among those deep contradictions that in América tear us apart politically, culturally, and in our everyday life.

The indigenous family compound was an *ayllu*, or Aymara community dependent on Toledo, situated close to Oruro (Bolivia), squarely in the Andean highlands. It included just a square adobe house and two *putucus*, or cylindrical constructions of the same material, all joined by a *pirca*, or wall, also made of adobe. We had arrived there with some students to conduct our fieldwork, and we succeeded in making connections with the Halcón family who inhabited it. The family was composed of the grandfather, his son, the son's wife and three children.

The grandfather caught my attention. He was leaning on the adobe *pirca* and was looking into the distance as we pestered him with questions. It was really the son who talked with us. He knew Spanish, so probably he had done his military service. He showed a degree of self-confidence. The interview in itself was average, though it was a bit slow and arduous. Once in a while the grandfather would turn and answer our questions with a smile. A smile can be useful when one does not want to say what one is really thinking and generally when one does not want to speak. But he showed goodwill. One could even say that given our questions, he took the effort to probe regions of his memory to give us the information we needed.

He informed us about the system of reciprocity (*ayni*), the *ayllu*, or community, and a thousand other things. But in reality he did not want to speak. He eventually began giving abbreviated replies. I remember his gaze as he returned to leaning on the *pirca*. He seemed to be saying to himself with a certain smugness, "Why is there a need to ask so many questions?" Besides, he must have been wholly preoccupied with his own concrete labor on his farm. He remarked, for example, that the earth had yielded very large potatoes in the past and that today that was no longer true, that before it used to rain more than now, and that before, everything was better. The world had gotten old with him.

It seemed pointless to keep asking questions. I had the reaction most people have in those kinds of cases. Indigenous people like the grandfather do not have any reason to become conscious of their customs, since they do not even know where the customs come from. They think only that they must be followed when the circumstances require it. Thus, the interview tended to be disorganized. The grandfather became fatigued, as was to be expected if one thinks that the questions required a great deal of effort from him.

But at that moment we found ourselves in a peculiar situation provoked by some members of our group. Someone took the initiative and asked the grandfather why he did not buy a hydraulic pump. His face became more impenetrable. Several institutions could help him. Surely he could make an agreement with his neighbors and they could pool together, buy the pump, and in easy installments, shared by all, it would be paid for in short order.

I looked around. The Andean plateau was dry and arid, the sheep thin. That was reason enough to buy the pump. We told him that the pump "would help you" and "it will fatten your herd." "Go to Oruro and stop by the Agricultural Extension Office." The grandfather did not answer. The son, to be agreeable, answered between clenched teeth: "Yes, we are going to go." Then a heavy silence. The grandfather kept on looking at the Puna. What was he looking at?

There was nothing left to ask and nothing left to propose. We left. In the distance we saw how the sky weighed on the *putucus*. What was the grandfather thinking? Maybe the son would try to convince him and would tell him: "Grandfather, we are in another time, these things are necessary. The *gringos* are right." But the grandfather would chew some coca, would offer some of his alcohol to the earth, and would not answer.[1]

What's more, he would surely think that to produce rain one of the common rituals like the *Gloria Misa* or the *Huilancha* would be cheaper and much more reliable.[2]

What are we to think? The grandfather belongs to a world in which the hydraulic pump lacks meaning, given that the grandfather relied on his own resources, such as ritual. Now, if this is true, the border between him and us appears immovable. Evidently, our tools do not cross easily to the other side. I remember that we were barely a meter away from him, but the distance between us was much greater.

Somebody, scandalized by the grandfather's attitude, called him ignorant. That is what we usually say in those cases. Why? Because naturally if he knew or simply *saw* the reality around him, he would be forced to buy the pump. The question for us rests on *understanding (conocer)*.[3] That is why a good literacy program would lead the grandfather to *understand* reality and therefore to buy the pump. Nevertheless, it is at this point that the grandfather would insist on having the *Gloria Misa* or the *Huilancha* to make a propitiatory offering so as to improve his land and his herd.

Evidently the grandfather does not complete all the stages of understanding. The problem of understanding, according to our Western point of view, seems to have four stages. First, a *reality* that is given *outside of* us. Second, an *understanding* of that reality. Third, a *knowledge* or *science* that is the outcome of the administration of understandings, and fourth, an *action* that returns to reality in order to modify it.[4] This is, in the end, the Western attitude from the fourteenth and fifteenth centuries onward, from Bacon's *Novum Organum* to the European Industrial Revolution, and it is also the feeling of the United States at this moment. They are also the principles of any given middle class situated on the Atlantic border of South América. We are speaking of four moments that enclose the ideal that everything is *outside* and that in order to resolve our problems, we must appeal to the external world.

Why didn't the grandfather do that? Is it that he did not find the solution *outside*? If we want to theorize, we would say that his understanding does not end in action; that is, it is not finalized in the external world, because he substituted the hydraulic pump with a ritual. He does not fulfill those four moments of the problem of understanding we enunciated above. But what does the Indian understand by *reality*, by *understanding*, by *knowledge*, and by *action*?

For us, reality is populated by objects. The term *object*, given its etymology, seems to be related to a *throwing in front, ob-jacio*, which implies placing a reality before the subject in a way that is to some extent voluntary. And what of the indigenous world? It appears to be different. Bertonio in his Aymara vocabulary from the sixteenth century indicates the terms *yaa* and *cunasa* as translations of *thing*.[5] *Cunasa* refers to "anything." *Yaa*, on the other hand, is related to "things of gods, of men, etc." Furthermore, it is used for an "abominable thing," *huati yaa, yancca yaa*, or "a thing of esteem," *haccu yaa*. One could say then that for indigenous people there are no things in themselves. They are, rather, always referred to in terms of their favorable or unfavorable aspects. It is not objects in themselves that are interesting, but their auspicious and inauspicious aspects.[6]

And this should not be strange. What the researcher Whorf says about the Hopi—that their language tends to register events rather than things—fits the Aymara just as well as it fits the Quechua. European languages on the other hand register things rather than events.[7] This is confirmed by Bertonio when he says in the prologue to the first part of his *Aymara Vocabulary* that the Indian does not look "so much to the effect as to the way of doing." For example, the form of the verb *to carry* in the Aymara tongue depends on "whether the thing carried is a person or a beast or whether the thing is long, heavy, or light."[8]

Now, what does it mean that in one language movement, events, the process of becoming are registered before things? Bertonio mentions "the way of doing" something and not the doing itself taken as an abstract concept. This indicates the predominance of emotional feeling over the act of seeing itself, in such a way that one *sees* to *feel*. Emotion is what drives one in the face of reality. The indigenous person takes reality not as something stable and inhabited by objects. Rather, he takes it as a screen without things but with intense movement in which he tends to notice the auspicious or ominous sign of each and every movement before anything else.[9] The indigenous person registers reality as the affect it exercises on him before registering it as simple perceptual connotation.

This must be the reason why in Aymara the term *understanding* does not have meanings similar to ours. Bertonio records as "understanding" the term *ullttatha* (to understand) but links *ullsutha* with "looking out," and then adds *ullattatha* as "to understand something" and also as "to point with a harquebus."[10] This term can also probably be connected to *ullinaca,* "the visage, figure, aspect, face."[11] It is also probable that in Aymara one finds a distinction similar to the one that exists in Nahuatl between a knowledge of the face and a knowledge of the heart.[12] The same seems to hold true of Quechua. Holguín records in his vocabulary the term *riccini,* generally used to refer to an understanding of people prior to an understanding of things.[13] But it is as if it were a question of an understanding of *publicity,* as Heidegger would say, referring to the community. And this would be accurate, given that the indigenous person is always deeply linked to community.

But it is natural that where there is no conceptual order of objects, there is also no understanding, with all that that implies, at least in the terms of Western thinking. This leads us to notice that the moments referred to above, which form part of the parable of understanding within a Western problematic, are proper to it and are not found in the indigenous world.

The Indian is not, then, the photographic subject, as Whaelens would have it, but rather he participates in understanding, and in greater measure than we do. His knowledge is not of a reality constituted by objects, but one full of movements or happenings.

The indigenous people will understand the sown land, the sickness of the llama, the breaking loose of the hailstorm, but the consequence of this understanding is different. And that, which is due to his own style of life, leads him neither to enter reality impetuously nor to foreground the will in his sense of life. That is why that grandfather did not want to go to the Agrarian Extension Office to buy a hydraulic pump. He does not see the solution to his problems outside of himself. And what happens to us? Why do we see the solution to our problems *outside* of ourselves? What is given outside?

Let's examine one more time our Western point of view on *understanding.* From Kant to Nicolai Hartman, the problem of understanding was given serious consideration. That led to magnifying the problem, but always in accordance with the true meaning assigned to it by our style of life. Above all, since Kant, the incipient Industrial Revolution underlies the truth of the philosophical problem of understanding. This revolution consists in installing and mobilizing a world of objects *outside* a subject. That is why, from simple sickness to the vicissitudes of our physical and spiritual life, we always find the solution or the *reason in this outside.* And an *outside* is always given: from the simple *reason* that explains to me the cause of my sorrow to a large administrative issue that could become concretized in an Agricultural Extension Office. We live as if a manageable reality plagued by causes were given to us with our lives as a *plus*. And our urban task consists in compensating on the *outside*, with the *plus* any lack of balance produced inside ourselves. Furthermore, any interior imbalance is confidently attributed to some failure on the outside. That is why, when someone like the grandfather appears who does not want that which is given *outside*, we experience a certain depression.

Understanding, moreover, does not even consist in recovering outside information about an object. It is, rather, reduced to a kind of compensation from the *outside* that does not refer to the reality of science but only to the management of remedies for our personal needs. To understand that which one sees and to see that which we need is to some extent the enigma of our life in the South Américan urban world. That is why it is not a question of understanding the world, as Whaelens says, as if it were an immense spectacle. It is not a question of the world in general, but rather only of the gadgets, drugs, and the management of them that will save us. To understand is to open oneself to a specific world in order to search for a compensation for our ills, and action is only useful to construct that specific world and in no way to *change* the world.

Now then, the grandfather does not work on the *outside* and we do. And what do we do then if our tools are not accepted? I remember the sensation we experienced when the grandfather answered us evasively. Our condition as researchers did allow us to take that attitude into account. But the truth is that we were invaded by a sensation of dispossession. Why? It is because the grandfather obliged us to move from the level of a self—one that offers objects and develops a system of compensation with that which is given outside and that knows how to manage the compensatory *plus* to benefit one's own life—to a lower level in which we feel simply helpless.

It is in the end the common experience in the Andean Highlands that generates that climate of hopelessness when faced with the Indian. In the face of this, we only have as a last recourse to classify the grandfather as illiterate. But even then we come up short. Isn't a pejorative qualifier like "illiterate" a magical means to subjugate the indigenous people? When we notice our dispossession, it is not we who modify reality, but rather reality, embodied in the Indian, that modifies us. And then the insult is our last recourse to reestablish the sense of our world. But this happens when we feel trapped, almost like a return to a womb. Here, to say *illiterate* is as if we said deep down "Look, grandfather, we were taught that hydraulic pumps are important. We beg you to accept them. Think about it, what would we do if you don't?"

Here we go back many years in history, as if there had been no evolution, because of the curious strength indigenous people put out in reducing our offerings to nothing. And it is useless for us to say that four hundred years of domination, colonial first and republican afterward, have brought them to that state. They could also ask us in turn, What have you achieved in those four hundred years? Perhaps you really dominate reality? And they would be right. In the end we have not resolved a problem of understanding but a problem of management. We have only managed European understandings and have turned them into an external *plus* so that we could be compensated. And offices and objects and professionals create the possibility of finding our balance. We think that all of that belongs to an epic of humanity with which we have little to do. We only use it.

The proof is that it really did not ever occur to any of us doing our fieldwork to modify reality, given that, in the end, none of us had invented the hydraulic pump. Even worse, we had simply used the referral to an office which seemed to be in charge of such modifications of reality. With that allusion we achieved peace. But it was no more than a simple allusion. In the end, it was the same as the one the grandfather made. He appealed to a ritual coined by his own culture. We resorted to a tool coined by the West. In this sense, the *huilancha* and the hydraulic pump were equivalent.

But our reference was a bit more *impersonal*: a simple office. The grandfather's on the other hand was *personal*. A ritual shows a commitment; an office does not. The remedy proposed by us depended on the technician's impersonal way of installing the pump. Now, to justify a life, which one was better? Is it better to use ways that commit one's self or ways that do not entail commitment?

Here one can adumbrate the crisis, not of the Indian, but our own. The grandfather stirred his interiority through the completion of the ritual without making appeal to an external solution. We returned home to what civilization has offered us, but we could only stir our own interiority with difficulty. We understand no other way.

If one has a field, and that field is arid, and one does not want to buy a hydraulic pump to remedy its dryness, then—as we know well—one enters chaos; that is, one enters a social and economic hole of unforeseen calamities. Here, misery, abandonment, in sum, civic death is produced. To avoid this it is necessary to assume a *limit* attitude that consists in evaluating the *objective situation*, such as the dryness of the field, in order to reach the solution. It is a question of reaching that moment in which—once one sees the aridity of the field—one says: "Evidently I take care of this with a hydraulic pump."

At this point I reach equilibrium, a sort of placid retreat, in which I say *that is how it is*, and with that I situate myself, and thus proceed and seek help from the Agricultural Extension Office. My *limit*, in sum, is in the objective situation, and from there I modify reality.

Now, why, instead of modifying reality, would the grandfather appeal to a ritual? Experience tells us that a ritual is not useful in modifying objective reality. In that case, we tend to believe that the grandfather must have another experience according to which reality can be modified through rituals. It is curious that we always attribute to others the understanding of any experience as the manipulation of *external* elements. Is this really the case with the grandfather? But if we think only that the grandfather did not have experiences in this sense, then how can we explain his attitude? Here the following perspective begins to open up: is it that the *limit* situation that he reaches—once he sees that the field is dry— is different from the rather visual, objective, and realist *limit* that we use?

It is a question of knowing what resources the indigenous grandfather uses once he sees the dry field and is satisfied with the simple ritual. Where does he find the ground to affirm *that is how it is*, the affirmative *is* of the formula? Will the Indian grandfather find that *is* in terms of a faculty other than the one we use? In that situation we invoke *reason* and it takes us to the hydraulic pump. And the Indian grandfather, what does he invoke? Surely, it could not be reason.

Once I asked an Indian from Kollana, a community near La Paz, whether in their magic rituals they used *mesas*. I received a strange response. The *mesas* are certain ritual preparations characteristic of and found throughout the Altiplano. They involve sugar, herbs of different kinds, generally with magic properties, ground stones, and other elements.[1] This Indian, who, according to the community teacher, was a *yatiri*, a witch, answered me with an air of self-sufficiency that they did use *mesas*, and he pointed to one in the room. Clearly, he changed the meaning of the word, and instead of the magic utensil, he referred to the piece of furniture.[2]

Naturally, he adopted a cagey attitude. How can we understand that? I take it he wanted to maintain his distance from me, an intrusive, prying *gringo*. One must recall that this community had changed its customs suddenly in the middle of the twentieth century. If before it had been rigidly closed—so much so that strangers were received at gunpoint and thrown out—this was no longer the case.[3] Nowadays, anyone who arrived was welcome, though in a curious way: in this case, through a change in the meaning of the word *mesa*. And that is not necessarily a bad thing. This Indian felt acculturated and had acquired first of all an objectivity such as we understand it, to such an extent that a term like *mesa* could not mean anything other than the piece of furniture. One more step and this Indian would cease to be Indian and would be ready to study symbolic logic. But without a doubt this was all a mask, and he hid from our view that which the grandfather used openly.

It was different in Copacabana, an indigenous family compound close to Toledo. An old Indian had invited us to go into a chapel, common in those compounds, to *present us* to the Virgin. When we sat down to talk, given the questions we were posing, he preferred that we go outside "so that *la Mama* would not hear us and become upset." After talking easily with us for a while, he put his hand in the sack of coca we had given him as a gift and laid out a handkerchief. After examining the coca, he said, "You are burdened with difficulty [*pena*]."[4] He clarified that we should be careful with "our little car," the Citroën in which we had come. It goes without saying that on the way back we had a small mishap.

It seemed to me that this Indian's attitude was freer than that of the one in Kollana, an attitude closer to that of the grandfather. While the one from Kollana simulated objectivity—feeling a stranger to it—the Indian from Copacabana accessed a different register. The one from Kollana was more precise, more perceptive, more intellectual, if you will; instead, the personality of the Indian from Copacabana was of a different modality, one that was to a certain extent the opposite.

What does this different register connote? From the point of view of an analytic psychology, his attitude was not wholly rational, and one could speak of an excess of affectivity. But to characterize it this way is clearly consequential. Lévi-Strauss would not classify it this way, since he is keen on demonstrating that primitive people are capable of using classificatory schemas that are perfectly adequate to *know* their surrounding reality—as apt as our own if not more so.[5] But it is not a question of demonstrating the ability of indigenous people in functions similar to ours. Their whole cultural tradition indicates that the *ability* of indigenous people may reside in the use of a mental function that our Western style of life does not customarily use.

Affectivity, for example, seems to be that function which from our perspective is always seen in a pejorative light. Researchers of the old school are in the habit of stressing affectivity. Bandelier, for example, points to the fear that affects the Aymara. He spends several pages indicating how fear besieges the personality of the Indian.[6] Rigoberto Paredes also refers to this same quality.[7] Tschopik takes this sense of things to an extreme and, as a good North Américan, notes the *anxiety* that affects the Aymara from Chucuito and classifies it meticulously, consequently giving a pejorative picture of indigenous psychology.[8] It is true that a Rorschach test done on the Otomies of Mexico shows the emotional background against which the Indian personality moves. Nevertheless, I think these observations do not emphasize the peculiarity of indigenous psychology, but rather provide evidence of Western prejudices about emotionality.

This urge to pigeonhole emotionality results from a complete lack of knowledge of this aspect of the psyche. Scheler has observed that since Descartes until the eighteenth century, emotional life was considered a confused stage of intellectual life. Kant considered affective acts simply sensuous or chaotic states.[9] Even Scheler himself ends up skirting the question of emotionality in the deep sense, inasmuch as he is interested in the intentionality of emotion to shore up his discussion of personality. Almost all of German Romanticism had already taken up the question of emotion, but only in Scheler's sense. When Heidegger touches on the topic of fear, he distinguishes it from anxiety, indicating that the former leads to flight before something that had made itself frightening by bringing itself close within-the-world.[10]

We might add that emotional life is not even understood in the field of psychology. For example, when the psychiatrist Wolff wants to define emotional life, he only mentions what it provokes, that is, the paralysis of control over rational life, but he does not define it; or more precisely, he defines it negatively.[11] The whole of Freudian psychoanalysis aims to channel emotional life in order to restore the free activity of the patient's intelligence. One could say that Western culture was erected on making emotional life disappear through sleight of hand rather than through overcoming it. This is the case whether the sleight of hand is used to evade the problem or as a way to deflate emotionality in order to restore the free action of intelligence—as is the case in psychoanalysis.

Now, how does the indigenous person face his emotional life? Or, put differently, can he show us other aspects of it, particularly in cases of extreme fear?

Sayres, in an article published in *América Indígena*, points to the psychological problems of the first generation of mestizos born to indigenous parents.[12] They seem to have a *magical fear* of breaking traditional norms in greater measure than their parents, to the point that the number of rituals for *fright* (*asustamiento*) increases. *Fright* is called *mancharisca* in the Andean Altiplano. *Mancharisca* comes from *manchay*, which means "having fear" in Quechua, and is attributed in this case to the loss of spirit.

Valda de Jaime Freyne refers to this when she discusses the Aymara doctrine of the soul. According to her, indigenous people conceive of a soul properly speaking (*jachcha ajayu*); a spirit (*jiska ajayu*) that sticks to everything and thus wears itself out; and finally a *kamasa*, or shadow, also called "courage," and which is generally represented by an animal.[13] I was told in Tiahuanaco that when someone suffers from *susto*, or fright, and manifests symptoms such as fever or delirium, it is said that he has lost the *kamasa*, or courage. It is then necessary to appeal to a ritual.

Morote Best describes how it is in the Quechua world. If the *fright* is not serious, one takes a pinch of dirt from the place the person fell and while consuming the dirt, says "*hampuy*, ánimo . . . *hampuy*" (return, spirit, return). But if the sickness is serious it is cured with a *despacho*. This consists of burning a bundle containing about fifteen different things, among them, tiny bits of lead, condor feathers, colored paper, etc. Once the *despacho* is finished "a patient must lead his cap on the ground with the right hand as if it were a person walking, with the earflaps serving as feet. In the left hand he carries some dirt from the place where the things were burned and a coin worth nine-tenths of a *sol*." He does this while "marching, murmuring the words *hampuy* . . . *hampuy* . . . ánimo. The assistant follows behind with a bowl full of live coals in which incense is burning." What is curious is that in the meantime, "at the sick person's home all lights must be out and all men must remain silent. . . . In the darkness of the dwelling, if one were to turn on the light—which must not be done— one would see a man applying pressure to the forehead of the patient while another man does the same to the toes, while the return of the soul is accomplished."[14]

Relevant here is the description of the same ritual by Dr. Olano, a Peruvian physician. He reports that in his youth he had been diagnosed by an indigenous doctor as suffering from *fright*. In order to cure him the doctor spoke to him with affection: while caressing him, the indigenous doctor recited the following verses in Quechua to effect a return of his spirit: "Why do you go to that dark mansion / Where the Sun does not reach / Where water does not exist! Return! Don't be afraid! Your parents are grieving!"[15]

Now, if we take Sayres's observation that magical fright is a natural consequence of the passage from a "primitive culture" to a "superior culture," we must classify this fear as a simple psychological problem. But, then, in the end we are not explaining anything.

We would draw another inference if we were to consider that indigenous culture constitutes an autonomous and parallel entity to Western culture. In this case it is fitting to affirm that indigenous people have ritual solutions to confront the extreme manifestations of their emotional life, manifestations unknown in the Western world.

That becomes clear in the difficult transition that the first generation studied by Sayres undergoes when it suffers acculturation, from being a culture like the indigenous one which works at the affective level to being another culture which, like the Western one, favors an intellectual level.

More than anything, the indigenous person does not see in affective life the sensuality or chaos that Kant saw, nor the paralysis of control of rational life as the psychiatrist maintains, nor does he feel an urge to overcome emotional life since he does not see it in terms of disintegration as does the man formed in the West. Rather, as he faces and ritualizes his fear, he simply accomplishes something that Western man does not.

Now, if indigenous culture appears to be structured around affect, what are its conceptual values? More precisely, around which concepts does a culture turn whose basis is understood as confronting or ritualizing affectivity? Are those values in total opposition to those of the Western culture of the average urbanite of South América? No doubt the Indian from Kollana confronted his affectivity, but he hid his rituals from me because he was in the midst of the process described by Sayres. The indigenous man from Copacabana, on the other hand, followed the old attitude of facing forthrightly his most ancient fear, as he demonstrated in his handling of the coca. This would also be true of the indigenous grandfather when he substituted the bloody sacrifice for the hydraulic pump. Surely the last two must be deeply connected with their old indigenous culture, even when, as is the case with the Indian from Copacabana, they are operating with a heterogenous cultural content, as embodied in the use of the chapel and the presence of the Virgin.

If the indigenous culture is autonomous and parallel to Western culture, one would expect that it has internal coherence, issuing precisely from the affective background within which it works. In other words, to return to a concrete case, what was the deep motivation or limit that provided safety to that Indian grandfather when he rejected the hydraulic pump? Above all, it cannot be an intellectual motive but an irrational one, and an irrationality frankly embraced.

Holguín records in his Quechua vocabulary of 1608 the term *ucurunan-*

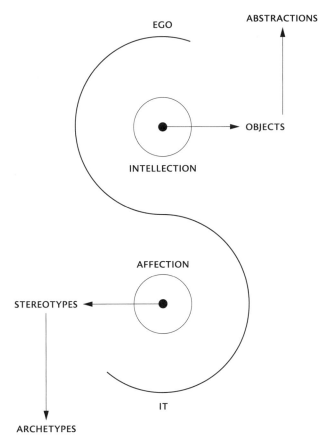

3   The correlation between the inward-directed (*entrancia*) and
the outward-directed (*saliencia*) aspects of the psyche.

chi which he translates as "the interior man or the soul." He opposes it in
the next line to *hahuarunanchi*, "the body, or the exterior man."[16] Bertonio
also points out a similar opposition in Aymara between *manqhue haquessa*
and *alakha haquessa*, respectively.[17] The first term Holguín uses must
surely be *uk'u-runa-nchej*, that is, "our interior man," and the other *hahua-
runa-nchej*, "our exterior man." Apparently this opposition is connected to
the behavior of a subject and whether he hides his decisions.

But why does Holguín record these words in particular, and why does he
record them together? We could think that he sets down the first one,
ucurunanchi, because it provides another sense in Quechua for soul (*alma*),
since he must have been thinking about how to teach the catechism. But

both of them must have been coined in the speech of the Quechua intellectual elite of their time, not only because they indicate two ways of behaving, but also because they refer to an opposition between what today we would call "interior life" and "exterior life." This would seem to be the case because of the presence of the term *uk'u* which means not only "inside" but also "cavity" and, above all, "body," almost as if it were referring to the affectivity that breathes within the cavity.[18]

If this is so, then it makes sense to think that Quechua culture, just like Aymara culture, valued the *interiority* of man taken globally as simply *inside* (*uk'u.*) Now, will this characteristic enable them to grasp with deeper understanding certain aspects of the psyche that we miss? Do indigenous people use different psychic functions from our?

More than anything, the term *uk'u* implies an opening to irrational aspects of personality. These aspects are forthrightly acceptable to a degree comparable to the rational aspects. Perhaps William Stern makes a similar comparison in the field of psychology. He speculates that the emotional aspects of personality are the counterpart or inward direction (*entrancia*) of the intellectual aspects or outward direction (*saliencia*) of personality (figure 3). They constitute moreover the intermediary between that *outward direction* and the deep life of the unconscious.[19] This way of seeing things, which Stern comes to from his structuralist and personalistic viewpoint on the psyche, approximates the psychology implicit in the indigenous world and opens up an understanding of the problem.

Only through the inward direction can one understand indigenous subjectivity. This contradicts the ideal of *objectivity* and the outward direction to which we are accustomed. The inward direction has its own solutions, which we disregard, such as the ritual to confront fright. Only from within inward direction can one understand the total structure of pre-Columbian culture. A structure like the Bennett Monolith cannot be understood on the grounds of a *salida* (a going out) to a world of objects, and even less as a creation of objects, or as an *outward direction* of the personality. Rather, it must be understood as an *inward direction*, facing emotional life in its deepest dimensions until it touches the unconscious with its archetypes.

The same thing happens in interpreting the Codex Borgia. A psychiatrist would always judge it strictly subjective and borderline schizophrenic. That does not keep it from having, to our way of thinking, a certain numinous aspect not usually found in cultural elements used in the West.

From what we have seen, in the indigenous personality the problem of the *limit*, where the magical decision is affirmed and achieves its harmony, is not located in the movement out but in the movement in. It is curious to note that one does not find in either Holguín or Bertonio many terms equivalent to *intelligence*. On the other hand, terms abound that relate to intelligent decisions, but that are translated into expressions where the term *heart* is present. The body, as we have already seen, is conceived as an interior cavity and within it the heart is held almost as a symbol. *Heart* in Quechua is *soncco*, and Holguín translates it as "heart and entrails, and stomach, and conscience, and judgment or reason, and memory, the heart of the wood and will and understanding."[20] Bertonio translates the equivalent Aymara *chuyma* as "the lungs proper, also applied to the heart and the stomach and almost to the entirety of the inside of the body. Everything belonging to the interior state of the spirit, good or bad, virtue or vice according to what precedes it." But he then takes the terms *chuyma-hasitha*, which he translates as "to begin to have understanding and discretion"; *chuymarochatha* as "commend to memory"; *chuymakhatara* as "wise or learned"; and finally *chuymatatha* as "trace in his thinking."[21]

Let us add information I received from Macrima Quiroz Sánchez in Oruro. According to her, when an Aymara patient explains his ailment, he says that "the *chuyma* hurt," even when that organ is not specifically involved. The Peruvian doctor, Olano, notes also the curious insistence in Quechua on the term *heart*, elevated almost to a psychic faculty.[22] Evidently, since ancient times the heart has been that which at the same time sees and feels. Its value is as the intuitive regulator of judgment. Judgment which issues from the heart is at the same rational and irrational. On the one hand, it says what it sees, that is, it participates in the intellectual world of perception. On the other, it feels faith in what it is seeing, almost like a deep register, like the affirmation of the whole of the psyche before an objective situation. It is a kind of coordination between subject and object, where the holistic subject predominates. That is why everything indigenous appears with that cast of the "just because" (*porque si*), almost irrational, which accompanies indigenous affirmations. But the patient does so because that attitude gives him the interior safety that is lacking in the average urban dweller in South América.

More specifically, could the issue of the heart have something to do with the symbol on the chest of the central figure on the Gateway of the Sun in Tiahuanaco? It is a larva with a feline head (figure 4). Does the

4   Detail of the Gateway of the Sun, in Tiahaunaco, Bolivia.

meaning of this symbol coincide with the one on the central figure on the side of the Bennett Monolith? The latter consists in the extension of the figure's face situated in the chest between the two breasts. Very peculiar signs are also present in the minor figures of the monolith, which Posnansky interprets as huts or hooks. But below we will provide their correct meaning.[23]

In his manuscript, Guaman Poma describes a scene that alludes to divination, in which a sorcerer pulls out the heart of a llama in order to predict the future.[24] Let us consider also that at present the *huatapurichi*, according to information I have received from Charazani, achieve their role as foretellers of the weather and of the year (predictions used for agrarian purposes) by showing ability at tearing out the heart of an animal and keeping it palpitating in their hands.[25] With this manipulation, the heart becomes a visual symbol equivalent to a sort of magic center. The heart has always been the fifth element of every live being, a symbol of integration or balance. It is manifest in divination but also in the structure of the empire, as in the four zones established by the Inca, with the city of Cuzco as the navel. This was also surely conceived of in terms of heart, or perhaps in terms of seed.[26]

But a way of thinking like the indigenous one must point to deeper limits. If the process of that indigenous grandfather consisted in using the *inward direction* of his personality to shore up the "interior man" and to elaborate his judgments with the *chuyma* or heart, there must be a background, also *interior*, which in the end guarantees the absolute safety of the whole procedure. Only there would the grandfather find the *is* of the *"that's how it is,"* the conformity, the safety, and the true and only salvation within his traditional world, even if this works only at the level of the simple teaching of the Achachilas, the snow-covered peaks or Grandfathers.

But only with the analysis of indigenous knowledge will we find that second, deeper, limit of indigenous thinking.

If indigenous thinking does not seem to follow our own habitual chain of thinking—moving from reality through understanding, accumulating in knowledge, and finally returning to
reality—then it is fitting to ask in what exactly does indigenous
knowledge consist, and where does it come from?

A blind witch from Tiahuanaco named Apaza Rimachi (figure 5) recommended a ritual which involved burning incense.
We asked for the names of the gods to whom the offerings were
being made. He said they were four, namely:

1   *Achachila*, or grandfather, which generally connotes the snowy
    mountain peaks;
2   *Kejo-kejo*, or lightning;
3   *Huak'a*, or ruins, probably the local ones;
4   the earth.

It struck me that three of these terms are related. The *yatiri*
said that the *achachila* creates us because he sends rain, but the
Ak'apana also creates us and so does the Puma Punku.[1] These
last two are *huak'as*, important ruins that lay just a few meters
away. He said the *achachila* confers upon the *huak'as* the power
to create.

But then he added, according to the translation provided by
Dr. Vilela, "The *kejo-kejo*, the lightning, says he is the *achachila*,"
and for the purposes of the ritual, "we are going to recite (the

5   The witch, or *yatiri*, Apaza Rimachi in Tiahuanaco, Bolivia. Photograph by the author.

prayer) to the Puma Punku." I asked whether it was lightning or the Puma Punku who created us, and the *yatiri* answered in Aymara that it was the Puma Punku. Evidently, he was posing a contradiction. In order to resolve it, we assumed the question was one of proximity.

The *yatiri* nevertheless continued to insist that the *achachila* is lightning or *kejo-kejo*. Is it that the three divinities, the *achachila*, the lightning, and the *huak'as*, were one and the same? Were we dealing with an unfolding trinity in which the *achachila* corresponded to the sky, or that which is above, the *huak'a* to that which is below and surely had characteristics of hell, and lightning served as an intermediary between them? Only thus could we understand the witch's contradiction that the *achachila* creates us but the *hua'ka* does, too.

In addition to these three deities, the earth was mentioned as something separate. Were we dealing with a four-part schema according to the formula 3 + 1, in which the fourth element acquires a certain autonomy?[2] I confirmed my suspicion when I saw the magical manipulation performed by another witch from Tiahuanaco, Ceferino Choque, when he performed a *Gloria Misa*. This is a propitiatory ritual to ensure safe travel, good luck, and it serves other purposes as well.

The ritual was divided into two parts. The first part was limited to the preparation of two *mesas* or offerings, which consist of two small boxes prepared by the witch himself. The first box was devoted to the *Gloria*, which seemed to incarnate what is for the indigenous people the Supreme Divinity and must be equivalent to the Catholic God. Nevertheless, its precise name is left vague and unstated, as if it were an unnameable god. According to the witch, Apaza Rimachi, the *Gloria* consists of twelve saints, six male and six female, with the following names: Santiago San Jerónimo, Santiago San Felipe, Santiago Pacha-paya, Santiago Pacha-lajari, Santiago Pacha-llallagua, Santiago Rayo Capitana; and Santa Cármina, Santa Bárbara-mama, Santa Concepción, Santa Elena, Santa Catalina, and Santa Cecilia.

In order to fulfill the obligation to each saint, Choque had prepared *tacitas*, as he called them, made from cotton and red thread. These *tacitas* were filled with incense and several green twigs called *pachankilli*. They were placed inside the first box.

The other small box was devoted to lightning-*achachila*. It contained a large *plato* also made from cotton and red thread. Inside, the witch placed twelve *pachankilli* herbs: one for each of the apostles, he told us. He completed the second box by adding incense.

The two boxes were then incinerated in a special brazier while the witch held it over the heads of each one of those present as he recited his chants and prayers. Interestingly, the first box, the one devoted to the *Gloria*, had to be *ch'allada*—that is, sprinkled with alcohol. The second one, however, did not have to be because "it is not worth it," according to what an informant told me in La Paz. To *ch'allar* lightning may result in bad luck.

The second part of the ritual consisted in making four more boxes. One of them was full of sweets, and was devoted to the *yanccas*, or evil ones. The *yancaas* are also called *tíos*, whose name is the equivalent of *supay*, or devil, who rules the mines and who is the object of special worship by miners. Choque, in reciting his prayer, singled out several *tíos* for special mention. These included *Anchanchu*, a head which rolls continuously throughout the Puna, and *Curumini*, or rainbow; he also mentioned a courtyard full of gold, a courtyard full of silver, and he also invoked *cahuallani*, *majarini*, *antalhuallani*, *sirinuni*, and others, all surely connected to infernal forces.

The other three boxes were devoted to, respectively, the *mallkus*, or snowy mountain peaks generally, the *mallkus* of Argentina in particular, and finally the home. Each of the three small boxes was filled with precisely forty coca leaves. Sweets were then placed over the coca. According to Cobo, the offering of coca was for the earth or *Pachamama*. If that is true, the three boxes were destined for the earth.[3]

In short, the four types of boxes were dedicated to *Gloria*, Lightning-*achachila*, infernal forces, and the earth, respectively. These four types approximate the division made by Apaza. In the Gloria Misa, then, three orders of the universe are united: the world overhead, the world-in-between, and the underworld. A fourth is excluded. This system coincides with the division of the universe provided by the chroniclers, according to whom there was a *hana-pacha*, that is, the sky or ground above, a *kay-pacha*, the ground here which we occupy or world-in-between, and a *uk'u-pacha*, the ground within, which the chroniclers identified erroneously as the Christian Hell.[4]

Both Apaza and Choque were using a knowledge subject to a principle of a priori ordering—it did not depend on sense data. This ordering consisted of a fixed schema divided into four quadrants, three forming a trinity with a segregated fourth. The latter unfolded in turn into three other units; it is as if the *mesa* dedicated to the earth formed another trinity. In sum, six boxes were organized into quadrants. The knowledge thus implied was rhythmic rather than a knowledge of things.

Such a form of knowledge is not exclusive to contemporary indigenous peoples from Tiahuanaco. For example, when Guaman Poma mentions the Legend of the Four Ages, he notes that the Quechua who lived in the second age, the *uariruna*, believed in a trinity: *yayanruna muchochic*, or "just father"; *churin runa cuya payac*, or "charitable son"; and lastly *sullca churin causaycoc micoycoc runap alliinnincap*, "the youngest son who gave us health, kept us healthy, gave us food, and sent water from the sky to give us food and sustenance." Guaman Poma remarks that the first one was also called *yayan illapa*, "resplendent father or lightning"; the second one *chaupi churin yllapa*, "middle resplendent son"; and the third one *sullka churin yllapa*, "resplendent younger son or lightning." He also indicates that this trinity signals that "the ancient Indians had knowledge that there was only one god, three people."[5] Does this mean that the father, or *yayan*, is the equivalent of the Father in the Catholic Trinity; the *chaupi churin*, or middle son, is the equivalent of the Son or Christ; and *sullka churin*, the youngest son, the Holy Spirit?

If that is the case, the Trinity is conceived in almost chronological form.

The opposites are first and a mediating third term follows. This middle term is cited at the end as the youngest son, but is understood sensually—visually. Because it is understood sensually, this third figure, the youngest son, is the one who offers food and life to man. In the same way perhaps Apaza Rimachi mentions the *kejo-kejo* in its function as intermediary.

In the *ceques* of Cuzco one notes the same principle of tripartite organization. The *ceques* were paths or lines, forty-one in all, on which were placed a total of 328 altars. According to Bernabé Cobo, one of these altars was referred to as *Chuquipalta*, and consisted of three stones. One of these stones was dedicated to *Pachayachachic* (the Teacher of the Pacha), the second to *Intiillapa* (the Ray of the Sun) and the third one to *Punchau* (the Day).[6] Could one apply to this schema what we observed in Guaman Poma? Are we dealing here with the father, the older or middle son, and the youngest son, so that *Inti illapa*, lightning, could be the consequence of the existence of a *Pacha yachachic* and a *Punchau*, a sun or day? We need to reflect on the importance of this altar. These three divinities are not only present in the Inca celebrations, but they also seem to be necessary in the numerous groupings of three stones placed along the *ceques*. In the *Qolla-suyu*, the *suyu* that stands opposite the one cited above, sixteen divinities were harmoniously distributed around the fifth *ceque*, the middle one, to the left and to the right of it, and only two appear in the *Conti-suyu* and in the *Anti-suyu*. In this we see a rare association of a tripartite schema with a four-part schema.

The same *ceques* can be further qualified: each of them can be *callao*, *payan*, or *collana*. Analysis of these terms leads one to note that *callao* is associated with "principle," *collana* with "principal" (in the sense of main or chief), and *pallan* with "fruit." Could it be that the principle of organization of the *ceques* is also a tripartite schema, so that the *ceque callao* is the initiation of a group, *collana* is the opposite, and *pallan*, the middle fruit resulting from the first two? This cannot be tested in the places of worship, but it is curious that the ten families descending from the ten Incas had each been assigned a *ceque*, which generally coincided with the one qualified as *callao*, or principle.[7]

The special four-part scheme of 3 + 1 is also found among the Chipaya Indians. They belong to a culture that preceded the Quechuas and Aymaras, and they inhabit the Carangas region of Bolivia, close to Lake Coipasa. In their village they have four shrines distributed to match four cardinal directions, but which are oriented in a peculiar way. The north, east, and west towers are all oriented toward the east, but the one that lies to the south is oriented toward the north.

The eastern and western shrines are devoted to two saints, Saint Jeronimo and Santiago, respectively. The ones to the north and south, on the other hand, correspond to feminine personages, Saint Ana and the Virgin del Rosario. The ones devoted to Santiago and Saint Jeronimo have in front of them small rectangular calvaries capped by a cone and crosses made of straw. Santa Ana's shrine, on the other hand, has a rectangular *pirca*, or adobe wall, with small niches in the corners. The Virgin of Rosario's shrine, which is the southern shrine oriented toward the north, has only one calvary placed asymmetrically on one side of the church. This recalls the strange distribution of altars in Cuzco. Nine *ceques*, or lines, are oriented toward the *Chinchay-suyu*, another nine toward the *Anti-suyu*, and nine oriented toward *Qolla-suyu*, but toward the south, the *Conti-suyu*, one finds instead fourteen. It works out to a 3 + 1 rhythm, similar to the one used by the Chipayas, as well as by Choque and Apaza Rimachi in Tiahuanaco. In each case the knowing is *rhythmic*.

To say that a knowledge is rhythmic means that it does not seem to have an exterior origin or an origin in sense-data, as ours requires, but rather has to do with the act of remembering and must contain an archetype. Indigenous knowledge does not emphasize the real content, such as the snowy peak or the plains or the fetish, nor the concrete material manipulated in rituals, but rather the fascinating and numinous aspects of the archetype. Thus, for example, lightning or thunder themselves are not so important to Apaza as the trinity which groups and connects the *achachila*/lightning, and the *huak'a*/thunder, with each other. The trinity, or the quaternity of 3 + 1, function as empty containers prior to any sense experience, and only a posteriori do they receive contents originating in reality.[8]

It seems that before the conquest, there was some consciousness that knowledge takes this form. This is evidenced in the use of the term *unanchani*, "to point or signal" in Quechua. The correlative term in Aymara, *unanchatha*, Bertonio translates as "knowledge," which makes one think that its meaning must have been *"knowledge of signs."*[9] In Holguín's Quechua *Vocabulary*, *unanchani* is connected to *unancha*, sign, and this term, in turn, is linked to "one" or "that which endures."[10] Does this mean "endure" like that which is divine?

Unanchani is mentioned by Santacruz Pachacuti in a hymn, where several verbal forms appear in order to express the idea of looking for Viracocha. He uses among them the verb form *unanchapty*. *Unanchan* is repeated five times in the ritual prayer which he transcribes in the upper part of his schema, and which he says corresponds to the main altar of the Coricancha of Cuzco. But they are repeated as signs of Viracocha.[11] This obviously has to do with knowledge as revelation, constituted as an enthralling and numinous archetype.

Indigenous knowledge is not therefore a "why" knowledge, or a knowledge of causes, but rather a "how" knowledge, or a knowledge of modalities. It is also not a knowledge on call that can be closed up or filed away, and even less a knowledge alienated from a subject. Rather, it demands the commitment of the subject who handles or manipulates it. In indigenous thinking knowledge is closely related to ritual.

This link is indicated by the Aymara term for witch, *yatiri*, which translates literally as "owner of knowledge." He seems to be both the keeper of rhythmic and traditional knowledge and a promoter of ritual. His capacity as keeper of knowledge can be noted in the word *yacha*, meaning "knowledge" in Quechua. The prefix *ya* indicates, according to Holguín, "the truth is that it is such," and *cha* indicates the idea of making.[12] This confirms that *yacha* indicates a knowledge not acquired, but determined, already existent. Middendorf translates *yachacu* as "it is known, it is understood, it is the custom."[13]

Bertonio's Aymara *Vocabulary* confirms that the witch is a promoter of ritual. Curiously, he translates a related term, *yataacha*, as "to raise, which is proper of God."[14] The same obtains in Quechua. The term *yacha*, to know, seems to have suffered a significant semantic transformation. In his translation of the hymns of Cristobal de Molina, Rowe indicates that the form *yachacuni* is translated by the chronicler as "augmenting." Rowe notes that in the sixteenth-century *Vocabulary* of Santo Tomas, *yachacuni* appears as "to multiply like the sown lands."[15] That is not how it appears in Holguín, who belongs to the beginning of the seventeenth century. Nevertheless, Holguín translates *yachacuni* as "learn, exercise," and the form *yachacu* as "power," *yachacuchini* as "to carry out," and, finally, *yacha chik* as "the one who *makes* it or *maker*."[16]

Is it that indigenous knowledge not only aims to determine things which endure, or *una*, but also has the auspicious meaning of "to multiply like sown land" or relates to the *maker*? One suspects this is the case with Apaza Rimachi. His report could not be taken as ordinary knowledge, but it rather must be placed against a background that commits the subject to the act of knowing, in the sense of making something *grow* in him. The contradiction implicit here is not due to his thinking in terms of a trinity—that would be a superficial explanation—but rather to the knowledge having to be given in an open and forthright way to promote such growth. In confronting antagonistic forces such as *achachila*, lightning, and *huak'a*, the ritual was necessary to complete the knowledge. Only through the ritual could a tear in the cosmos be integrated in the subject; that is, only then could it "multiply like sown land." Apaza, in communicating his knowledge, announced only the first part of a drama whose second part consisted of the ceremony.

This contributes to the peculiarity of indigenous knowledge and limits it to a certain sphere. It is not a scientific knowledge of reality, given that the latter is not understood by indigenous people in the way it is conceived by us, but rather it is a knowledge related exclusively to the pure fact of living. This can be demonstrated through analysis of ritual. In the following chapter, we will see of what ritual consists.

In Pupikunka, Bolivia, an indigenous community located in Chuquichambi, four hours west of Oruro, the *yatiri*, or witch, an old man, dressed in rags, with blackened teeth, read us our fortune. Following the custom, we had given him a bag of coca leaves as a gift. He reached inside, withdrew a fistful of leaves, and examined them without moving them about. He repeated the procedure constantly.[1]

He had developed a dislike for one of those present, someone who had perhaps not shown enough respect for the ceremony. It caught my attention that the witch told the disrespectful participant, according to the translation Alconz Mendoza made of the taped version, "You are burdened with great *pena* [trouble]. You must *do part of your duty*. You must do some ablutions. *Remember* well." Alconz wrote me the following gloss: "He must *remember* the road he travels."

To express the idea of *remembering*, the witch had used the Aymara term *amtaña*. Bertonio writes the same word in the form *amutatha*. In another part of his *Vocabulary*, he translates the first part, *amu*, as "bud of the flower."[2] The witch had used the Aymara verb *pukhachari* to say "fulfill your obligation." Bertonio uses the term *phuccasitha*, which he translates as "to pay, to fulfill all your debts," and adds *phucca*, "full." In the Aymara vocabulary published by the Canadian Baptist pastors, *phokha* means "full, complete," and *phokhaña* means "to fill, to complete, to fulfill."[3] So, in what sense can the ritual, that is, the ablutions recommended by the witch, *fill* the subject? And, does this *filling* mean to achieve the "bud of the flower"—the *amu*, referred to in *remembering*? If this were the case, language would be being used in a highly symbolic manner, since the "bud of the flower" refers to the integration of the original rending of the cosmos. From this rending or tearing indigenous wisdom is conceived. The bud of the flower also provides the exact meaning of the term *yachacuni* insofar as the knowledge seems to point to a "multiplying like the sown land" but through ritual and only at the conclusion of it. Let us consider the terms in which a ritual is carried out.

Alconz Mendoza de Oruro, born in Turco, near the Chilean border, gave me the following description of the *qharira*. It is a blood sacrifice performed the day before a celebration "to provide meat for the guests" (figure 6). It begins in the morning and lasts the whole day. During the entire ritual an emphasis is placed on *remembering*. In this way, they *remember* the *huihuiris*, or young. They evoke a trinity composed of the *father*, *mother*, and *son*. This trinity is composed of the *huihuiri malku* and the *huihuiri tayka*, the lord and lady of the young. They *remember* them and evoke them so that together they issue the *huachu huihuiri*, or young, as their fruit and so that the young be good, *asqui huihuiri*. The participants are incited during the ritual to "perform the whole ritual with all their *heart.*"

The aspersions are always performed *remembering* the snowy peaks and the sacred places. To that effect they are grouped in three circles: a large one devoted to the *apus*, such as the Illimani, the Mururata, the Tres Cruces, the Sajama, the Huayna Potosi, the Tata Sabaya, that is, the most important mountains; a second, smaller circle that includes the smaller *apus*; and finally the third circle with the local *apus*. During the ritual a tall, rustic guitar that has wooden pegs and is strung with gut is used to accompany the Aymara verses. This instrument was referred to as a *guitar-rilla* by the informant.

Alconz said to me that in another version of the ritual the offering is made in the middle and in the *depth* or center of a large circle. It is useful to remember in passing that, according to Lira, the Quechua word for *depth* is *pacha*, which also means, as we will see later, "the here and now of daily life."[4]

Returning to the ritual, after the dedication each man cuts the throat of

6   The slaughter of a black sheep during a *qharira* in Toledo, Bolivia.

a llama. The *yatiri*, or witch, gathers the blood in a large bowl and in other smaller ones and sprinkles it in the direction of the three circles. Those present prepare a *mixture* with the usual ritual elements which are then used to *cuscachar*, to place on the same footing, according to Bertonio, *inviting* the *apus* and *sharing* with them as they have done with the blood.

The informant also told us that they remember the *illas*. According to Bertonio the *illas* are "anything one keeps as provisions for the house such as desiccated potatoes, corn, money, clothes, and even jewelry, etc."[5] Nowadays, they are votive places where ceremonies are performed and where propitiatory offerings are buried. They seem to be oriented to the four cardinal points surrounding an *estancia* or the seat of an *ayllu* or community linked to the *samiris*, whose literal translation is "for luck or happiness." It is worth noting that *huilanchas*—also blood sacrifices—are dedicated to these *illas*. Sometimes during the *huilanchas* the heart is torn out of the animal. This operation is performed by the *yatiri*. Those present eat some of the meat of the animal grilled and without salt. They burn or bury the rest.

The *qharira* continues with the skinning of the animals and with their legs and heads placed ritualistically next to each other. The *sajsa* is performed at this time.[6] Men and women wear the skins as blankets and dance, imitating the animals. They pursue each other as the llamas do when they are in heat. They imitate the llamas' gestures, moving the lower lip forward and even simulating spitting their food. At the same time, they sing the following verses to the animal accompanied by the guitarrilla: "May this be a good time; may you shake [meaning, perhaps, "come back to life"] as if you had not been sacrificed; may you be *remembered* well as if you had not been sacrificed; you are the one who creates us; what am I for? why do I exist?; I am merely the one who *impersonates* the llama, the one standing here; now you will take care of the guests and of everything so they will serve themselves." After that the musician plays on the guitarrilla the appropriate *huayños* corresponding to the slaughtered animal, whether a sheep, a cow, a mule, a donkey, etc.

The example speaks for itself. The *yatiri* from Chuquichambi, like the one from Tiahuanaco, recommended a traditional "knowledge" (*saber*), alluding to the ancestors, but understood in terms of "things that endure" (*una*), with the purpose of *filling* someone's existential *void*. In the same manner, the traditional character of that knowledge has the standing of a *remembrance*, a reminiscence, with archetypal structures, without any relation to reality, but in the character of "the bud of the flower" (*amu*), integrating the vital feeling of the subject through the ritual, in order that the subject does not *go around empty*.

Such a knowledge distances itself from what we ordinarily understand as knowledge. In our case, instead of being reminiscence, knowledge is completely acquired. Instead of taking vital feeling into account, our knowledge tends toward a rigorous objectivity at the margins of all existential valuing. We completely lack ritual and have no appreciation of totality, whether empty or full. Can one claim, then, that the distance between indigenous knowledge and ours is similar to the one that exists between a knowledge of salvation and one of domination, to use the duality created by Max Scheler?[7]

When the participants in the ritual during the *sajsa* formulate the question "What am I for?" it must be the moment of culmination of the *pukhachari*, or filling, recommended by the *yatiri*. But what is the sense of *filling* in this case? The term *sajsa* does not seem to be Aymara, but rather Quechua, and it means "rags" as well as "satisfaction." Is it satisfaction due to absence? If it were, it must be an absence of visible things, and as such it will mark the limit, especially in the moment of the ritual mentioned above in which the visible is substituted by the pressure of divinity. This pressure is already given at the beginning, at the moment of conception of knowledge, as when Apaza Rimachi opposed the divine forces. This pressure reaches its plenitude only through ritual, but it accomplishes it through something such as the rags of the *sajsa*, almost as if an absolute absence were given validity.

Something similar happens in ritual divination through coca. The *yatiri* demands a Bolivian peso, which he calls *nayrajja*. According to Bertonio, *nayrajja* means "without time" or "ahead of time."[8] It is also related to "first," to "eye," and to the "grain of some seed." Among indigenous Peruvians, the eye, or *ñawi*, of the potato is connected to the growth of the plant. Evidently *nayra* means something like "seminal center," which has the status of the center of the world, and which in the case of foretelling is manifested in the bill used.[9]

Two leaves are laid on the bill to form a cross. This cross is called Tata Lindo or the Lord Jesus Christ by the *yatiri*. The cross consecrates the cloth where the ritual will be held. Around the cross, the *yatiri* places the problems and the people connected to them, each symbolized by leaves (figure 7). Next the foretelling itself begins. The *yatiri* casts more coca leaves onto the ones already on the cloth. Depending on which side faces up, the green or the light side, and according to the shape the leaves form, their position and their orientation with respect to Tata Lindo, the witch makes his prediction. During the whole ritual he sprinkles the leaves and the area with pure alcohol, almost always in a circle, invoking the heavenly and infernal deities. The foretelling rite develops as if it consisted in an exploration of the difficulty, or *yaqui*, or perhaps in finding the *huak'a*, which, in this case, means "to fall into bad times."[10]

The way the ritual elements are placed naturally leads one to think of a microcosmos centered around the Tata Lindo and the *nayrajja*. These in turn will create that negative *filling* where the divinity applies pressure to show the difficulty or *yaqui*. Thus, it constitutes a ritual that is the inverse of the *qharira*. While in the foretelling rite the divinity's pressure is required at the beginning of the ritual, and from that moment on the duality is explored, in the case of the blood sacrifice one begins from the duality to reach, only by the end of the ritual, that same end. The coca divinatory rite is performed starting from creation; the *qharira* instead begins with the rending duality in order to return to it.

If indigenous knowledge points to ritual it is because it is not a connotative knowledge, but rather because it is knowledge expressed through

7   The initial moment of the foretelling ritual with coca leaves
performed by Ceferino Choque
in Tiahuanaco, Bolivia. On the
folded bill, or *nayrajja*, is a cross
made of two leaves, the Lord
Jesus Christ or Tata Lindo. To the
left of it a leaf symbolizes that
the one consulting the leaves is a
widow. The leaf to the right symbolizes the person about whom
the inquiry is being made, and
underneath, hidden by the hand,
a leaf stands for the one consulting the leaves. Later, Choque
added another upturned leaf at
the base of the cross to symbolize
the problem. Photograph by the
author.

yachacun. Yachacuni, as we have seen, is related to growing, multiplying, bringing into existence—that is, a knowledge for living. It is not knowledge of an object, such as a plough. Rather, it transcends the object. It enters the religious background that lies behind the object and it seems to be linked with the foundational reason for their being objects at all, and even for the existence of community and life in general.

For that reason it culminates in ritual. Ritual manipulates the invisible limits of a transcendent and sacred world. It is not only the medium to *fill* the *emptiness* of a subject, but it also transcends it and balances the *yaqui* and the *hisqui*, the ill-fated and the auspicious, with coca, for example, but acting as components of the cosmos. The indigenous cosmos consists of an organic totality whose center is not in the ego of every person, but rather in an unknown place that can sometimes be visualized temporarily in the stone hit by lightning, in a sacred place, or in the *nayrajja*. Living beings revolve around this center. Its symbol must be like one of the characters who, according to Gamboa, accompany Viracocha the *Tahuapaca* 4-Eagle, which suggests the centralization of four regions around a seminal center, of which the Inca Empire is an example.[11]

In a universe so understood, organic, total, an animal-cosmos, distinctions among its elements are of little importance. What is important above all is its internal equilibrium. The auspicious and the inauspicious predominate over any object. Therein lies the continuity of knowledge into ritual. One and the other converge to balance the cosmos. In this sense, the knowledge is as distant from ours as the distance Scheler sees between knowledge of salvation and knowledge of dominion, but with a single caveat. He sees salvation as it was in the Middle Ages, but with European eyes, as marking the distance from scientific knowledge. The European sees the world as spectacle; the indigenous person instead sees it as an organism whose internal balance depends on each person.

That is why this knowledge almost always inhabits a ritual to maintain the cosmic balance, a revealed knowledge, according to which the contrary—not knowing or ignorance—must be conceived as it is in Eastern philosophy: as an absence of revelation. It is difficult to prove this last point, but in any case it is worth noting that to reveal, according to Holguín, means "*Reuelar. Suticharcuni mastararcuni paca simictan tocyachicuni.*" Elsewhere he adds: "*Simicta ttokyachicuni.* To discover what is secret, to let a word escape without wishing to." But then he translates *ttokyani* as "to explode; to bloom (a tree); to open (a flower)."[12] One could say that revelation in Quechua is related to the flower, the same as the *amu* in Aymara. Is this the cosmic flower that reconciles opposites?

Do the strange pieces of painted cotton placed, according to Wiener, in the mouths of mummies fit within this revelation?[13] These cotton pieces consist of a figure with open arms in the style of the central figure in the Gateway of the Sun, surrounded by fretwork consisting of what Posnansky called tiered signs. What is curious is that these signs follow each other in opposing rhythms, and they appear to hook onto one another, sometimes in obvious ways and others signaling an opposition through absence or negation. The drawing symbolizes an organic cosmos that shares itself between the auspicious and the inauspicious in such a way that the central figure would be the divinity that puts back together the originary rending as *amu*, or flower.

Given this account, understanding has no other end than to apprehend this flower that balances the duality. And the only way to achieve this is in terms of a "bursting or sprouting"—that is, as a violent eruption of the sacred that can only be achieved through ritual or, in the case of the mummy, when the dead person has achieved definitive transformation and become sacred.[14]

The analysis of knowledge (*saber*) has led us to ritual and thus to divine pressure as that which moves indigenous thinking. But the road we have followed has been both too direct and not very indigenous. It was probably motivated by a thoroughly Western prejudice, that of examining their thinking from the angle of a theory of understanding (*conocimiento*).

What is missing is something much more important: determining the categories that intervene or condition their thinking. Only these categories will introduce us to an exclusively indigenous point of view.

When Ceferino Choque was asked about the meaning of the world, he referred to the Catholic Trinity, to the sky, the earth, and the sown fields (figure 8). When pressed, he limited himself to saying in Aymara: *ucamahua mundajja*, which translates as "That's the way of the world" (*el mundo es así*).

A world taken in terms of *its así* (its way) is seen as pure succession of events and not as a stage populated by things. The favorable or unfavorable tonality of things is of much greater interest than their material solidity. That tonality has become embodied and has created a parallel world with its own behavior and laws, almost like a network of relations that acquire a solidity similar to that of matter.

In his early-seventeenth-century *Vocabulary*, Bertonio rec-

8   The *yatiri* Ceferino Choque during a ritual of divination using
coca leaves, Tiahuanaco, Bolivia.
Photograph by the author.

ords the term *yancca,* meaning an unlucky event.[1] When Choque performed his Gloria Misa and burned the *mesas* or offerings dedicated to the
evil ones, also called *yanccas,* he indicated that no one should watch because the *yanccas* could appear and kidnap anyone who was nosy or
voyeuristic. This is the same degree of solidity as the world of the *achachilas,* the old ones or the snowy peaks. Choque himself would say that were
he not to perform the ritual correctly, the *achachilas* could *tie him up.* In
order to avoid this, it is always necessary to *pay the Lord.* Father Monast
cites many examples in this vein. According to Monast, an indigenous
man, when asked why he does the blood sacrifice, will frequently answer
that it is *to feed the achachilas.*[2]

These answers, which have been put in excessively visual terms, are in
no way explanations, except for the one who asks questions. The indigenous person is not interested in thinking of them as such. But they do
indicate the degree of solidity acquired by the world of magical relations,
as well as the degree of presence of the *así* of the world. A world that is *así*

cannot be thought about except with the *así* of the senses, within that margin of sensory immediacy that is part of daily life.[3]

In Choque's turn of phrase, in a world that *is así* the true attitude of indigenous people is hidden. Thus, what motivates their thinking is also hidden. Above all, it confirms the complete availability and openness of the subject, which leads one to suspect a constant fear in the face of the *upturn* or the fluctuation of the *así* of the world. The old Quechua and Aymara term, *kuty*, which means "to change, turn into, overturn or revolutionize," attests to this. Let us try to analyze its meaning.[4]

I met Elvira Gutiérrez on Linares Street in La Paz, Bolivia. It was a typical alley where the *chifleras* sell all manner of things related to witchcraft. She was a very likeable elderly woman, who spoke Spanish fluently. She gave me an interesting description of the so called *mesa negra*, which is used to *overturn* evil spells once one boils the ingredients and washes oneself with the water.

The *mesa* included the following elements: two objects of mineral origin, one called *maza*, which is also used for fright (*asustamientos*), and another, reddish from rust, called *macaye tacu*, which also can be used as a remedy; a dried piece of starfish; two *misterios*, or sugar tablets, which are usually imprinted with a variety of symbols such as Catholic saints, animals, common scenes of indigenous life having to do with travel, the mines, court, and so on. In this case one represented the Virgin of Copacabana, the other a table with two high glasses and a pitcher drawn in perspective. The *mesa* also included a small, grey bluish stone similar to those used by the indigenous people to chew coca, which—according to the informant—was made of ash; a type of seed called *margarida*; a piece of carob tree; *chaq'eri*, which seems to be the dung of an animal she could not specify; garlic from the mountains, which is "good for the stomach," *k'uru*; four small pieces of dried root from Puerto Acosta, two grey and two yellow; *mashi*, a piece of a tree trunk good for *aire* (a bout of stiffness); *pujlulo*, used on Tuesdays and Fridays to prevent illness—but that must be consumed before evening because otherwise it would do harm; another unspecified element that consisted of five small seeds; a piece of black incense; a *calaverita*, a seed with dark dots that resembled the eyes and mouth of a skull; and, finally, two large seeds, one called *kuti-avilla*, used to "overturn sickness," and another one called simply *kuty*, which had to be boiled and which was then used to comb through one's hair and which protected against "ill will."

Father Lira has the following entry in his Quechua dictionary for the word "*kuti*": "It is a systematic cure through the use of certain herbs—usually thirteen—also called *kuti*." Later on he points out that *kutichi* is the "counterproposal practiced to counteract the effects of evil spells or witchcraft so that the intended effects will be nullified." He also indicates that *k'uru kuti* and *pacha kuti* are two vegetables connected to the *kutichi*.[5] It is not difficult to think that the thirteen other elements of vegetable origin of the *mesa negra* coincide with Father Lira's observation on the Quechua world.

The folklorist Flora H. de Verduguez has also found several objects called *kuty*. They were included in *mesas* devoted to the Pachamama (*kuty ch'uru*) and the evil wind (*kuty waynitu* and *kuty-k'elluana-yuraj*). It is curious that in all of those cases the word used is *kuty* and not a word merely signifying withdrawal.[6]

This leads us to think about how sickness is conceived. Sickness does not consist in an alteration of the body. It is, rather, the result of a turn (*vuelco*) in reality, an inversion from the auspicious to the inauspicious. According to R. Paredes, when an Aymara decides to travel and a fox crosses his path on the left as he sets out, he turns back.[7] How should we interpret that? We are accustomed to say in these cases that the indigenous man had a superstition motivated by an object, the fox. This is our way of conceiving of the world, as a spectacle. But for the indigenous person there is no spectacle. There is a reality completely committed to the trip, a travel-reality that hangs by such a thin thread that the smallest event may turn it from auspicious to inauspicious. Much more important than the fox is the fear of the turn in reality, that is, the *kuty*.

But it is in the pre-Columbian world that the term *kuty* acquires real conceptual importance, especially in the compound form *pacha-kuty*. The sense of the term *pacha* is extremely complicated, even though at first sight it seems to be connected with time, for example in the chronicle provided by Fernando de Montesinos.[8] He includes a list of 104 names of kings, of which nine carry the qualifier *pachacuti*. They are symmetrically distributed throughout the list. Four of them, according to Imbelloni, coincide with the turn of the millennium, and the other four with the end of a five-hundred-year period. In addition, in the case of the millenarian *Pachacuti* cataclysms occurred such as earthquakes, lights in the sky, monsters, sicknesses, or wars.

Historic time was conceived strictly symmetrically, as if the list slid on a panel. For example, the name Huanacauri, the title of a king, is repeated in positions 3, 42, and 73. Names like Cayo occupy places 20, 25, 48, 62, and 68. In this case indigenous time is not empty, but rather qualified and concretized partly as a visual space. In this sense the narrative of the ages consists generally of four segments with a fifth one in which the indigenous people place historical time.

Imbelloni notes that *pachacuti* means the turning of time "in the double sense of the loss of the old time and the renewal of the new time." Generally, a personage named Yupanqui, a young hero, defeats the enemy and fights against a mysterious race, the Chancas, and thus begins the new time. In order to do so, he changes the calendar and installs new times of worship.

In Mesoamérica this myth of the renovation of time is preserved in a more primitive form. The legend almost always takes the shape of four great ages within which four humanities are created and then destroyed by each of the elements: water, earth, fire, and air. Before the beginning of the fifth age, it is said that a pair of hero twins are born of a marriage between heaven and hell. They descend to hell to balance that which is opposite and then create the fifth humanity which, in the Mayan case for example, is made from four species of corn, each a different color.[9]

The same conception of time in five ages can be found in Guaman Poma.[10] He reports in his chronicle that there were several generations of Indians before the Incas, all descendants of Noah. They are the *uariuiraco-charuna*, the *uariruna*, the *purunruna*, and the *aucaruna*, each one an age or a humanity within a specific passage of time (figures 9a–d.) They are called *viracocha* because this was how foreigners are identified. And since they were descendants from Noah, they had long beards and white skin.

In the first age, that of the *uariuiracocharuna*, he adds a drawing of a couple dressed in leaves. The man handles a *taklla*, or indigenous plough, while the woman assists him. During this time women "gave birth in twos" and everyone worshiped only one god.

In the second age, the age of the *uariruna*, they appear dressed in furs and build *pucullus*, circular stone huts. The inhabitants of the third age, the *purunruna*, are represented as a couple that spin. Behind them sits an Inca-style house that has a roof with two slopes. A cataclysmic plague takes place at the end of this age. All the characteristics enumerated by the indigenous chronicler Guaman Poma seem to refer to the "*chullpas*,"

9a First age, that of the *uariuiracocharuna*, according to Guaman Poma.

9b Second age, that of the *uariruna*, according to Guaman Poma.

9c Third age, that of the *purunruna*, according to Guaman Poma.

9d Fourth age, that of the *aucaruna*, according to Guaman Poma.

adobe tombs common in the Altiplano and which are generally considered by the indigenous people to have been built by distant ancestors.

The people of the fourth age are the *aucaruna* or men of war. They appear in the drawing divided in two groups, one atop a *pucara*, or fortress, and the other one attacking the first from below. In spite of its name, this generation does not seem to have been very belligerent. Instead, they lived in a happy age; Guaman Poma marks the development they had achieved. Finally, the fifth age is the one of the *incaprunan*, the age of the Incas. It coincides with their dominion.

Guaman Poma gives the story a curious rhomboidal structure. He points out that the *uarivuiracocharuna* gave birth to two lineages from which sprang both great noble lords and principals of this kingdom, as well as bastard, lesser offspring. The latter engendered the common people and multiplied quickly and were called *uariruna* and *purunruna*. Are the second and third ages conceived as having a higher and lower part the same way that indigenous people structure their villages today? If this were true, would the fourth age, the *aucaruna*, be linked to the ritual struggles annually played out between both parts even today? The conception of "ages" in Guaman Poma seems to have a spatial dimension. That is not strange if one thinks that each of the five ages in Mesoamérica encompasses not only a temporal segment, but is also linked to a particular place.[11]

Guaman Poma himself assigns to the first three ages a list of ten kings and, for the fourth age, another list of twenty-eight. They add up to thirty-eight which is not far from the thirty-six that results from multiplying four by nine. Nine is as meaningful as ten according to the use that the Incas made of these numerical signs. Let us remember, for example, that the shrines of Cuzco were grouped in forty-one rows. These in turn were regrouped in four zones, three of which had nine rows each.

It is probable that Guaman Poma's conception was a two-part rather than a four-part one. This can be seen in the location of the only *pachacuti* in the aforementioned lists. It appears only once and at the end of a series of four times nine names, almost coinciding with the *aucaruna*. Is Guaman Poma pointing to a coincidence between the "turning of time" and "the men of war"? Betanzos also refers to only two creations carried out by the god Illa Ticci Viracocha.[12]

This kind of thinking is also found today in the Altiplano. Ibarra Grasso provides several examples of a dual conception of time among the indigenous people of Sur Lipez, Bolivia. I was told a story of the creation of the world by the sorcerer Huarachi of the Chipaya community in Carangas. He made reference to two ages, the first being that of the ancestors of the Chipayas, who were also known as the *Chullpas*, just as in Guaman Poma's account. They were twenty people, ten men and ten women, who worked through the night and hid during the day in the water. The present age begins after that, when Christ appears and they are baptized. To achieve this, the father "ties them together" and places them in a wide rectangular area and sets fire to the four sides.[13]

Whether the division of time is a two-part or four-part one, as it is for Guaman Poma, it is certain that the revolution of time acquires its exact dimension in the concept of the *pachacuti*. On the one hand, facing the Spanish, Guaman Poma adopts an aggressive and dynamic attitude for his polemical ends; on the other, he uses his indigenous inheritance, a knowledge accumulated from seeing the world *así*, to pose a completely contrary, passive, and contemplative attitude. As we shall see below, the intertwining of the two concepts leads Guaman Poma to lose the indigenous tone. But he does not achieve the required Western efficiency in his polemical attitude.

That he does not achieve it can be seen in the use he makes of the term *pachacuti*, insofar as it appears as the qualifier for a king situated just at the end of the story of the four ages. It can also be seen insofar as he notes that he is a descendant from those who were kings prior to the Incas, and that the fifth age occurred because the Incas usurped power. It can be seen insofar as he adopts a clearly messianic attitude simply because he sees the Spanish as the ones who cause a revolution in time. All of that is indigenous and fits the conception of *pachacuti*. In fact, he uses all that in terms of the legend of the four ages as if it were the same concept. It is probable then that the *pachacuti* constitutes in Guaman Poma a structure consisting of the *reality-in-which-I-live* tending to *turn*, in the sense of *kuty*, be it because of the Spanish, or as happened with the coming of the Incas. This *reality-in-which-I-live*, in turn, is the habitat stated as a global vision of the *here* and *now*, as we will see in the next chapter. It is wedged in by tradition starting from a simple *así* before the world, sustained with extraordinary stability. In spite of that it can collapse (*vuelco*) just as the *reality-for-travel* *turns* for that Aymara man that Paredes mentions above.

It is clear that Poma's *kuty* has lost the association with fear that it must have had in the pre-Columbian world. The Aztecs, for example, sacrificed human beings constantly and tore out their hearts only in order to maintain the fifth age, so that it would not *turn*. Even today as part of their *huilancha* the indigenous people of Carangas, Bolivia, conduct sacrifices, though not with human beings.

The truly agonizing dimension of the *kuty*, however, as it was lived before the conquest, is reflected in the legend of the red being, as told by Fray de Murúa. He tells us of "a person dressed in red ... with a trumpet in one hand and a staff in the other. Before he appeared it had rained day and night without stopping for an entire month during the grazing season. They were afraid that he wanted to overturn the earth, which they call Pachacuti. This person had come over the water that begins four leagues from Cuzco. When this prince (Inca Yupanqui) came to meet him, he asked him not to play the trumpet because they were all afraid that if he played it the earth would turn and they would be brothers."[14] According to Fray de Murúa, this figure appears in Chacataca, also called Sapi in Cuzco, which is a shrine that, according to Cobo, "was a large quinoa root which according to the sorcerers was the root from which Cuzco came to be and by means of which it maintained itself."[15]

It is curious that in Tiahuanaco's Gateway of the Sun, in the fourth lower line, one can find in the decoration a kind of fretwork with nine heads or masks, each with a symbol on top. It could be said that all of them show a movement from left to right, returning in the opposite direction, and at both extremes, both the left and the right, a small personage appears with a trumpet very similar to the one about which Nazca Jiménez Borja wrote.[16] Is this the same personage cited by Murúa? Could it be that in becoming corporeal the *pachakuty* has turned into the figure in the red outfit and in whom is lodged the terror in the presence of the *kuty*'s mutation? (figure 10).

A reference to the red sorcerer who lives in the nether world, *uk'u-pacha*, also figures in the Inca hymns compiled and published by Cristóbal de Molina, a chronicler from Cuzco. Was this figure also related to the fear of the *pachakuty*? If this were the case, it would be very significant since this would have taken place in the capital of the Inca empire, what was considered by them to be the "world's navel." Thus, this fear of the *pachakuty* would be intimately related to the indigenous conception of the world.

10   Personage appearing on both sides of the fret on the lower part of the Gateway of the Sun, in Tiahuanaco, Bolivia.

Numerous shrines in Cuzco seemed to refer to the *pachakuty*. In the region devoted to Chinchay there was a report of a shrine consisting of a flat surface called *cutirsaqpampa*, "which was made into a shrine because the Incas achieved a victory there." The next line of the report mentions another shrine called *Queachili*, "which is located like a door between two mountains and is revered because it is the location of the victory."[17] Is this a reference to the Inca Yupanqui who, according to Murúa, faced the figure dressed in red? *Cutirsaq* seems to be composed of *cutiri* plus the sufix *sa* and the ending *j*, which could mean "the state of turning" or "the one turning." Close by is another shrine called *Cutimanco*, which marks the burial place of a principal lord to whom children were offered in sacrifice.

Murúa adds at the end of his account that the red personage did not play the trumpet and "after a few days turned to stone and for that reason was called Pachacuti, which means to turn the earth." Several shrines in Cuzco mark figures who turned to stone. One of them is called *Omana-man*, "a large stone said to be the pururaucas," to which a "universal sacrifice was offered for the health of the Inca." *Omanaman* could be *umanpamanta*, which translated could mean "turned upside down," "of the head," "head down." It is not difficult to imagine that instead of *uma* it would be *umu*. According to Holguín *umu* means "sorcerer." Sarmiento de Gamboa mentions a figure called Humanamean, who had a connection with Manco Capac.[18] De Gamboa does not mention what we are discussing here. But that is probably because his attitude is excessively concrete and literal, which would impede his collecting the account of the legend of the *pachakuty*. No doubt if the red sorcerer had turned to stone he must have been venerated in some holy sites in Cuzco; otherwise all the shrines would be connected to the fear of facing the *turning*.

It is worth noticing that other shrines in Cuzco are also probably connected to the concept of the *pachakuty*. Five of them are called *cuipan*, which Jijó and Caamaño translate as *quepan*, that is, "conch trumpet." Two of them are found in Anti-suyu, two in Qolla-suyu, and one in Conti-suyu. They are always distributed with extraordinary symmetry. One of them shows evidence of having been a place of child sacrifice.

To this group of shrines one can add the four called *churucana*. According to Jijón and Caamaño *churucana* means "the one who restores," in Aymara. All of them received abundant sacrifices associated with the important deities of the Inca pantheon.

It is evident that the term *kuty* is found in abundance not only in the pre-Columbian world but also in the modern indigenous world, as we saw above. This leads us to think that we are not dealing just with a simple word, but rather with a mechanism that forms an intimate part of indigenous thinking, almost a category. No doubt *kuty* is related to seeing the *así* of the world. This is centrally what distances indigenous thinking from ours. But it is difficult to understand *kuty* and the indigenous *así* without analyzing the concept *pacha*.

We have said that *pachakuty* means the overturning or the metamorphosis of the *pacha*. But we will not know what is overturned or transformed unless we analyze the concept *pacha* as part of another word such as *pachayachachic*. *Pachaya-chachic* means "the one who teaches the *pacha*" or "the teacher of the *pacha*." An initial comparative analysis between *pacha-kuty* and *pachayachachic* leads us to notice that, on the one hand, the *pacha* could be *unsettled* or *converted* and, on the other, it could be *taught*. *Pacha*, then, must not just mean "time" or "ground," as it is usually translated. Rather, it must mean something much more involved in the life of the indige-nous person.

Santacruz Pachacuti uses the term *pachayachachic* to de-scribe the highest deity, the one who is both unreachable and unnameable, according to the Inca hymns cited by him and those transcribed by Cristóbal de Molina.

Bernabé Cobo also mentions *pachayachachic* and links it in an unclear way with Viracocha in the forms *Ticci viracocha* (Viracocha of the Foundation) and *Viracocha yachachic* (the one who teaches about Viracocha). This leads us to suspect a relation between the Teacher of the *pacha* (*Pachayachachic*) and Viracocha.[1]

But only in the *ceques* do we find the whole theological

architecture connected to Pachayachachic, or Teacher of the *pacha*. In Cuzco, as we have already seen, three hundred and fifty or more shrines were divided into four large regions that coincided with the four regions of the empire, and which were aligned from the Coricancha in a radiating shape oriented to the four cardinal points (figure 11). Cobo says, "Certain lines emanated from the temple of the sun as from a center. The Indians call these lines *Ceques*. These lines became four parts corresponding to the four royal paths that came out of Cuzco. In each of the *ceques* were the *guacas* and shrines, each in their appropriate order in Cuzco and the surrounding region. They were like stations in pious places, universally venerated. Each *ceque* was in charge of the respective factions and families of Cuzco, from which came the lords and servants who took care of the *guacas* of their *ceque* and who tended to the sacrifices so that they were offered at their established times."[2]

Among these *guacas*, or shrines, was one of which Cobo writes that "it was called Pucamarca: it was a house or temple assigned to the sacrifices of Pachayachachic in which children and everything else were sacrificed." But the deity was not limited to that temple. Rather, it seems as if all the *guacas* were a place of unfolding for the Teacher of the *pacha*. That unfolding was accomplished through triads, in the same way as Apaza Rimachi joined heaven and the netherworld with an intermediary, or as Guaman Poma describes the descending rhythm of the Just Father, the Son, and the Younger Son as the trustee of food, health, and fecundity. Cobo expresses the same idea when he speaks of the grouping of three of the divinities according to the schema of Father, Son (middle, *chaupi*), and Brother (*guauque*, or Younger Son, *sullca*.) Let us see the way in which he does so.[3]

The Teacher of the *pacha* appears to be made up of a trinity with the day (*punchau*) and lightning (*inti-illapa*), each represented by a stone in the fortress or Sacsayhuaman. If we apply the triad schema, we could affirm that the first had the rank of Father, the second surely that of the Older Son, and the third that of the Younger Son, whose role was that of mediator, as if he were the visible aspect of the divinity at the level of daily life.

Yet we have seen that the Pachayachachic, or Teacher of the *pacha*, is unnameable. Thus, he surely must show himself through a nameable god, and this must have been Viracocha, but as Ticci Viracocha, or "Viracocha of the Foundation or the Fundamental." Cobo observes that when the

11   The church of Santo Domingo del Cuzco was built on the Coricancha. The lower part, which is Inca, must house one of the 328 shrines mentioned by Cobo when he refers to a "stone, called *subaraura*, which used to be where the lookout of Santo Domingo is now, and which was believed to be a principal among the Pururaucas." Photograph by the author.

indigenous person sought grace from a religious source, he would invoke first Viracocha, as if this god were present in all of the shrines.[4]

Viracocha of the Foundation is, then, the first emanation of the Teacher of the *pacha* and also a member of a triad. He is worshiped as such on a mountain at the east end of the valley, bordering with Angostura, and also on a round mountain to the west, above Carmenga, bordering old Cuzco. Finally, he appears as *guauque*, or brother of Viracocha of the Foundation, in the center of Cuzco in "an almost round stone which was located in a window next to the said temple of the sun." "Universal sacrifice was devoted to him because of all the *pressing necessities*."[5] Linked to this shrine was "an enclosure beside the temple of the sun where sacrifices were made for the *universal health* of the Indians." This enclosure carried the name Chiquinapampa, "pampa of misfortune."[6] Could it be, then, that everything referring to Pachayachachic, the Teacher of the *pacha*, turns into a "foundation" (*ticci*) to which Viracocha is related; and he, in turn, attended to the *needs* and *misfortunes*? If this were so, how did the unnameable deity fulfill these *needs*?

Cobo mentions that the Teacher of the *pacha* "had given to the Sun together with the earth the ability to grow all the food." The sun, in turn, was not conceived as a unity, but rather as another triad whose first member was the *sun* proper (*Apu-Inti*), the second was the *day* (*Churi-Inti*) and the third was the *brother* (*inti-Guauqui*) who had the "ability to beget." He must have been represented in the temple of the sun as a human figure whose belly would be filled with the gold powder kneaded together with the hearts of the Incas.

It is curious that the shrines were related to the three above-mentioned members of the trinity to make nine, also organized in groups of three, probably also according to the rhythm or pattern of Father, Son, and Younger Son. The first group consists of a shrine made of three stones worshiped "so that the sun would not lose its strength," a wall "made by the sun," and a gorge.

The next group consisted of three houses or temples "where the sun would lay down to sleep," probably related to the day, or *Punchau*, the second term of the triad. The third group must be related to the sun's "ability to beget." In effect, the three shrines consist of stones that "when the sun reaches them" mark "the arrival of the season to sow the land." In short, the second unfolding of the unnameable deity that corresponds to the sun seems then to fulfill the *need* of indigenous people insofar as it gave the signal to sow the land.[7]

The third member of the triadic unfolding of the unnameable god must be thunder. According to Cobo, it was part of a trinity that included flashes of light, thunder, and lightning rays, that is *Chuquilla, Catuilla,* and *Intiillapa. Chuquilla* was worshiped in Pucamarca itself. Pucamarca contained the shrine to the Teacher of the *pacha,* or Pachayachachic. The second member of the trinity is in the main square, Aucaypata, "next to the Cabildo where thunder bathes itself," and the third member is represented by a statue of gold imposed by the Inca Yupanqui as his *guauque,* or brother. *Guauque* is used here as a double, and it is the statue that each Inca had sculpted after himself.

Those shrines that are linked to and that have some affinity to thunder, such as hail, wind, and storms, are symmetrically distributed in the circle of shrines surrounding the temple of the sun. Now, what is the meaning of thunder? Everything said up to now corresponds to the reality of the unfolding or emanation of the Teacher of the *pacha* in his most benign aspect, but when thunder is related to hail, the wind, and storms, it seems to take on another aspect. No doubt thunder is an intermediary emanation between the part of the sky related to the Viracocha of the Foundation, and the part of the sun visualized as present in the stone piles. Thunder, with its flashes of light and its lightning, is the indisputable intermediary between sky and earth.

To the indigenous person, thunder, because of its relation to hail, storms, the wind, and the earth tremors, constitutes an element of tension and perturbation. Let us remember, for example, that today one does not *ch'alla*, or sprinkle, the offering devoted to lightning because it would bring bad luck. Is it that everything connected with thunder is also the unlucky unfolding of the divinity, as if the divinity were disturbed by an antagonistic force?

If this antagonistic force existed, it would eradicate the third part of the indigenous world, the *uk'upacha*, or inside ground, which is different from the two other grounds, the *cay-pacha* and the *hanan-pacha*. This "inside ground" represents the hidden level, in a certain way hellish, though without the characteristics of the Christian Hell. It is an equivalent of the *huak'a* mentioned to me by the witch doctors of Tiahuanaco, Apaza Rimachi, and Francisco Cruz, or an equivalent of the *yanccas* of Choque, understood as generators of grief, or *yaqui*. It is necessary, then, to locate the principal instigator of the *chiqui* of the "plain of misfortune" mentioned above.

The Inca hymns cited by Cristóbal de Molina can help locate the source of tension that comes from the *uk'upacha*.[8] This can be seen not only in the contents of those hymns but above all in the rhythmic order in which the divinities are mentioned. From the first hymn to the last, a certain descending dialectic seems to be followed which goes from Viracocha, passing by the Pachamama, until it ends in the eleventh hymn with the mention of a mysterious character, a red sorcerer, who inhabits the "inner world." In the same manner, the hymns maintain among each other a rhythmic correlation. It is curious that the fifth is devoted to fruit and the tenth to the Incas. Are they each the result of their respective series? If they are, then hymn eleven would specify the two prior series of five hymns, as if it reflected the final point in the descent of the divinity. It is devoted to the *huak'a*, or shrine, where the sacred and the profane mix. Moreover, it is where the pressure of the divinity becomes agonizing; it is expressed in the translation that Tschudi makes of the term *huak'a*, a "place of weeping."[9]

This hymn is one of the most enigmatic ones. It mentions first a quality of Viracocha which for Urteaga means "great elder our creator, of our constant needs."[10] Does this coincide with the *guauque*, or brother, of Viracocha of the Foundation worshiped in the form of a stone located in the temple of the sun as we saw above? This stone was devoted precisely to the indigenous people's needs, and solemn sacrifices were made to it for the universal health of indigenous peoples.

The second part of the hymn is more interesting. It speaks of the necessity of living in peace and safety with the food available like corn, llamas, and all things. But the hymn appeals simultaneously to Viracocha to free them from the forces of witchcraft. Is this related to the concept of necessity or misfortune (as in *Chiquina pampa*, or "pampa of misfortune")? Is it that which is favorable, such as "corn, llamas, and all things," opposed to the unfavorable, like witchcraft? The hymn indicates as much when Viracocha is petitioned, "You who have placed the Red Sorcerer in the netherworld." Is this the sorcerer who provokes the disfavor?

When Rowe comments on the hymns of Cristóbal de Molina he is surprised not to find any prayer devoted to the Guanacauri. But according to legend, all that happened on this mountain seems to be linked with certain demonic forces that correspond to a "Red Sorcerer of the netherworld." According to Sarmiento de Gamboa, Manco Capac went to that mountain because he had seen the rainbow above its summit. When Manco Capac arrives there with his brothers, one of them, according to Cobo, turns to stone. This is the main reason why this mountain is worshiped.

Let us look at the details of the episode in Gamboa's account. The brothers were trying to reach the summit where the rainbow was when they "saw a guaca, a shrine in the form of a person, beside the rainbow. . . . When Ayar Ucho reached the statue, or guaca, he sat on top of it very spiritedly, asking himself what it was doing there. At these words the guaca turned its head toward him, but because it was weighed down by him, it could not see him. Then Ayar Ucho tried to turn, but he could not because the soles of his feet were stuck to the *guaca*'s back." Ayar Ucho then turns to stone, but not without first asking his brothers that he "be the first one to whom you make offerings, because I stay here for you, and when you make the *guarachico,* worship me as you would worship your father who stays here for everyone."[11] Santacruz Pachacuti attributes to what is probably the same *huak'a* the following words when it sees Manco Capac's brother: "You have done well in coming for me, you have finally found me, I was also looking for you; *you are finally within my grasp.*"[12]

This episode made the Guanacauri very important since it constituted one of the prominent oracles along with the one in Pachacamac. It was also the main shrine where the young became initiated into the warrior clan. But even if its meaning has always been uncertain, one can infer that being transformed into stone is an act of witchcraft. Because the episode involved the rainbow, it is also probable that Guanacauri is linked to lightning.

The first part of the name, *guana,* which can be rendered *huana* or *wana,* means "lesson, punishment, example, correction or suppression."[13] It is strange that *cau,* in Aymara, according to Bertonio, refers to "the hem of the blanket" or "robe with *red* thread."[14] Thus, Guanacauri would, on the one hand, be related to guilt or responsibility and, on the other, with the transformation of certain people into stone. It is almost as if he stopped the vital flow of time of a subject in terms of the *kuty,* structural change or conversion through metamorphosis. This surely must coincide with an essential sense of witchcraft in the indigenous world.

Lightning is always related to witchcraft. Valda de Jaimes Freyre says that today the Aymaras believe that "when lightning strikes a person, it kills them with the first strike, it breaks into pieces with the second strike, and with the third, if no human being is present where the event is taking place, it gathers the pieces together and returns them to life. Such a person acquires clairvoyance, the gift of divination and premonition," and causes misfortune to those who "cause him or her tears or suffering." These people are known as the "children of Santiago."[15]

If there were a relation between the red sorcerer and the Guanacauri, it would be a deity. Or it would be an antagonistic force corresponding to the "inner ground," that is the *u'kupacha,* the third order of the indigenous cosmos. It would confront to a certain extent the gods of the *hanan-pacha,* or the ground above, the Pachayachachic, or the Teacher of the *pacha,* in short. Thunder would be the intermediary between them, as if it reconciled the demonic with the celestial.

Proof of this confrontation seems to lie in that Guanacauri and the sun each had a farm whose produce was devoted to the respective deity. Guanacauri's farm was located in Chinchay, to the west, and the sun's farm was in Qolla, to the east. That is, each farm was located in a region counterposed to its opposite. The four shrines, moreover, *Cumpuguanacauri*, *Ataguanacauri*, *Chacaquanacauri*, and *Maychaguanacauri*, distributed in all the *suyus* except in the one in Chinchay, were apparently parallel to and correlated with another four shrines which carry the name of Viracocha and may be secondary shrines. Do they constitute two parallel and opposing structures?

Everything related to guilt, stones, and witchcraft must be linked to the Guanacauri. In that vein, it is not difficult to link a series of other shrines with Guanacauri, such as the large quantity of *pururaucas*, or warriors converted into stone, who had helped the Incas in their struggle against a legendary race, the Chancas, and the numerous graves symmetrically distributed in the four regions.

Before continuing, it is fitting to ask about the earth's position in this schema. The only reference to Pachamama is found in a shrine consisting in a plain in the Anti-suyu, situated relatively close to the temple of the sun. The plain is called Aylli-pampa, which undoubtedly is hayllipampa, "the plain of victory."[16] The relative isolation of this flat country with respect to the other *huak'as* leads one to think that it represented a fourth element of a four-part scheme whose other three members would be the fundamental Viracocha, thunder, and day. It is probable that these three deities belong to the order of the *hanan-pacha*, or sky, and the Pachamama belongs to the order of the *kay-pacha*, the "ground from here." It furthermore makes sense that the planes of the cosmos maintain a connection. Undoubtedly, this is all made concrete in the above-mentioned stone piles that mark moments of sowing and harvesting.

The *collca*, or granary group, mentioned four times, is related to this *huak'a*. The first appearance is the Collca-pata, which is where it is said that Manco Capac built his palace; Collca-pampa, a plaza that lies to the south of Cuzco; a fountain called Collca; and finally Mama-collca, in Membilla, a village also south of the city.

Corn, which must also belong to this group related to the Pachamama, is also cited several times. Three of them are tied to the sun and to the sowing of the earth. A fourth makes reference to the mountain Mantocalla, to the north of the city, where great celebrations were held at the

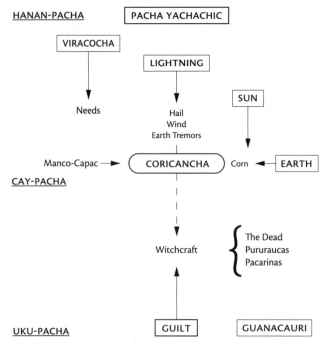

HANAN-PACHA

PACHA YACHACHIC

VIRACOCHA

LIGHTNING

SUN

Needs

Hail
Wind
Earth Tremors

Manco-Capac ⟶ (CORICANCHA) Corn ◀— EARTH

CAY-PACHA

Witchcraft

{ The Dead
Pururaucas
Pacarinas

UKU-PACHA   GUILT   GUANACAURI

12   The fundamental concepts and triadic structures of pre-Columbian
religion as inferred from the analysis of the list of shrines in Cuzco
cited by Cobo.

time of threshing. Another refers to Lima-pampa where a ten-day celebration was held after the harvest so that the corn would "last and not rot."[17]

The more than three hundred and fifty *huak'as* in Cuzco surrounding
Coricancha, the temple of the sun, measured the extent to which the
Teacher of the *pacha* was favored with offerings so that he would attend to
the needs of the Indians with sun and corn. They also measured the extent
of disfavor to which that divinity was exposed due to the Guanacauri.

According to the *ceques*, the schema of the Inca religion seems to
consist in two opposed poles. At one pole is an unnameable positive god,
known simply as the Teacher of the *pacha*. At the other pole is another
unnameable deity, the Guanacauri, the one that provokes the *kuty* or the
overturn of the *pacha*. Thunder seems to be in the middle as an ambiguous intermediary, since through lightning, hail, and storms it would
overturn the favorable and provoke *needs*. But as its order is already visible,

it would regroup within another trinity consisting of the Fundamental Viracocha, lightning, and the sun. A fourth element, the earth, maintains a certain autonomy from the others (figure 12).

This schema is not far from the religious schema of the witches Apaza and Choque, whom I observed in Tiahuanaco. Apaza's Gloria, composed of six male and six female saints, corresponds to the unnameable pole of the Inca pantheon, the Pachayachachic, or Teacher of the *pacha*, even though it seems that it is kept separate by the Aymara witch. It is not difficult to determine a clear equivalence between the Guanacauri and Choque's *yanccas* or Apaza Rimachi's *huak'a*, as well as that of another witch doctor, Francisco Cruz, also from Tiahuanaco. The latter two also promote the *kuty* and constitute the lowest level of the trinity which they compose together with the *achachila* and lightning. It is curious that the earth maintains autonomy in both schemas. The thinking from the past has persisted through the present in the Andean highlands even though the doctrine is considerably impoverished because there is now no established priesthood for witch doctors. The differences lie in that the Fundamental Viracocha is replaced by the *achachilas*, and the sun also disappears as a minor trinity. With it has gone the theological subtlety one notices in the concept of the "sun who begets" (figure 13).

Finally, we must determine the constitution of the *pacha* which must be taught by the Teacher, or Pachayachachic. With it we come to the center of indigenous thinking.

Only through analysis of the *ceques* do we understand the true meaning of the legend of Manco Capac. He is the initiator of the Inca dynasty, and he also belongs to a group of eight characters, four women and four men, who, as we saw above, suffer significant vicissitudes in the Guanacauri. They suffer them again as they approach the center of Cuzco, where Manco Capac builds the temple of the sun.

This character figures in numerous shrines according to Cobo's list. One can follow his path through Qollasuyu, the Conti-suyu, until the Inti-cancha, situated in the farm of Santo Domingo at precisely the central point of the Inca cosmos. Here begin the *ceques* that align the shrines. The dramatic conversion into stone of the members of the group and the installation of the temple of the sun point to a reconciliation of the *hanan-pacha*, or ground above, with what belongs to the *uk'upacha*, or ground within. This reconciliation is almost a meeting of the two unnameable

Apaza	Choque	Ceques	Bennet	Guaman Poma
Gloria	Gloria	Pacha Yachachic	Eagle	Just Father
Achachila	Lightning Achachila	Ticci Viracocha	Eagle	Just Father
Lightning	Lightning Achachila	THUNDER (Sun that begets)	Feline	Older Son who gives life
Huak'a	Yancas	Guanacauri	Fish	Older Son
Earth	MALLKUS Argentina House	Earth		

13   Comparison between the religious ideas of the present-day *yatiris* (witch doctors) of the Andean highlands and the triadic structures of Inca religion, the symbols of the Bennett Monolith, and Guaman Poma's trinity.

extremes of Inca theology. According to Sarmiento de Gamboa, the reconciliation is consummated when Manco Capac and his descendants reside for a long time in the Coricancha.

Is Manco Capac the repository of the *pacha* who taught the Teacher or Pachayachachic? Imbelloni translates *pacha* as "human life and the universe in its generic spatial and temporal dimension." According to the *ceques,* and also according to what we have seen from the analysis of the witch doctors, *pacha* means, rather, "state of affairs" or "habitat," a vital *here* and *now* which also includes food. This is a given. All of this can suffer an overturn or a change, in sum, the *kuty*. The *kuty* requires a consecrated character such as Manco Capac, who, linked as he is to the symbol of the center, consecrates this "state of affairs," or *pacha*, by proposing a ritual. The ritual allows one to avoid the collapse of the *kuty* of the state of affairs; thus, one avoids such things as a bad harvest, an unlucky event, or being turned into stone.[18]

The ritual must not only be an efficacious solution to reach peace; it must also be carried out through a face-to-face encounter with fear, almost as an immersion in the domain of the *kuty* to take on the demonic forces which foster the *kuty*. In this way one succeeds in crossing a threshold of mutation that leads one to a vital catharsis that aims at attaining the totality of man and all his mystery. This is attained just as the lower world is reconciled with the upper world—the two unnameable extremes: the Pachayachachic's and the Guanacauri's, the *pacha* and the *kuty* simultaneously.

That is why Manco Capac does not limit himself merely to building the stone temple or the temple of the idol. He first sets up the numinous in general. This is what turns all the shrines into a mystical epic of conscience. Through natural elements such as stones, springs, mountains, or gorges, the steps are placed that lead to salvation, at the end of an archetypal struggle among opposites, but confronting fear so as to achieve the prototype and reach the point where psychic integration is produced and peace is won. Manco Capac represents in this sense the *gnosis* of the Inca world or the *yachacuni* as a knowledge of provocation and salvation. Such knowledge is the other sense of the term *pacha*, "the foundation" of existence in Lira's terms.

This concept is confirmed by the link that each of the Inca families maintained with the *ceques*. Each *ayllu*, or family, upon the death of the Inca founder, had to take on the responsibility for a *ceque*. The *ayllus* of the first Incas, those of Manco Capac and Cinchi Roca, took responsibility for the *ceques* of the Contisuyu, and the next three kings took care of certain rows of the Qollasuyu. Perhaps because the sixth Inca initiates the second series of five, his *ayllu* receives a *ceque* from Chinchaysuyu. That is, the dynasty crosses the line that separated the lower region, or Hurin-Cuzco, where the Contisuyu and the Qollasuyu are located, from the Hanan-Cuzco, or upper Cuzco. Was this done in order to reconcile symbolically the opposites, in particular the Guanacauri with the Pachayachachic? The families of the seventh and eighth Inca receive the Anti-suyu rows, and the ninth and tenth receive those of the Chinchaysuyu. The ten *ayllus* take responsibility for ten *ceques* arranged in a way that radiates out, encompassing the four regions of the indigenous cosmos. Likewise, they tend to occupy a *ceque*, generally called *callao*, or source. Upon this *callao* each of them seems to give rise to a group of three rows with a certain structural unity, if one takes into account the adjacent ones called *collana* and *payan*.

The distribution of the *ayllus* among the *ceques* gives shape to a sort of seminal unity which Manco Capac initiated and which ended with the penultimate king. This order gives a certain coherence to the plurality of shrines, including a distribution within indigenous time, in the shape of four segments since the kings distribute themselves in four regions. From the center, installed by Manco Capac, the dynasty moves in spiral form until they reach the Chinchay-suyu, the world of the Teacher of the *pacha*. History is thus mixed with ritual to maintain the fifth segment with the aim of avoiding the *pachacuti* and the appearance of the Red Sorcerer, and to maintain the deep sense of the *pacha* as a habitat of the *here* and *now*, or better, the *foundation* of existence.

Does the concept *pacha* imply a form of understanding specific to the pure fact of living? It follows from the analysis of the *ceques* that life is besieged between the two unnameable extremes, the Teacher of the *pacha*, on the one hand, and *Guilt*, on the other. Thus, it does not achieve any satisfaction or peace as it turns into immediate, nameable, daily reality. To achieve equilibrium or harmony in saying *my house, my work*, or *stone, tree*, or *sown field* seems to imply a rest or repose typical of someone urban, but not of the indigenous person, since the unnameable lays siege in a way that adds a constant margin of relativity to that which surrounds each one of us. That is already expressed by the *ucamahua*, the *así* of the world, insofar as it notes the mere event of *ucamahua* in the presence of which there is no place for rest. If the indigenous person says *my work* he does not express an unperturbed possession, but rather casts a magical spell through words; that is, he expresses the urgency that it really continue to be *"my"* work. *My work* enters into the *así* of the world and is thus relative, such that it can be lost through sickness, death, or dismissal. There is, then, no faith in the naming. Because it always flows into the unnameable extremes, the *pacha* or the *kuty*, naming is useless. It is always necessary to appeal to those extremes ritually to secure a line of understanding. Thus, the conciliatory knowledge of opposites opens itself always to new contradictions, as in the case of Apaza Rimachi. In his case the *achachila*, lightning, and *huak'a* referred just to the original tearing of the cosmos, including the mystery that the three of them exist. To say that there is nothing more than *pacha* or *kuty* is the same thing as to say that there is no more than one Teacher of the *pacha* and the black world of *Guilt*.

The pure fact of living is reduced to its minimal possibility. Because of that, the indigenous person cannot affirm without remainder the concept of man, because he knows, just as the existentialists of today know, that it does not exist. Bertonio confirms this when he translates the word *haque* as "man," but also as "the score counters in a game." It is curious that Holguín also translates *runa* in the same manner as "person, man, or female and male," but also as "the score counters in a game, as in *chuncam runay . . .* I have ten points." Does this mean that there is a lack of faith in man? No. It is simply a question of a torn conception of man, which is not far from the concept in the West. Here we have also reached the same point at the end of the euphoria provoked by the Industrial Revolution. Today in the West one appeals to the antagonism of the unnameables, as we will see below. The crisis consists in that one does not reach an understanding because of an excessive preoccupation with naming everything.[19]

A way of thinking that constantly points to an absolute tearing of the cosmos must nevertheless have some concept where it rests, even if transitionally. It seemed to me that Santacruz Pachacuti revealed this concept. As I demonstrated in my book *América Profunda*, the ordinary elements of the indigenous conception of the world appear in the drawing he includes in his chronicle. The split man is shown as a pair dressed in the style of the seventeenth century. They are pictured above the four elements: water, earth, fire, and air. As if this were not enough, he adds above the cross of cosmic fate, with the "pot of corn" and "the pot of weeds" (*saramanca* and *coramanca*) as symbols of scarcity and abundance, or their equivalent, the *pacha* and the *kuty* (figure 14). This is the same concept of man which Holguín and Bertonio record. But it is curious that he inscribes the whole figure within a framework which seems to represent a house with a gable roof. Yet there is more.

The name of the ancient wise people of the pre-Columbian world was *amauta*. According to Middlendorf, *amauta* comes from the Aymara verb *hamuta-ña*, which he translates as "thought, order, manner, mode." But surely this translation is not altogether precise, so it is worth mentioning what Bertonio contributes. First, he provides the graphic representation *amaotta*, which suggests a word composed of *ama* and *otta*. He links the particle *ama* with *amajasiña*, which is related to "to love," "to be fond of," "to remember," and "the dead." He also relates it to the idea of foretelling. This is not strange since, according to Garcilaso, the knowing of the *amauta* included astrology. In turn, *otta* must be *uta*, which in Aymara means "house." If this is correct, would it be related to the cosmic abode that the *amauta* had to offer his disciple? Is this the meaning when Santacruz draws the house?

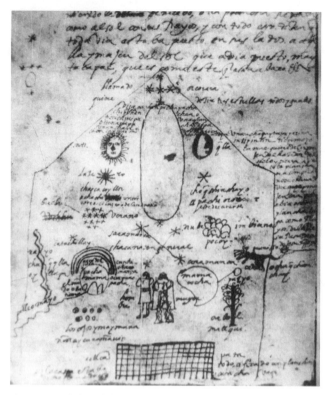

14   The presumed altar of the temple, named Coricancha del Cuzco,
according to Santacruz Pachacuti.

The same root *uta* seems to fit in the Aymara word *utcatha*. The second particle, *ca*, has a demonstrative value, so that if the word in question were *uta-catha*, it could mean "the way of the house," in the sense of its inhabitability, which is not far from *estar*, Bertonio's translation. Let us consider other senses. *Utcaña* means seat or chair, but also "mother or womb where woman conceives." *Utkhatatha* refers to "fulfilling *mita*" by keeping house or coming to someone's service, and *ut.ttaatha* to "expose or to take out things for sale as the peddlers do, or those who sell bread or other things in the square." *Tiyani* is the Quechua equivalent of this term. In the Quechua texts collected by Farfán, consisting of audio recordings gathered in the contemporary indigenous tongue, this verb occurs with remarkable frequency, even when it is used to mean to live or reside in a place.[20] When this verb forms *tiyachicuni*, according to Holguín, it means "*estar* selling";[21] *tiya* is translated as *hearth*.[22]

The first term, *utcatha*, is associated with *estar* in the sense of inhabit, but also with seat, womb, *mita*—that is communal work—and, finally, with the communal center or plaza. The same is true of *tiyani*, though with less richness of meaning. Do both terms enclose a basic feeling in indigenous life, what we termed *pacha* above? *Pacha* may be linked to the idea of growth (womb), community (*mita*, plaza), and, fundamentally, with place of residence, though in the sense of that cosmic house drawn by Santacruz Pachacuti.

It is natural that this vision comes to the indigenous people after seeing only the *así* of the world. This is confirmed in the Aymara verb *cancaña* and the Quechua *cani*. According to Bertonio and Holguín, respectively, these terms could be translated as "being or essence"; nevertheless, these verbs do not define but instead simply point, as the Quechua root *ca* makes particularly clear.[23] It is what Choque said when he referred to the *así* of the world.

Is the finality of indigenous thinking exhausted by this dwelling in the world found in the face of the *así*? It seems not. *Chuymani* is among the meanings Bertonio provides for the concept of the sage. Translated it means "owner of the heart." He also mentions the expression *achankhara chuymani*, where *achankhara* refers to a "flower of many colors," and *chuymakhtara*, where the term for heart appears once again.

A world torn between good and bad events is undoubtedly inhabitable. But its inhabitability will not be found merely in an *estar*, in an *utcatha*, but rather in being the owner of the heart, *chuymani*. Its inhabitability will also be found—as we saw several pages ago—through placing the *nayra* ahead of time in an object for the foretelling rite.[24] It will also be found remembering, *amutatha*, but this is done with the aim of attaining *amu*, or the bud of the flower, always tracing the *una*, or divine signs.

It is interesting to note that even when the *amu*, *una*, or *nayra* are achieved, at the end of the process there will always be a place of residence left which is exposed to the overturn or *kuty*. This will always happen as expressed in the Inca hymn transcribed by Guaman Poma. This hymn asks after the unnameable and unlocatable divinity:

> Viracocha of the Foundation and limit
> Where are you?
> In the *ground* above,
> In this *ground*,

> In the *ground* within,
> In the limiting *ground*?
> Creator of this *ground*,
> Maker of man,
> Where are you?
> Listen to me![25]

This poem outlines the indigenous cosmos admirably. I have translated the term *pacha* as "ground" to make it more intelligible. But it is evident that this term is thought of as habitat or residence. There are then four *pacha*, the one above, the one here, the inner one, and the one of the limit. Moreover, the unnameable god creates the *kay pacha*, that is, this *pacha*.

Indigenous philosophy does not separate knowledge from life. To the contrary, it revolves around precisely this life. It is what we call the *pacha*. *Pacha*, as *kay pacha*, is not existence, but rather what Heidegger rejects as "mere living." *Kay pacha* is linked with nameable things, what we call habitat, in a *here* and *now* not far from worries about food. The *pacha* sustains itself between a tearing of two unnameable extremes: one auspicious, the *pacha* from above, characterized in religion as Pachayachachic, Teacher of the *pacha*, and the other inauspicious, the inner *pacha*, Guanacauri.

This *pacha* can turn over at any moment because that is the law of the cosmos. Thus, man is conceived as chance, and ritual is necessary to maintain the stability of the habitat. This is not far from pre-Western thinking like that found in Buddhism. The theory of causations in the Wheel of Life also contains a conception of the *pacha*, but it is intermixed with other concepts such as reincarnation. Buddhism, like the Inca religion, is fundamentally a phenomenology of daily life. This is the basis from which the religion is structured.

Surely the common man of the empire did not achieve this form of gnosis. It would be attained only by certain personages. The Anonymous Jesuit and Fray de Murúa mention the *huancaquilli*, who devoted themselves to prophesy and philosophy. "From sunup till sundown they looked at the wheel of the sun intensely, no matter how bright, without moving their eyes. They said that in that resplendent, bright red wheel they saw and reached great secrets. They would stand during the whole day on one foot on the burning sand without feeling pain."[26] He then also mentions their frugality, health, and asceticism.

All of this gives the impression of an ascetic and rending conception. But it seems that it was not entirely so. Near Chiquinapampa, "the plains of misfortune," in Cuzco, was Cusipampa, the "plains of happiness," where the Inca Yupanqui was born, who was named Pachacuti, the one coinciding with the revolution of the *pacha*. He established new rituals and shrines.

The proximity of the *chiqui*, or misfortune, with the *cusi*, or happiness, is curious. Was there, then, some possibility of confronting the mere wordly succession of events with happiness? This is not far from indigenous wisdom. Ceferino Choque, the witch doctor, told me as much. Coca was useful not only to foretell but also to advise. I remember the time when one of our people consulted him as to how he was going to do in the United States. Choque said: "Why are you going?" And he recommended that he "quiet his heart, you will be fine right here, always." After a while he returned to the same person and said: "He does not want to go, but he does not want to stay here; his heart is split, his thinking is split."

That day we had given him too much alcohol as a gift. He was still sober when he told us that he was going to die within ten years. At a certain moment, while he showed us a leaf which symbolized death, he said to us: "You are going to do fine, but when I am dead," and laughed: "That is how it is, *ucamahua*," he added. With his death his *pacha* would reach its culminating point. His death would transform the *here* and *now* of his life, but also *his* hut, *his* community, in short, everything that was *for-his-life*. One could say that there was no death, only a mere overturn.

Chiuchis can be bought in any Bolivian market.[1] They are small lead figurines. As far as I could ascertain, there are more than fifty types. The most important figures seem to be: *sun, moon, star, mermaid, Santiago, couple, arch, plaza, tower, eagle, hen, lion, llama, weasel, bull, cow, sheep, key, wave, cane, musician, trumpet, charango, palm, amphora, fork, spoon, knife, bottle, chalice, plate, chair, table, platter,* or *pot* (figures 15a–d). Sometimes they attach to them silver or golden thread or paper, small sugar cubes, or pins. The presentation and shape of the figures vary according to whether they come from Oruro, La Paz, Puno, Sicuani, or Cuzco. Their range and the way they are duplicated also depends on their origin. For example, the sample from Oruro seems to keep a greater internal coherence. In La Paz the number diminishes, even though others are added. These also all show a certain popular style with elongated and simplified shapes. In Puno they are similar to those from Oruro. In Sicuani the shapes acquire great perfection, and this is true to a lesser extent of Cuzco.

I was able to observe some of the aspects of their manufacture in Oruro. The *chifleras* use as molds sheets of slate in which each shape is cut and repeated four or five times. The ones in La Paz seem to be manufactured differently, since some of the time whole series are stuck to each other, which surely

The *chiuchis*, or lead pieces, that are sold in the markets of the Andean highlands.

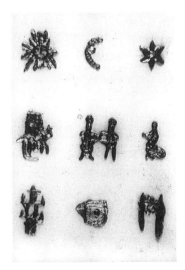

15a   From left to right in each row: *sun, moon, star, Santiago, couple, mermaid, tower, plaza,* and *arch.*

15b   From left to right in each row: *eagle, bird, hen, lion, llama, weasel, bull, cow,* and *sheep.*

15c   From left to right in each row: *fork, spoon, knife, bottle, chalice, plate, chair, table,* and *platter* or *pot.*

15d   From left to right in each row: *cane, wave, key, charango, trumpet, musician, amphora, huayruru,* and *palm.*

indicates that only one mold is used for a whole series. It is worth noting that these have elongated shapes, as if made with a burin, maybe to facilitate the work. In every case the casting is made by pouring the metal into molds. They are sold in small packages which are divided into two classes according to whether the *chiuchis* are *simple chiuchis*, which include only one series of figures that tend not to be repeated, or *chiuchis dobles* that include two copies of each figure, that are symmetrical opposites. Naturally, new molds are used in that case. The price of each envelope is 500 bolivianos for the *simples* and 1,000 for the *dobles*.

Tschopik points out that in the ceremonies of Chucuito the *yatiri*, or witch doctor, places each figure in front of its symmetrical image. The operation lasts a long time. An informant from La Paz told me that in Copacabana the *yatiri* smeared the *chiuchis* with grease and then would pick them up one by one with a stick to read someone's fortune.

Choque, the witch doctor from Tiahuanaco, did not know exactly either the name or the meaning of each of the figures, but he said that they were used to "feed" the *yancças* or *tios*.[2] He added, "It is for men," as if letting us know that, for example, it was not offered to divinities such as the Earth. A chola from La Paz gave me the same information.

A statistical analysis of the frequency of each figure in each region leads us to note that as one comes closer to Cuzco, some figures are lost, but the ones left are very significant and include *animal, bird, knife, fork, spoon, plate,* or *pot*; and also the sacred group, *sun, moon, star, mermaid, couple, Santiago, tower, plaza,* and *arch.*

They evidently seem to be offerings to infernal deities such as the *tios*, since they eat metals. The *tios* are the deities of the mines. The miner represents them through a small anthropomorphic clay statue placed in the first corridor of the mine and makes frequent offerings (*ch'alla*) to them. In general, as a *callahuaya* informed me in Oruro, they are used in negative rituals, that is, black magic, and they must not be mixed with the offerings of white magic. They are used to do evil. They bring misfortune to those who hold them in their power, even though they may also bring luck as Oblitas Poblete notes.[3]

Their use must be ancient. According to Bernabé Cobo, some of the shrines in Cuzco received as offerings gold and silver figurines representing adults, children, or animals. This is the case in very important *wak'as* such as the one of *Chuquipalta* which was devoted to the *Pachayachachic* trinity, which was composed of *Pachayachachic*, *intiillapa*, and *Punchau*, as we saw in the previous chapter. The shrines of *Guamansari*, surely a deity in the north of Perú, *Catongue*, *Pururauca*, *Saucero*, the farm of *Huanacauri*, and the landmarks devoted to the sun also received these offerings.[4] Bandelier has reproductions of some drawn from the Titicaca Basin.[5]

The thinking that accompanies indigenous people when they use these kinds of figurines must be different from ours. Thus, the question arises as to what extent it is possible to ascertain these differences.

The group from Oruro lends itself to an interesting analysis. The figures are distributed in threes. These in turn form four large groups that constitute a total of thirty-five figures, plus the red-and-black seed known as *huayruru*. If one adds to this the dual configuration such as one finds in the *chiuchis dobles*, then it can be affirmed that they follow the following numerical schema 2 x 3 x 4.

This principle of numerical organization is followed by all indigenous products even in the case of the unforeseen or unpredictable. If we gather those *ceques*—first those whose number of shrines is a multiple of five, and then separately those that are multiples of four, and finally all the rest, we also obtain three groups of fourteen *ceques* each. Moreover, the *ceques* with even and odd numbers of shrines are grouped in an eminently rhythmic manner. In Chinchay-suyu there are six *ceques*, with a number of even shrines and three odd ones. In Anti-suyu it is the opposite: three even ones and six odd ones; in Qolla-suyu, six even and three odd ones; and in Conti-suyu, six even and eight odd ones.

Let us look at the *chiuchis* grouped in threes. We have already dealt with the concept of trinity in Apaza Rimachi and Choque and in some of what Guaman Poma discusses. It is now appropriate to see whether a sort of dialectic is present in these groupings. This is the case with *eagle*, *bird*, *hen*, or *sun*, *moon*, *star*, or *church*, *plaza*, and *arch*. The *arch*, for example, has a great deal of significance in indigenous celebrations, since the Indian hangs offerings to the saint from the arch. How is the dialectic organized such that from church and plaza, the *arch* is the result?

Santo Tomás mentions something that allows us go deeper into the matter. He notes that the "sound of thunder" was *curaca yllapa*; "the minor thunder" was *chaupi yllapa*; and "thunder with lightning" *sullca yllapa*. That is, the *chief* thunder, the *middle* thunder, and the *minor* thunder.[6] They are three elements ordered in terms of increasing visibility. *Curaca* (chief) and *chaupi* (middle) are heard but not seen. *Sullca* (minor) is visible as lightning. The third term of the divinity belongs to the order of visible reality.

Guaman Poma adds to the third term the word *churin*—son—as in *sullca churin yllapa*, "minor son." Generally the last two terms of the trinity are considered as offspring of the first one. Cobo agrees. In relation to *churi*—son—Lima mentions *churiyakk*, which he translates as "the one that begets," or as the progenitor. He notes that *churi* must be understood only in relation to the progenitor.[7] Also in Cobo, father and son appear as completely dependent on and in opposition to each other, as if they entered two different orders of the indigenous cosmos. One can think, then, that the trinity, insofar as it moves from father to son, implies a fall of the divinity to a visible order. The opposition rests in that the less visible order is opposed to the more visible, almost as if the sky were opposed to the earth.

In turn the order of the fall of the divinity into the visible assigns to the third term functions entangled with daily existence. Cobo mentions that the third term of the sun trinity (*inti guauqui*) was the brother (*guauqui*) of the second term and also "had the virtue of begetting" as we have seen. Guaman Poma says of the third character that he was "the youngest son who gave and increased health and fed and sent water from the sky to feed us and to give us sustenance."

The third term was also considered to be *guauque* (brother) as we have seen. But Jesús Lara maintains that the chroniclers confused *guauque*, "brother," with *huanqui*, "statue."[8] When Cobo mentions that the *guauque* of Ticci-Viracocha was a mere stone, should we understand that as *statue* or as *brother*? In Chinchay-suyu there is "an idol of solid gold called *Intiillapa*. . . . It was made by Inca Yupanqui, and he took it as his *guauque* or brother." Cobo adds that "each of the kings and lords of the Inca line would build a statue of himself during his lifetime. With a certain solemnity and ceremony they would take the statue as their brother, calling it *guauque*, which means brother."[9] Evidently the visible order of a statue is confused with the third term of the trinity. Be that as it may, whether it be statue or brother, they are both given at the same order and with the same hierophantic meaning.

Holguín translates the term *guauque* as "brothers and all males," but also as "cousin, or second or third cousin or nephew when he is of the same age or older than ego." He adds later that *huaoque* is said of the "acquaintance or friend," and he relates this to the *ayllu*.[10] The concept *guauque* contains then not only the idea of brotherhood but also that of friendship and community. In sum, the third term is visible, promotes fecundity, and is also related to community. It fits in the *pacha*, that is, the here and now of existence. The *guauque* is, then, the visual presence of the divine in the tactile, physical plane of the idol or the sacred object.

But it is not a *guauque* without the two prior elements in the order, the father and the older or middle son. The *guauque* of Ticci Viracocha is related to two other shrines, as we have seen. The sun, according to Cobo, is preceded by *Apu-Inti*, Lord Sun, and *Churi Inti*, the sun's son. We could cite other examples. Does this mean that all that is visible is preceded by two terms, one the equivalent of a father that coincides with the "above," another a middle or older son that corresponds to the "below," these two considered opposites, resulting in turn from a divinity that descends and commits itself, or becomes tangled, or torn in an opposition at the heart of which is the cosmos? Behind everything that exists, or *is seen*, an original duality operates against a background, a duality that only at the end of reflection is thought of as a divinity that has fallen into triads. Does this constitute a category of indigenous thinking?

It is not difficult to prove that this schema holds in every case. The indigenous person notices an uneasiness long before noticing an object. The object is no more than a symbol in the manner of the *guauque*. Afterward there is the reference to the original tearing of the cosmos which goes from the simple possibility of alternating the favorable and the unfavorable, *yanoca* or *hisqui* in Aymara, to the conception of a Pachaya-chachic and a Guanacauri as unnameable extremes which tear the cosmos. Both a simple witch doctor like Apaza Rimachi and the priesthood who ordered the *ceques* in Cuzco have used this schema.

This is reflected even in the written histories and legends. Santacruz Pachacuti transcribes in his chronicle a story common to several authors of the time. He tells us that Tunupa arrived in "a village called Tiyagua-naco. It is said that in it people were drinking and dancing. Tunupa preached to them as he was accustomed to, but they did not listen. They say that in his anger, he lifted his eyes to the sky and spoke in the language of that land. And as he left the place all the people who were dancing turned into stones, and that they can be seen there until today."[11]

In this narrative there is a restitution or compensation of opposites. Tunupa is the intermediary in a cosmic duality that transcends him. The mistreatment to which he is subjected and which constitutes an injustice is compensated by the petrification of those at the party. Behind the story lies a cosmic balance that stabilizes the everyday world. The two unnameable poles function to fix what man spoils and vice versa.

This can be seen in another legend which tells of a character called Inkarrí. It was transcribed by Arguedas and Bourricaud from an audio recording made among the Peruvian Indians.[12] Inkarrí, who is the equivalent of Inka-king, is a character who had imprisoned the wind in a mountain. He had also tied the sun to the same mountain, "so that time would last, so that the day would last." The founding of Cuzco is attributed to Inkarrí, but he is imprisoned by the Spaniards: "They say that only Inkarrí's head exists. He is growing from the head down, they say that he is growing toward his feet. Inkarrí will come back when his body is complete. He has not come back to this day. He will come back if God gives his consent. But we do not know, they say, whether God will agree to his return." Another indigenous man gives the following version: "They took his head (Inkarrí's) only his head (to Cuzco), and they say his hair is growing, his small body is growing down. When he is reconstituted the judgment may take place." This tale consists of a visual symbol, Inkarrí, which must surely contain everything that the indigenous person feels toward his race. That is why his head grows until the day of judgment, surely to restitute something which has been taken from the indigenous people. Now, why does it grow? This can only be understood if one understands Inkarrí as a consecrated visualization, the equivalent of a *guauque* which points to a background consisting of a dual cosmos. Inkarrí will restore the equilibrium between the opposites that was originally torn by the foreigners.

The structure of thinking here is the same as in the case of the *chiuchis* or the *ceques*, with the difference that instead of following a descending logic which goes from the Father to the Older Son and ends with the Younger Son, the tale begins with the fallen divinity at the level of the Younger Son, or *guauque*, and appeals to the numinous torn duality between the unnameable and opposed extremes. That duality affects the conception of time that in the tale ends in a judgment, almost in the manner of a cycle. This cycle also depends on that duality.

The tearing is not suffered only by that which is susceptible to visualization, as in the case of the characters in the story. Everything that can be thought, including concepts, is subject to the cosmic tearing. For example, it is curious that according to Bertonio the term *hatha* means "cast," "family," or "*ayllo*," but also "seed of plants, men, and all the animals."[13] *Hathasina* is linked to semen. He translates *haccu* as "thing worthy of esteem or value," but also as "innumerable." When *maa* is added, or when the word appears in the form *haccutatha*, it implies something conceived by a woman. *Utcatha*, "to be seated," also means matrix. *Hila*, translated as "older brother," is associated with *hilaatha*, "to raise as mothers do," or *hilatha*, "to grow, to become older." According to Bertonio *viñaya* means "always," but it is associated with a plant or tree, and in Quechua, according to Holguín, it is translated as "growth." In the *rezalipiches*, the prayers painted on leather by the indigenous people, the term eternity is represented by a tree.[14]

Other concepts are even more significant. *Nayra*, as we have seen, means "eye," but also "antiquity." Similarly the Quechua term *ñawi*, according to Kuzcinsky Goddard, is a symbol of germination, or is a fountain of *mana*, as Valcárcel adds. The eyes of the potato are very important. Varcárcel mentions the word *pacarina*, or place of birth, as a germinal fountain of favor and disfavor for a subject. Aymara and Quechua are flexible in turning nouns into verbs and vice versa, and they have an abundance of particles that indicate the idea of realization or completion. Without doubt we can go to what Whorf says about Hopi in order to explain this. Hopi is one of several languages that reflect events rather than objects. However, in saying this we would not be saying anything, because the explanation is external and superficial.

Where does this link come from between concepts and the idea of growth? It must be that a concept, insofar as it becomes concrete in a word—as Leenhardt interprets in the primitive case—belongs to the order of the intelligible, of the connotative, of the nameable; it becomes, in short, of the order of the *guauque*. But as it has not fallen into the visible order, it still grazes against the numinous sphere and acquires the same rank and function as the third element of the trinity. That element is what we saw in Cobo as that which *begets* in connection with the sun, or "that which gave or increased health" in Guaman Poma. In short, it has acquired the generative function of the *sullca churin*.

Everything that belongs to the *kay-pacha*, or "ground from here," and which has to do with the *pacha*, that which the unnameable Teacher teaches, the here and now of our life, the everyday, has the possibility of growth as a primordial quality simply because it belongs to the order of the *guauque*.

Where does this obsessive insistence on growth come from? The question leads us to the schema of the fall of the divinity. Evidently the order of the *guauque* is present when the divinity crosses a barrier of mutation from the terrible or transcendent toward the intelligible or quotidian. The terrible rests in turn on the monstrous and inhuman but transcendent play of opposites. Is growth then a way of compensating with what is intelligible and perceptible for a cosmic game that is unintelligible and unnameable?

I got that impression from a tale I taped in Oruro and which was similar to the one of Inkarrí cited above. The informant said that the Aymaras from Carangas think that "the Inca has turned into money, into silver." They say, "the Inca king, without a body, like money . . . like a treasure . . . like a *powerful* thing."[15] He added that he had heard a boy (*chango*) sing a song that often mentioned the money associated with the Inca and others had immediately forbidden him from singing it.

This concept of the Inca is conceived on the order which we have called that of the *guauque*. It is as if it grazed against the numinous and terrible background of the unnameable. Growth, centered on "that which is powerful," is the intelligible extreme of a background that transcends it.

Toward what and within what limits does everything of the order of the *guauque* grow? Evidently growth is not unlimited. Nor is there a general trend toward growth since the opposite, decline, can also happen. One can see this in the concept *huiñay*. It points to growth, according to Ibarra Grasso, but also to diminishing or wearing away.[16] Thus, the question may not center on the concept of growth, but rather on the mobility between opposites. This mobility seems to depend in great part on the play of opposites against the cosmic background. This is expressed through the symbol of the pot with coca and the pot with weeds which Santacruz places beneath the fundamental circle of the creator Viracocha.

In this sense it is worth emphasizing the great importance that seminal symbols such as *nayra* or *amu* have for the indigenous person. Are they manifestations of the numinous at the level of the intelligible? In short, are they signs, or *una*, of the cosmic background which, given their well balanced structure, suggest the idea of equilibrium between opposites?

The indigenous person comes to intuit the mechanism peculiar to his conception of the world through a criterion that must not be very far from what is expressed by the term *chamakani*, "owner of the darkness." It is the term he uses to name the highest witch doctors.[17] Behind the faculty of seeing clearly and distinctly lies the background of darkness. The demonic margin that conditions the world is surely deposited in that background. The indigenous vision does not become concrete, then, in the simple tree, but in the numinous margin which surrounds the tree. The anti-object frame makes the existence of the tree relative to it. The faculty of seeing is made possible by absence, like an immersion of the existent in the nonexistent, as if reality were viewed in the negative.

This is confirmed by how the *chiuchis* are organized in four groups. Each seems to correspond to an order of reality. Two of them are made up of sacred symbols and animals, respectively. The other two do not maintain a particularly marked internal coherence. But one can say that one joins together the symbols of the home and the other encompasses those that refer to community (rule, entertainment, and appeasement).

The symbols linked to agrarian activity are nevertheless missing. It is also intriguing that the Virgin and other symbols are also missing. Would this be a question of seeing through absence, as we just discussed? It is evident that a fifth group is missing. This fifth group would complete the circle encompassed by the *chiuchis*, specifically those symbols that refer to the *pacha* of indigenous people.

The absence is explicable in part because the figures in question are offered to infernal deities "so that they can eat." This is done to save the *pacha*, the environment or state of things. In any case, indigenous thinking operated in this case also through subtraction. What would this mean? Or more precisely, to what is this "seeing through absence" due?

It is surely based on the *ucamahua* of which Choque spoke. To see the *así* of the world is to turn it into a pure succession of events. That is, it is to place it at the level of the *guauque*, as victim of the unnameable gods. In this way matter and antimatter are combined, since things are always accompanied by the pressure of the divinity as the divinity plays with them. This is what we have called "facing fear" or the opening to another dimension of man where the imponderables have weight and where thinking, whether one likes it or not, transcends perception and escapes in search of unnameable terms. It is worth noting in passing that only because of this does the indigenous person conceive a perceptible world, the *kaypacha,* or ground from here. Behind it are the torn or rent background, the *hanan-pacha,* or ground from above, and the *uk'u-pacha,* or ground from within. This is also why Apaza Rimachi places the *achachila* and the *huak'a* behind the visible order of lightning, or Choque distinguishes between the Gloria and *yanccas.*

What, finally, in all of this, is the real situation of *Pacha-mama,* generally connected to the earth? Its literal translation is suggestive, "mother or lady of the *pacha.*" Did the generation of this *pacha,* or habitat, depend on this divinity? It is a question of the habitat but at a perceptive level, the visible, such as that which *is seen growing.* And because it is of the visible or everyday, she is segregated from the major trinities. In short, it is the microcosmos situated in the *kay-pacha,* or ground from here, which is what we argued in our discussion of the *ceques.* It corresponded to the order of Choque's *así* or *ucumahua* and required a thinking in terms of threes to achieve a transcendent explanation. The *así* falls into the logic of the *guauque.* Thus, the tearing of the cosmos into the opposed good and bad omens must be behind the *pacha* as habitat that grows, as expressed by the term *pacha-mama.* This three-part thinking offered the indigenous people a deeper understanding of their lives, an understanding that simple perception of reality could not give them.

This fits the citation of the hymn transcribed by Guaman Poma that I discussed in the last chapter. He mentions four *pacha*: first, the one above; second, the one inside; third, the one from here; and fourth, the one of the limit or the one nearby, according to the other meaning of *cailla.* There are four slots, three of which are ordered in a trinity and a fourth considered as nearby or marking a limit. The first three correspond to the cosmos divided into opposites in dialectical conciliation, and the fourth one, the one of the *guauque,* to the *así* that is perceivable. Thus, indigenous thinking goes from this *así* to the tripartite group where one finds the ultimate and transcendent explanation of all events.

At first sight the ornamentation of the Bennett Monolith seems to follow a criterion of symmetry which, from an artistic point of view, consists in two parallel and inverted shapes. But behind this concept of symmetry there must be much more.

Cuzco was divided symmetrically into an above, the Hanan-Cuzco, and a below, the Hurin-Cuzco. Chroniclers insist that the division is not due to social but to religious categories. These are given to us by the Aymara; it is in the Aymara that we can trace the true meaning of this opposition.

According to Bertonio the part above is called *alasaa* and the one below, *maasaa*. *Ala* must be linked to *alakh* which means "above" since together with the term *pacha* it translates as "the sky, abode of saints." *Maa* means the number "one when referring to things other than men, angels or God." *Saa*, in turn, translates as "the stature or size of a man." It seems to follow that *alasaa*, the part above, has the meaning of a sky reduced to the size of man. *Maasaa* is the world of happenings, populated by things, and also reduced to the size of man.

The two parts are opposed as the sky is to the earth. Actually, it is as if the original duality of the cosmos were joined in a unity. From that point the ritual sense of the struggle emerges, *ti'inku* in Quechua, carried out annually between the two parts. This ritual is practiced in the whole of the Andean highlands and usually ends in a bloody way. Also from this unity comes the sense that everyday life acquires from the simple fact of inhabiting a village structured according to this somewhat cosmic model.

Even more significant is the symmetry in Santacruz Pachacuti. Everything on the left side of his drawing is related to the masculine, such as the sun, or Imaymana Viracocha. Everything on the right is related to the feminine, such as the moon, or Tocapo Viracocha. If on the left is inscribed the idea of the abundance of all things (*ymaymana*), he also added disease, *usu*, in Aymara. And if on the right is the figure of Tunupa, a symbol of dispossession, rain is also there, ultimately a symbol of fecundity.[1]

Left and right do not correspond to good and bad omens. Instead one finds good and bad omens simultaneously and on the same side. One could say that Santacruz's thinking intertwines antagonistic elements in such a way that each element linked to habitat, or *pacha*, is related to some form of its opposite: the overturn, or *kuty*. Clearly, this is the question of immersion in darkness I discussed in the last chapter.

Symmetry must not be understood, then, in terms of inverted and equal forms, but rather as a monstrous vision in which the auspicious and the inauspicious, the *pacha* and the *kuty*, or even worse, the unnameable polarity of the cosmos, are given simultaneously.

Returning to the Bennett Monolith, can we affirm without qualification that it reflects in its ornamentation the indigenous vision of the cosmos?[2] If that is the case, we would have to give up the prejudice of seeing in the monolith a simple, static block of stone (figure 16). Let us see.

In the region of the thorax one finds three great levels, a superior one, a middle one, and an inferior one. Are these three bands to be identified with the *hanan-pacha*, the *uk'u-pacha* and the *kay-pacha*? Do they contain symbols equivalent to the Pachayachachic and the Guanacauri, that is, the unnameable extremes?

Something like this seems to be indicated by the lower band, particularly on the sides of the monolith. One finds a skeleton with a corn plant on the rear. Does it refer to the *uk'upacha* or the world below, that of the Guanacauri? Another important aspect is the central figure on the back of the monolith. It has its arms raised and points to two opposed faces, one surrounded by felines and the other by eagles. To the left and right of this figure appears a head hanging from a trident, which evokes the Mayan symbol of the "sun that falls." In general, the ornamentation on the

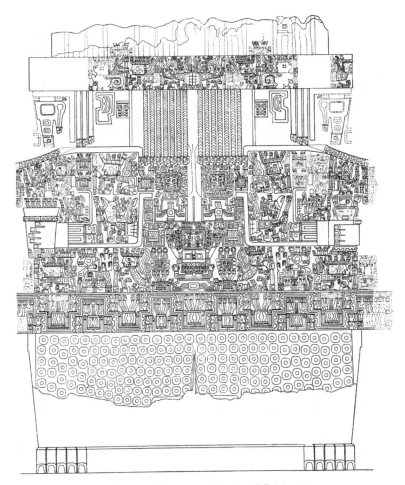

16   Unfolded decoration of the monolith uncovered by Wendell C. Bennett
in Tiahuanaco, Bolivia.

back is highly integrated relative to the dispersion on the front of the
monolith. Is it that a problem opens up in the front of the monolith and
closes in the back? In this sense it seemed to me that the process described
in the monolith, from a structural point of view, must not be far from the
tale of the Popol-Vuh. I am thinking in particular of the legend of the twin
heroes introduced before the creation of the fifth age, the flower age. The
legend tells of the descent of two characters who have celestial qualities,
which makes them good musicians. They are clumsily unable to resolve

the enigmas posed to them at the entrance to hell, the kingdom of Xibalbá. Because of their failure, one is sacrificed and his head remains hanging like a fruit from a tree.

An infernal character appears before the tree and is spat upon by the skull who says: "In my spit and spittle I give you my descent." From this union twin heroes are born. They have, among other things, magical gifts such as the ability to tear a man to pieces and then put him together again. They create the fifth man out of corn. The fifth man then has to be blinded because of his excessive wisdom, and consequently he can only see things that are very close by.

Were the three levels in the Bennett Monolith represented in order to indicate a descent into hell so as to achieve the ultimate integration, something like a fifth humanity made of corn, or at least simply the creation of corn? This is nevertheless not how it appears in the Popol-Vuh, but rather in the Codex Borgia.

In the Codex, the descent into hell is told in two moments. In the first one, after Quetzalcóatl's death, the young corn is born. The second one is more important since it shows the elaborate participation of a priesthood. Quetzalcóatl is sacrificed in the same manner as the Aymara do in their *huilancha*, by removing his heart. Once Quetzalcóatl is dead, he is associated with feminine symbols, whether it be the goddess of sin, or the *tzitzimimes*, who are she-devils that appear at the end of the fifth age. The death of Quetzalcóatl is then linked to his metamorphosis, which also coincides with the appearance of corn.

In the final leaf, Quetzalcóatl is identified with the god Nanahuatzin, since Quetzalcóatl is inside a pot, accompanied by four female characters. Seler points out that the hero initiates his itinerary in the East and marches to the West where he meets the original mothers upon whom plants depend in order to grow.

In the Bennett Monolith there is no central character except for the general process from which corn originates. The central character on the back of the monolith does not seem to be a warrior, but a feminine character, since the breasts are marked. On the left and the right appears the theme we have already seen: the sun that sets, associated with corn which sprouts from the feet of the central figure. If this is correct, the monolith is not a mere object, but rather a cosmic cube in which the three grounds of the indigenous cosmos are symbolized and a fourth "world from below" is linked to corn. The consecration of this process is shown on the back. The back of the monolith belongs to the divine order, while the front belongs to the human order, that of mere events.

The ornamentation is even more significant. It consists of three elements: condor, fish, and feline. The condor is clearly connected to the sky, and the fish to the world below. These are distributed among the figures as opposed, since the condors and the fish appear in the anterior face, and on the left and right sides. On the back, on the other hand, the number of fish diminishes, and the felines figures predominate. Do the felines represent the point of union of the unnameable opposites of heaven and hell?

To these elements two other signs are added. One consists in a square with other inscriptions, and the second is represented by two interconnected hooks. The first must surely represent the *center* in the sense of the center of a mandala. It is a symbol of integration since it is primordially associated with the condor and appears on the breast of the central figure in the Gateway of the Sun. The other seems to represent opposition or revolution in the sense of the *kuty*, and is usually associated with the fish. It appears four times on the back, surrounding the central figure strategically. We shall call the first the symbol of the *center* and the second the symbol of *duality*.

Twenty-eight other characters figure on the monolith. They carry staffs. Some represent birds, others men. Almost all are kneeling or standing in worship. According to a particular criterion, diverse symbols are added to each such as snail, bird, fish, etc. Yet the symbols for the center and for the duality are only shown on the chest and at the center of the staff. The ten characters drawn on the monolith's headdress carry the signs of duality on the chest or on the dart thrower. The same is true of those on the first row of the chest, except for two characters, near the back, who, instead, carry the sign of the center on the chest. In the intermediate line, four characters carry the signs of duality on both sides, except for the one next to the back on the right, on whose scepter appears the symbol of the center. The four apparently human characters in the lower part have scepters with signs of the center, and two of them, next to the back, also carry the sign of the center.

Could the symbol of the chest, associated with the heart, be interpreted as something that integrates opposites in the sense we saw in the *chuyma* or *soncco*?[3] Let us remember what Wilson wrote regarding the attributes of

Ptah in Egyptian mythology. Could it be that the symbol on the staff is associated with rule or word, that is, with the aboriginal *aro*, or *suti* in its sense of commandment? If this is so, the drawings on the Bennett Monolith acquire great significance. The characters can be divided into those who are turners of time and those who are conciliators or integrators, depending on whether they carry the symbol of the center or that of duality, respectively. Is this similar to Siva and Vishnu?[4] We add that throughout the length of the body, excluding the headdress, are distributed seven characters who carry only the symbol of duality and another seven who carry the symbol of integration, whether on the heart or on the scepter. The rhythm of the three bands on the body has a very similar meaning to Guaman Poma's. The first band represents the premise of the *father*, the intermediate one that of the *just son*, and the last one that of the *giver of life*, since the characters tend to carry the symbol of integration or center. If we think that a scepter with a symbol of the center represents something like an integrative word, we can refer to the Popol-Vuh, in which the successive humanities were destroyed because they could not *talk* to the gods.

The theme of the fish as it appears on the belt and that accompanies the symbol of the center in five cases invokes the theme of the *chamacani*. *Chamacani* was the master of darkness, a characteristically ritual symbol. This symbol was almost a radical union of opposites, something equivalent to Quetzalcóatl as a union of *quetzal*, referring to the sky, and *cóatl* meaning "earth."

The scepter held by the monolith is opposed to the *k'ero*, or pot. The left hand is represented correctly; the right hand seems, however, to be inverted. This could mean that there is no right hand; it is the same left hand, but inverted, which holds up the symbol of the scepter. This would fit in with the wisdom of the primitive. Besides, the *k'ero* seems disintegrative, something that stirs things up, as evidenced by the abundance of fish. On the other hand, a small symbol, probably of the center, appears in the scepter. It is six condors surrounded by five fish. Is this an integrative symbol, a mandala, within the Tiahuanacotan thinking? The theme of the monolith must surely be that of reaching an integrative unity that previously passed through the world of the fish. It is worth noting also that the symbol of the center, with its eagles, appears specifically at the corners of the monolith. This symbol of the center is next to the two aforemen-

17   Detail of the back of the mono-
lith uncovered by Carlos Ponce
Sanginés in Tiahuanaco, Bolivia.
Photograph by the author.

tioned heads on the back. Another two appear beside the head of the main
character, which is located a little farther down.

The ornamentation on the whole seems to consist in a tale in which the
theme of the condor faces the theme of the fish; towards the back, the
theme of the feline is featured as conciliator of opposites and as the result
of the bad energy of the fish united with the virtues of the condor. All of
this is interwoven with the themes of the revolution of time and integration. In short, it is possible that it expresses no more than the idea of how
the world of the condor must pass through the world of the fish to achieve
the feline plane, almost as if it were a tale of hierogamy. This could be
confirmed by the Ponce Monolith on whose back appears a bird with a
feline head accompanied by two characters (figure 17). The feline is, then,
the symbol of the union of opposites, as if it carried magic and power.

The Ponce Monolith and the Bennett Monolith teach about the play of
opposites mixed with a style of thinking that tends exclusively to show
where salvation lies. All of this is subject to a pattern or rhythm of inversion. The Bennett Monolith is, then, not static. It is dynamic. It partici-

pates in the same mobility as the Inkarrí, Santacruz Pachacuti's tale of Tunupa, and Guaman Poma. But in the Bennett Monolith the fundamental points of a theology are made explicit. This theology would be useful so that man as a forsaken being, plunged into everyday living, consumed by uneasiness, can reach the order of the feline. Behind reality breathes the opposition of the cosmos, torn between condors and fish. One finds this in the tales as well. The tale of Inkarrí or the tale of Tunupa place us in the feline plane and *open* us toward the world of the original rending of the cosmos, even though neither fish nor feline are mentioned. This is also true of the *chiuchis*, where condor and fish are equivalent to the sun and the moon. The morning star would certainly have the same virtue as the feline, but without the support of a priesthood which builds monoliths or organizes an empire.

The imposing vision of the monolith, and, above all, that conceptual solidity with which it must have been made, makes one think of the concept of truth in the Quechua world. Holguín contributes the term *sullull* in his *Vocabulary*: "truth or true house." But he later notes for *sullull* "aborted dead fetus." Desiccated llama fetuses are called *sullu* in the Andean Highlands today. They are sold for use in witchcraft.

I remember when I attended a *qharira* in Toledo: on a small table, ritually arranged, was the fetus of a recently sacrificed llama. It had a lot of *truth* in the Quechua sense.

Our truth is of Aristotelian origin. It is the coincidence of judgment with the objective situation. But the Quechua truth was other. One could say it is of a seminal type, torn just like the fetus from the depth of the subject and put forth here and now on the level of *pacha*, with an enviable sincerity, the blood still steaming. This is, in the end, the deep reason that always encouraged their thinking. A cosmos subjected to a constant reversal cannot but incite each subject to achieve its integration at the level of the *sullu*. Let us see up to what point this can be confirmed in the indigenous economy.

In Toledo, near Oruro, in Bolivia, I had a very educated and distinguished neighbor, who, he confessed to me, was of pure indigenous descent. He charged the Indian with being illiterate, since he could not get accustomed to a cooperative system. He based his idea on the fact that though the Indian entered into cooperative arrangements readily, when things did not go well, he demanded the return of the profit, or at least the capital invested. For that reason, according to this informant, who had worked in an office of the United Nations in La Paz, all cooperatives fail among indigenous people. It is worth noting that the members of various North American firms who aimed at organizing the indigenous Bolivian people in cooperatives must think the same way. Faced with the sterility of their effort, they suspended their activity in 1967.

All of this is very serious if one considers that the indigenous people of the high Andean plane use a system of communal contribution or reciprocity called *ayni*, which is several thousands year old, and which has a great deal of similarity with the cooperative system. It is constituted by an economic relation prior to a money economy. It is based on common property in land and tools. Every job is entered collectively, so that even today, according to reports, when someone wants to build a house, the whole community helps. Sowing and harvesting the land are also done in common.

If the cooperative within a liberal economy constitutes the system of reciprocity closest to the indigenous one, and if indigenous people nonetheless resist it, then the neighbor's disappointment is understandable, as is the disappointment of the Left in the Andean highlands. One believes the forms of the economy are flexible, but nothing can be achieved with them.

What happened in Toledo has continued to repeat itself with the same curious persistence from the outset of the Conquest. Garcí Diez de San Miguel speaks to this when he describes his visit to the Province of Chucuito on Lake Titicaca in 1567.[1]

The ancient kingdom of the Lupaca had survived there. The people had preserved the ancient customs since, given its prosperity, the Crown had conceded certain privileges to it. The kingdom was composed of seven cities: Chucuito, Acora, Ilave, Juli, Pomata, Yunguyo, and Zepita. Each city had a large number of satellite villages. As was the custom in the Andes, the population was grouped into two large segments, the Hanansaya and Urinsaya, and each was headed by a *mallku*, or chief.

This kingdom had a system of communal contribution which consisted in ceding to the *mallku* at his request a certain quantity of *tupus*, or parcels of land and labor. The indigenous people who did the work received hardly anything in return, just a little "food to eat, coca, *chuño* [dessicated potato], corn, sometimes meat and what they need to subsist."

It is curious that Garcí Diez, who meticulously recounts everything that happens in these communities, does not emphasize the almost free contribution by the indigenous person, for which he or she was not, in the end, properly remunerated. This must be because the resulting production, even when it seemed to be to the exclusive benefit of the *mallku*, was used, John Murra tells us, "to satisfy the demands of the Dominican clergy for the construction of churches and to buy ornaments."[2]

The otherwise objective and calm exposition by Garcí Diez is disturbed when he gets to the problem of the weavers. First, Garcí Diez says that the men "take a month and a half to complete a piece." And "they make clothes for women to wear for themselves and for the care of their homes. They take care of their farms, land, and raise and house their cattle, which do not have another hacienda to go to. They go forty, fifty, or sixty leagues once or twice a year for two or three months to get food from the valleys and they also go the same distance for wood for their homes, which is twice what half the Indians ordinarily walk outside of that province."[3] In spite of these difficulties, these indigenous people made their textiles only at the request of the *mallkus*, not when requested by a Spaniard. And what is worse, and here Garcí Diez becomes indignant, "is that these Indians have never received anything for this work because everything was taken by the cacique (or *mallkus*). I learned this during an inquiry I conducted during the trip and from the declarations of the caciques themselves. They confessed forthrightly, even though they absolved themselves by saying that though they have not given anything to the Indians, all that they received in terms of manufacture of clothes and the work of the Indians had been spent on the construction of churches and church ornamentation. Given the sumptuousness of their works, they have quite absolved themselves." Venting his indignation, Garcí Diez advises, "Your Excellency should order that no cacique should be obliged to make clothes . . . but whoever wants clothes made (a Spaniard, for example) could arrange with the Indian or Indians who will do the work and pay them directly."[4]

The problem is understandable. Garcí Diez wants the weaver to receive what is just. Thus, he proposes that the weaver make arrangements directly with the Spaniards. His reaction belongs to our modern form of conceiving the economy. The product manufactured by the worker must be paid for. This constitutes one of the most important issues of our time. Almost all the problems of the modern world revolve around this question and above all around the question of how much one should pay.

The proof lies in that Garcí Diez does not pay much attention to the contribution of labor to the *mallku*, nor to the fact that the indigenous worker is only repaid with food. His irritation is due to an object, the woven cloth, and only then does he invoke repayment and the importance of the time the Indian has spent. Money and production, and above all, the objects produced, are the pillars of economic science.

But the weaver resists working directly for the European. Why? The resistance seems to us irrational. It seems as irrational as when Guaman Poma, in his constant diatribe against the Spaniards, tries to affirm the right to life and property of his contemporaries by invoking the ancient myth of the five ages. He writes, "The Christian Indians have learned such a false law because the ancient law was God's and of the saintly works of mercy of the Indians from that time—of *uariuiracocharuna*—and of *uariruna* and of *purunruna*—*aucaruna*—*yncapacharuna*. They have until this time the law of mercy. No generation of Christian Spaniards—Moors—

and Turks, French, Jews, English, Indians from Mexico and from China, Paraguay, Tucumán have ever eaten in the public plaza nor do they have celebrations in them such as the Indians from this kingdom have and all their relatives from that *ayllo*, or group who fed the poor."[5]

One is tempted to characterize the reaction of the weavers and of Guaman Poma as simply resulting from "custom." But to say "custom" is to give an external description of the phenomenon that fails to account for the root of these reactions and claims.

For example, Jesús Lara, in his book *La cultura de los Incas* (*The Culture of the Incas*), gives us a detailed and well-documented account of the system of reciprocity, and cites about ten versions of this system.[6] Nevertheless, his presentation is distant from our middle-class scholarly attitude, at the level of indigenous customs, given that the intimate and deep mechanisms that must have held up such a system are not noticed.

From that position it is useless to want to remedy or explain away the irrationality of custom and to affirm, for example, that "there was a rational distribution of labor," or that "the call for the contributions was made paying attention to the needs and predilections of the state."[7] The use of such terms as "rational" or "state" responds to a criterion that belongs to our Western culture. Without this criterion we would not understand the "custom," since only the rationality of Inca organization was apparent; as we will see, the organization was actually quite irrational. Besides, there was no such "state," since this term belongs to Richelieu's rationalism. It corresponds to a typical moment of European evolution, precisely that moment which reified the concept of state and distanced it from the religious background in which it had been immersed. This is completely the opposite of what was happening with the Inca system of government.

It is therefore clearly preferable to interpret the assumed "customs" of the pre-Columbian world in light of the categories of a cultural system parallel to ours and think that it moved within a strictly irrational plane. Yet this use of *irrational* does not attribute to it the usual sense of original chaos. Only then will we be able to understand the indigenous system of reciprocity and also Guaman Poma's apparent "naïveté" when he invokes the four ages where we would invoke modern economy.

In Bertonio's *Vocabulary* the concept of "reciprocity" has its Aymara equivalent in the term *ayni*, which means "the one obligated to work for another who worked for him."[8] This implies a criterion of compensation and of obligation. If we add to this the meaning of *maytha*, or request, that is, the request made by the *mallku* so that the system of reciprocity can begin its functioning, the concept becomes wider. *Maytha* is translated by Bertonio as "to give and lend anything." He adds *maysitha*, "to request that something be given or lent." It is intriguing that later Bertonio adds the term *mayhahuatha*, "to do good, to answer someone else's need." With this, reciprocity seems to be ruled by a kind of moral canon that obliges indigenous people to lend their labor.[9]

In short, reciprocity was carried out on an irrational basis, but the concept "irrational" is to be understood above all as an implicit system in Inca life. It is natural then to infer that reciprocity was not a response to coercion by the state, nor to a tacit contract between the state and the individual. Rather, it was carried out within that freedom achieved when, as Hegel puts it, the subject identifies with or subordinates himself to a moral law. Besides reciprocity and on the same moral plane, the obligation of the Inca was to refrain from interfering with the stockroom of the domestic sphere. Murra says in this regard that "the traditional income of the lords consisted fundamentally on access to the *energy* of the peasants ... who cultivated the land of the state, grazed their flock, wove the cloths for the Crown, and fulfilled their *mitta* in *public* works, but the peasant stockroom remained untouched."[10] The Inca evidently avail themselves of only one irrational element, the simple energy of the community.

Garcí Diez affirms that "in the Andes the lands had no value without the people; they were structurally nonexistent."[11] He adds an important definition of reciprocity: "a set of mutual 'favors' in life, taking as a model the pattern of reciprocity existing at the level of *hatha*, or the village."[12]

These new concepts take us to the background which we have already seen and on which the system of reciprocity was developed. The term *hatha* is translated by Bertonio as "cast, family, ayllo," but also as "seed of the plants, men, and all animals." *Hathasitha* is "to beget," and *hathasiña* means "semen." Evidently, the community on which the system of reciprocity developed was understood not in contractual or in statistical terms as the sum of individuals. Instead, it was understood strictly as a living organism, a habitat where the activity of man and everything alive yields fruit. The community in turn had to concretize the *pacha*, which seems to refer to a concept prior to what we separate analytically into the two categories of time and space, and which is placed before an "objectified" world, a world understood in the third person. *Pacha*, instead, refers to a concept more properly related to what we call a subject, and it is located in a terrain prior to that of the perception of things. Here we have a subjectified, private space and time that refers to a vital habitat where *our* time and *our* space melt into the pure fact of living here and now when this involves the time of *my* life, *my* work, *my* family, and in this place, the place of *my* community. All of this implies naturally an indiscriminate vision of external reality. This vision is incorporated into that vital feeling German philosophy terms the *Gefühl*, which translated means something like "feeling." That is why the indigenous people, as we have observed, tended to *feel* reality before *seeing* it.

That is the reason why in a world inhabited by qualities prior to objects, there could not be a fixed eternity, but rather an eternity that grows, that is *huiñay*, an eternity interwoven with the vital subjective feeling; that is, an eternity that is thought or, more precisely, felt at an affective level. Eternity is understood as duration limited by the unlucky aspects of the world. One cannot understand otherwise the indigenous obsession with ominous signs, or with the regulation of behavior that such an obsession carries with it. The same is true of space, which is no more than vital space, where life lives (*utcatka*), that space of the *hatha*, or community, which is considered a magic seed, the center of the cosmos, the fountain of all sustenance.

This explains in part the natural trust a system of reciprocity presupposes. It seems as if the work were placed as a seed in the earth in order to yield its fruit, a seminal cause that grows and germinates organically toward the effect.

Returning to the problem of the weavers, it is natural that in such a cultural environment, ruled by a seminal criterion, the weavers would fulfill their obligation with the *mallku*, but not with the Spaniards, despite the assumed exploitation to which the weavers were subjected. In the weavers prevailed the bond that united them with the *mallku*, that is, the bond of reciprocity and its fulfillment, over and above the object itself. Why? Because maintaining the organic nature of the communitarian group was indispensable. This does not imply that the weavers were conscious of what they were doing.

In what terms did Garcí Diez think? He thought in terms of causality within a world that is quantified. He belonged to the Spain of the Golden Age. He had gone through the process of substituting a world with a religious basis with another world moved by mechanics. In Italy the divinity had already been turned into a simple first motor, as Alfred Weber notes.[13] There, instead of a religious vision of the world, a mercantile vision began to predominate. It was bourgeois Europe already initiating its ethics, its cult of work, quantifying man and consequently reducing his image. It was a reform which, in the north of Europe, already was trying to translate this new imaginary at the level of religion, but with a view, as some authors have observed, to provide the bases of capitalism and the Industrial Revolution already crystallizing in Bacon's ideas.

The good Garcí Diez was not totally identified with these new ideas. Spain itself would remain at the margin of this process. But the state could not avoid that one of its officials, "an envoy of His Majesty," would think in some way in terms of the new conception, at the very least regarding a rigid money economy. This was the only role remaining to the poor Spanish middle class, by virtue of the underdevelopment that already hovered over Spain.[14]

In short, the difference between the weaver and Garcí Diez rests in the former's beginning from an approach that was to a certain extent affective, while the latter already defended an intellectual and mechanistic point of view. One required an interior beginning, invested in an intense desire to *feel* reality and to see it in seminal terms. The other carried out an external beginning, invested in objects and in the quantitative standard of money. One was, then, irrational, and the other rational, if we want to carry the differences to an extreme.

But let us consider something else about the irrationality of the weaver. I insist that we are accustomed to see irrationality as a form of original chaos when it does not seem to be so, as one can see precisely in the relation that seems to have obtained between the curious dual organization of the community in Hanansaya and Urinsaya, on the one hand, and the system of reciprocity, on the other.

We have already made reference to the predominantly affective tonality the indigenous people contribute to the world. When at the end of his long conversation with us, the witch doctor from Copacabana consulted the coca assiduously and told us suddenly that we were carrying "grief," he was evidently no longer interested in our visual presence, but, above all, in

18 Two *campesino* informants from the community of Copacabana, in Toledo, Bolivia. The text refers to the one on the right. Photograph by the author.

the affective shading—auspicious or inauspicious—our presence provoked in him (figure 18). I would add that it was a question of being on the lookout for this auspicious or inauspicious aspect generally, as if our interview were being conducted on an excessively visual and conscious level. Since this reaction was repeated on two other occasions, it made me think that it would not be premature to affirm that the natural tendency of the indigenous people is to withdraw from a strictly conscious attitude in order to access what is not conscious. The unconscious element conceals itself in foreboding or prediction and issues from a certain lack of censure, from a constant commerce of the indigenous person with the torn duality of the cosmos divided between the auspicious and the inauspicious. It is almost like a scale in which each pan alternately predominates as the night follows the day, the winter follows the summer. This also settles at the level of the community when it is divided into two parts, the *hanansaya* and the *urinsaya*.

We have also seen that indigenous people live not only in the imbalance between favor and disfavor. They also feel accosted by an almost anguished and obsessive zeal to reach equilibrium. That is, to reach the center that remedies the anxiety of the partition of the world. This zeal must already crystallize in a peculiar form of conceiving action. The action I perform must be balanced by compensation. If we want to understand this at the psychological level, one more familiar to us, we could say that the action which I deliver assumes available energy, that is the fracture of equilibrium. The resulting unevenness must be leveled because it is demanded by some ancient law. Which law? This is the problem.

In the name of this *law* a community was organized in parts or factions. Each faction had its *mallku*, almost as if it were a balance between opposites, but fixed as something static and trapped through magic. This balance remained fixed so long as each part of the community made all the contributions that sustain its organic nature, including fulfilling reciprocity.

Morote Best describes a strange celebration, in his work on the community of Sallaq. In it two factions battled each other, each pulling on one side of a long rope. The outcome would predict how the farm year would go. The strange part is that the triumph of one side would bring a malaise, but not if the other side won.[15] This is evidently a question of a community organized on the model the cosmos must have had since antiquity. This is one part of the law.

The other part must be the Inca. By virtue of the sacred nature of his person, and because he is the intermediary between sky and earth long before he is a mere head of state, he was the visual symbol of equilibrium between opposites. As a symbol, he coincided at the religious level with the strange sign which Santacruz Pachacuti placed at the apex of the so-called altar of Coricancha, as a gesture of autogestation by Viracocha.[16] We have already seen that the old conception of the world of the *amautas* (philosophers) consisted in a descent of the divinity. The descent was conceived as a passing from unity or balance to imbalance or disintegration of the everyday world. In all of this man had the mission of reintegrating the unity of the god within his own human level.

The Chinese conception was similar, according to Granet.[17] Action was also considered as a break in the balance between opposites in which the world was divided. Only the ceremonial, that is, the rigorous regulation of conduct, could restitute harmony. Man was considered a miniature form of the cosmos, and anything he did reverberated throughout the universe. It could be said that this is the same law as the Incas'.

But in what did that law consist? Surely it must be the law that results from seeing the *así* of the world and its presence at the level of the *guauque*, and leads one to notice the play of unnameables, and thus the typology taught by the divinity. The law surely reduces itself to the division into factions or parts, to an Inca who unites opposites, and to rituals that place a hold on chaos.

In a world organized by such *law*, weavers prefer to deal directly with their *mallku* rather than with Europeans, even when time is lost and energy is spent in the manufacture of textiles for which they receive nothing in return except for a bit of food. Why? Because of the satisfaction they receive in acting this way amid such a world; because the "law" guarantees that a limit will be achieved in which they will reach the plenitude of the fact of living, the *pacha*. It is at that point where the weavers feel from the *soncco* that what they are doing is fine. It is a divine law. It short, it is always learned through "revelation" and regulated by *amautas* (philosophers) and priests.

That is why the indigenous people felt that there was a fixed goal for their actions, a point where their labor became entangled with the mystery of the world, where it, no matter how humble, acquired all its sacredness and consecration. Guaman Poma also had this feeling. He ingenuously invokes the five ages in which his contemporaries still believed because it was the central theme of that conception of the world. The myth was central as it illustrated the heroic avatar of a humanity manufactured by gods, one which always failed because it did not "speak with the gods." That is, it had not succeeded in capturing the whole organization required to live in accordance with the law.

The Popol-Vuh, the Maya-Quiché bible, says it better than Guaman Poma does. After recounting the creation and destruction of the four humanities which "did not speak" with the gods, it describes the fifth humanity that is created from corn. So perfect was it, the text reads, that "it was able to see too far away." It had to be blinded so that it would only see things nearby. One could say that Maya wisdom points out that man in his effort to see that which is far away again will graze each day against the divine verb. That verb maintains the implicit organizing *principle*, the one that allows that a weaver reach his life's culmination delivering the textiles to his *mallku* in an environment of faith and plenitude. Bertonio and Holguín both record that the term *life* is associated with food or sustenance. This enables us to understand that in the Andean highlands the world was conceived in the same way.[18] It stands to reason that life and sustenance are considered to be the same. It is not so reasonable then that Garcí Diez separates analytically one from the other and that he feels himself obliged to recommend to the authorities that they pay for the product of labor.

This is one of the most important ways in which Garcí Diez distances himself from the indigenous world: he implies a meticulous discrimination between the productive subject and the product of labor, and, in the deepest sense, an analytical division between man and food, a division which constitutes the crux of our modern economic ideas.

Murra surely proposes the same problem, though in another field, when he refers to the unity formed by the lands and the people who work them. This leads him to affirm that "land and the people who work it on the basis of reciprocity form a single unity. Social scientists can divide it into these elements only for analytical purposes, but we must join them again if we wish to understand this unity according to the Andean criterion."[19] What was this "Andean criterion"? It cannot be other than that which the indigenous person selected for his thinking, what we saw as *sonnco* in Quechua or *chuyma* in Aymara: the heart, in short.

Only on this basis can one understand, for example, that land and man constituted a unity; that the weaver carried out his duty to the *mallku* and not to the Spanish; and also that in ancient times the *tupu*, or parcel of land, lacked precise measurements. Instead, it was delimited informally to be as large as necessary to satisfy the needs of a domestic unit.[20]

Holguín translates *muchuchik soncco apu* as "just."[21] One notices specifically the psychological symbol that the term *soncco* represented insofar as it indicated a peculiar use of faculties simultaneously conscious and unconscious. The "heart" was where truth is achieved in the double sense (and all truth has this double sense), in its intellectual connotation and also as faith. Truth is an amalgam of the intellectual clarity of judgment and the necessary faith that confers certainty upon that judgment.

From this point of view it is evident that Garcí Diez must have faced a world structured differently from his. Murra highlights the failure of understanding Garcí Diez manifests in making his proposal to the authorities. But really it is the same lack of understanding found today in people like my neighbor, the man in Toledo who, by virtue of the complexity of our modern world, thinks that Indian world is unredeemable.

But the Indian redeems his old conception of the world in his own way. We have proof of this in the *ayni* as it is practiced today in the Andean highlands by mestizos. The organizer of a celebration demands that everyone present, including the next host, pay twice what he had already invested. What I saw in Untavi is that then he makes a long necklace with a great quantity of bills, which he presents to the audience in order to carry out the *ayni* and to reimburse the money spent on the celebration.

This custom appears to be different from a system of reciprocity, but in reality it is no more than the translation of such a system to a money economy. The same criteria of compensation and equilibrium function in this custom, no longer on the level of faith, but rather on that of quantity. Furthermore, if previously the custom had the individual at its disposal and the custom motivated the weaver, now the individual has the custom at his disposal. It is a natural inversion that appears at the social level of the mestizo. To use Kuzcinsky Goddard's expression, the mestizos no longer want to live "like Indians." Even though they feel incorporated into an urban economy, the mestizos do not succeed in shedding their customs. In this way they do violence to their conscience and censure increases with the attendant neuroses of resentment and susceptibility. The mestizo has entered what is understood as a modern economy, but his incorporation is marginal and twisted. He is acting as if he were a Western citizen. But he represses a background which is still within what we have called *law* or limit and thus what provides satisfaction in work and implies a deep knowledge of why one works. This knowledge motivated weavers to fulfill their obligations to their *mallku* even when they would lose an enormous amount of time.

But is this not the problem of the whole of the South Américan middle class? This is a continent located in a liminal cultural zone. On the one hand, a quantitative economy elaborated in the U.S. and Europe exercises only a marginal influence in this zone. Because of that, this quantitative economy is rigorously imposed and uproots whatever our economists concede to it. On the other hand, the continent receives at the doors of the city the impact of a qualitative economy such as the one of the weaver. What should one expect from this contradiction? Does a mestizo attitude not arise naturally from this situation, an attitude which simultaneously magnifies the "modern" economy and wants to overturn it without remainder?

Here, then, is a fitting question. Does the indigenous system of reciprocity really affect the present economy of Latin América? What could be the outcome of the impact of a qualitative economy based on the truths of *sullu* or *soncco*, that belongs to a strangely irrational organization, on a quantitative economy in an apparently contractual society, with individual property owners, as Rousseau conceived it, a society that is rigorously analytical? Will the result of the contact of these two modalities only be that apparently surpassed episode of a Willca who—as Ramiro Condarco testifies—at the beginning of the century, when the whole of Latin Américan people lived the "belle epoque," had tried to abolish private property?[22] What is the true meaning of the present revolutionary agitation in the Américas? Is it only a problem of infiltration? We will come back to this question after comparing the two styles of thinking which one finds in América.

The last chapter leads us to compare the indigenous way of life and thinking with our own, even when this may not seem to make much sense. Indigenous people in Bolivia and Perú today look to public institutions to solve their agricultural problems. This seems to acculturate them completely. Indigenous people tend to act as if they were Westerners.

In the Kollana community I discussed in chapter 3, I perceived the mental attitude of indigenous people who just thirty years ago were totally hostile to white people and who show today instead a high degree of acculturation. The attitude, the use of Spanish, and their general conception of their way of life lead one to think that the Indian has really ceased to exist as such.

It is natural to believe that the indigenous people have come to approximate what is demanded of them. Acculturation can be understood as the straightforward use of indigenous energy, whether in the consumer market or as enlisted men. The calculus used in these cases is what any bourgeoisie, especially the Andean one, makes of the indigenous people. But it does not respond to a real understanding of the problem. Because when one scratches the surface one finds that neither are the indigenous people totally acculturated, nor are whites really in control of the situation. Let us examine the opposition between the two.

We can trace it in language. We have already seen that when Holguín wants to find an equivalent in Quechua for the concepts of *being* and *essence* he proposes the term *cani*. Bertonio also proposes the Aymara *cancaña*, which Ibarra Grasso considers as borrowed from Quechua. But these two terms do not in any way describe completely what happens in the case of indigenous people. The closest term to their way of life, as we know, is *utcatha*, to be sitting down. Let us add to it *cani* in Quechua, which is rendered *cancaña* in Aymara. In Quechua *cani* is linked to the demonstrative *ca*. *Ca* has to be thought in terms of extension rather than definition. In other words, it is limited to pointing to the existence of things. Oddly enough, the terms in both languages are related to *roasting spit* or *roasted meat*; that is, they suggest inhabiting or dwelling in the philosophical sense of *feeling protected* in the world, just as do *utcatha* or its Quechua equivalent, *tiyani*.

I have no doubt that the basic concept on which the indigenous view of the world seems to rest does not at all indicate the existence of an attitude similar to the Western attitude. This is what I have been demonstrating throughout the book. Where we use a conceptual and abstract thinking, the indigenous people have their own particular way of thinking, due to the absence of objects in their conception of the world. We aim in our Western culture at defining rather than pointing.

But the opposition seems to be much more drastic. The three terms *irrationality*, *community*, and *dwelling* take us back to the meaning of *utcatha* and of *tiyani*. If they correspond to the way of life of indigenous people, then their way and our way of conceiving of life are opposed. One of the basic reasons for the distance between the Bolivian and Peruvian middle class and the indigenous people is that they wield contrary terms: the middle class opposes *community* with *individualism*, *dwelling* with *solitude*, and *irrationality* with *rationality*. *Individualism*, *solitude*, and *rationality* are abstractions that are evidently the culmination of European thinking at the end of its evolution, influenced, maybe, by economic individualism. Those who oppose this individualism—those on the political Left—are not far from the same basic formulation.

Heidegger in the European world realized how to crystallize perfectly our official and public way of life, in which both Left and Right fit. The articulation of an empty self, the necessity of confronting time as the only solution, and the rejection of an irrational way of thinking—all face the

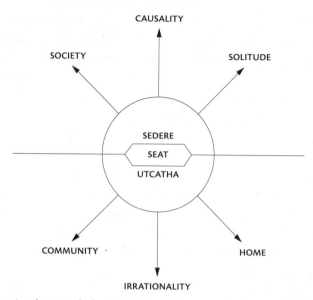

19   Comparison between the basic principles of Western and indigenous thinking.

very essence of this present form of our conception of the world. The economic, social, and political approaches in the Américas magnify these concepts. They seek to restore to man his individuality, his intellectual ability, and his facing a certain concept of solitude. These are the bases of our contractual society, a society that could not have been endured without ideals such as these. We conceive community in terms of contract, and we suppose that each person is placed in this society through a free decision. Government in Argentina would be impossible unless that attitude were wielded publicly; it even had to be wielded when the government was tyrannical. This attitude constitutes the very basis of our nationality and it belongs to the conventional order. It is with this attitude that one achieves a position as professor or as public servant. This convention has been carefully elaborated since Mitre, through Martínez Estrada, to even the latest essayists who exhibit precisely that extent of mental lucidity and casuistry to which we are so devoted.

It is clear that we wield the terms *individuality*, *rationality*, and *solitude* as external. The exaltation of the individual is always done within the limits of that pride typical of every middle class in keeping an attitude of honorable and gentlemanly isolation when face-to-face with other people.

Rationality is seen in many ways as a dogma we use when facing problems at the level of everyday life. And with respect to the dwelling, in the sense of an existential inhabiting of a friendly world, we also wield a solitude deeply impregnated with a certain romanticism, perhaps inherited from the old generations, and one implicated in the romantic origin of our republics.

No doubt the ideal of a culture based on individuality, rationality, and solitude is reinforced when economic issues intervene, such as land disputes over farmland in the Andean plateau or in the relation between bosses and unskilled workers in the large cities. Here an abyss inevitably opens between us and the indigenous world. Besides, industry and commerce as wielded by Argentina and Brazil promote an attitude of turning their back to an autochthonous América. Even the peasant invasion during Perón's time reactivated this antagonism. *Praxis* in América leads us to distance ourselves from our national roots. But does this magnify the contradiction in which América finds itself?

Something lingers—something makes one think it is useless to resolve the problem through segregation as when Martínez Estrada thinks that in the Argentinian case everything becomes concrete in the Pampa, and that the rest is the Balkans; or when a sociologist measures the problem with a statistical standard and reduces the indigenous world to a mere number, and thus avoids the antagonistic relation that exists toward them; or when anthropologists think, as the latest technicians do, that the indigenous people are becoming acculturated and that there will not be any more problems in the future. This may not be true. The only thing that is certain is that in 1968, after four centuries, the contradiction is still there, without any marked weakening from the other side. Everything leads us to foresee that neither the development of a capitalist bourgeoisie nor that of a redemptive Left will solve that opposition, because we do not know what will happen with that bourgeoisie or that Left once they triumph. We do not even know whether our position has any solidity. It is evident that the resistance offered by the indigenous world does not make assimilation easy. During the four hundred years of indigenous resistance since the Conquest, our nations have not achieved the level believed to be the goal of any democratic republic. In all of this it is worth pointing out that neither the opposition nor the similarities between the two cultures are very clear. Perhaps we will achieve better results examining what is Indian

20   Circular Chipaya huts, Bolivia. Photograph by the author.

and what is white in light of an opposition between two ways of thinking, rather than through the reductive leveling of economics or sociology.

I had a direct experience of this opposition when I visited Chipayas, in Carangas. On that occasion, Huarachi, the witch doctor, took us to his cylindrical hut, which had a domed roof. A member of our group asked the witch doctor why the hut was built this way (figure 20). The witch doctor was going to answer, but our group member anticipated him, suggesting that it must be because it was very windy in that region and a circular house would be warmer in offering less resistance to the wind. The witch doctor agreed. One could say that he confirmed the judgment. Our companion had formulated a *cause* superimposed onto the object, the circular hut. Moreover, he framed it in terms of a "correct solution."

Was the witch doctor really in agreement? Did he really accept this as the cause, and not another? The truth is otherwise. Ponce Sangines has made excavations in Huancarani and has confirmed that in the culture to which the Chipayas belong huts have been built in the same manner for fifteen hundred years. The persistence of this type of construction caught his eye.[1] According to Ponce Sangines the motive for the circular construction was not related to utility, but rather to tradition: it had irrational roots. Had we urged the witch doctor to speak, maybe he would have answered, "It is the custom." In saying that he would have done nothing other than hide from the nosey questioner the irrational act of building circular huts. He would be saying that his culture does not dwell on causes, but rather in a world that is *así*, like Choque's *ucamahua*.

What is the distance between seeing the *así* and seeing *causes*? From Jung's point of view the former could be understood as the consequence of the *concretism* of the primitive world. He writes, "Primitive thought lacks self-confident independence."[2] It is worth noting that "self-confident independence" led in the aforementioned case to coming up with causes when not necessary. Can this almost obsessive insistence on seeing causes be healthy and evolved? If we obsess over causes, could it not be because *concretism* in us is inferior and immature, and a great deal more evolved among the indigenous people? Could it be that there are superior forms of concretism that civilized people do not achieve? Insofar as concretism consists in "always being towed by perception," then a perception that comprehends the *así* of reality can take two paths: either causes are invented and, consequently, reality is distorted or excessively simplified, or, as in the indigenous case, that which is concrete is turned into the *presence* of the *así* of things. Consequently, it creates an opening to an interior path, one not resolved with abstractions or with causes and through which is channeled a strong zeal for salvation.

But not even abstraction is achieved except through that interior path which starts from a concrete presence in the world. Euclidean geometry, which emerged during Hellenism, the time of Greek decadence, was not an abstraction except after having been for centuries, since Pythagoras's time, a means to channel a form of salvation that began with an *así* of the world. In that sense, Euclid does not *surpass* Pythagoras. He instead represents the deflation of a mystical attitude. Since concretism accepts the *presence* of a world which is *así*, it constitutes the inalienable point of departure to achieve salvation, at least in terms of what differentiates the human from the nonhuman. It must have been a primordial attitude that differentiated the Neanderthal from animals. As a system of abstractions, science is no more than the epilogue to this differentiation. If we follow Ibarra Grasso, science joins man with animal again in the end, but on a higher level.[3] One notices this in the way in which science is deployed at the popular level in the Western world. This is especially evident in what constitutes the limit of that world in the North American environment, where in an author such as Gordon Childe science returns to the basic level of the animal wanting to survive.

This coincides with one of my experiences, avowedly subjective, doing fieldwork in the Andes. In the high Andean plateau one has the sensation that though he seems to be in command of abstraction and causes, the urban middle-class man, whether from Oruro, Bolivia, or Buenos Aires, Argentina, lives subject to reflexes that are much more biological or animalistic than those one observes in the indigenous man, even in someone such as Huarachi, a witch doctor who belongs to the ancient culture of the Uru-chipayas. It is worth recalling the Aymara courtesy, along with the circumspect attitude of the indigenous functionaries and that strange air of dignity the Chipayas showed when we asked for information.

It is probable that when Jung formulates the opposition between concretism and abstraction, he concedes a presumed advance coined by the European.[4] Is it that the European world, restricted to France, England, Germany, and Italy, really lives a world of abstractions, of causes and effects, and in no way a world which is *así*?

Western thinking seems to be hounded by a fear of losing a sense of action and progress, a fear of implosion. One cannot otherwise understand Gusdorf's contradictory announcement of the absence of dwelling in the modern world, Eliade's thinking that the absence of the sacred in everyday work is irremediable, or Heidegger's pompous affirmation that being is immersed in time. Jung, for example, defines the *one-oneself* as something that objectively *lives me* when faced with a subjective *I live*, in order to note the importance this process has to the integration of the psyche. With prejudice, Jung's disciple Henderson schematizes the idea and points to the Navajos, who perform their rituals to achieve "a *permanent repose* where the two contradictory aspects of human nature find their equilibrium."[5] Evidently Henderson has reduced the value of the concept. The *one-oneself* is seen by him as simple *permanent repose*. Could this *repose* be one the European does not allow himself? If this were the case, the primitive world would be being used here to make a social critique.

When Choque asked for the *nayrajja*, he evidently achieved a moment of repose, but this was understood in terms of a *lives me* and not in terms of *I live*. Choque did something the average Western man does not do, nor, it seems, should do. Why? Here two observations are in order: There is an evident fear that the benefits produced by the long effort of the Western bourgeois elite for one hundred and fifty years would be squandered by a *mass* it tries to ignore. Also, the vital tension required to maintain those benefits has met its limit. The European is thus testing the opposite possibility, of appealing to a salvationist thinking, but because he lacks the vital forms to adopt it, he sees the opposite as a uterine regression. Jung's ignorance of the primitive mind, for example, as denounced by Radin, is proof of the natural lack of understanding the Westerner has when faced with what afflicts us in South América.[6] It is strange that Western thinking is grounded in great measure and at these moments in a supposed exaltation of man's evolution; nevertheless, it seems to be motivated by nothing other than a defense of a particular state of affairs. One can see this in Neumann, who speaks of five thousand years of consciousness for just this reason.

The fear of implosion denounced by Western thinking answers to the fear of losing the profits of the Industrial Revolution. That is the reason behind the fear of embarking on an inverted path, of touching a limit where matter and antimatter alternate, where man meets his experience of being purely human. This is the point of departure of the hierarchies of psychological evolution, from *concretism* to *abstraction*, or the zeal to remove the *dwelling* in the world, or the proposition that man will be absorbed by time. But there cannot be man, or even objects, if there is no margin of internal safety that gives him a *home* to withdraw to from the events of the world. Western people are missing a seminal spring that would provide such safety, even the one that allows the indigenous person to say, "It is the custom," without worrying about causes.

Proof of the Western crisis can be found in Hartman's concept of the trans-intelligible, as a zone which marks the limits of knowledge. With this he opens the path to a mutation toward its opposite. But, unfortunately, he lacks the necessary faith to be able to foresee an overcoming of the contradiction at the level of the *así* of the world.

The Reform in the north of Europe meant revitalizing religion at the level of the Nordic way of life, pointing to a restitution of the *así* of the world; that is, the formation of those traditional bases that constitute a ground from which the abstraction of science can acquire meaning. The European scientific attitude cannot be explained without taking into account the religious drain that Europeans suffered for centuries. The European elite do not believe in religion, but cannot think too far from the masses insofar as the masses have stabilized a coherent vision of a world that is *así*. Only on this ground can the experience of abstraction arise, even when it takes pains to show, in the name of solutions, the failure of the acceptance of a world that is given in terms of salvation, that is, a simple religious *así*.

Everything leads one to think that there cannot be a culture in terms of mere abstractions and schemas that point exclusively to solutions without also including large domains where the world is accepted in its simple *así* with a view to salvation. If this is so, then the problem would not reside, in América, only within the indigenous people, but also within the urban dweller. Is it that our crisis consists in an exaggerated development of the system of abstractions accompanied by an almost childish deficit of its opposite: the concrete vision of *a world that is given así*?

It would have been very difficult in Carangas for anyone in our group to accept the world without the causes of the witch Huarachi. The absence of abstractions of the indigenous world naturally leads to populating it with contradictions. This clashes with the rational monism that every average urban dweller demands. The urban dweller's voluntarism is missing in the indigenous person. Taking the contradiction into account leads to the dissolution of all action-oriented volition.

We can schematize that opposition, saying that the indigenous person rejects Aristotle's logical principle of the excluded middle, while the urbanite accepts it. When Apaza Rimachi told us that we were raised simultaneously by the *Achachila*, or grandfather, and the *huak'a*, he was contradicting himself with enviable impudence. With the same impudence he would affirm that a mountain is an *achachila*, or grandfather. Between the judgment "the mountain is made out of stone" and its contradictory "the mountain is not made out of stone," neither is denied. Both are accepted as true, and he is left with the excluded middle: "the mountain is a grandfather."

The acceptance or rejection of the third term is not only a logical but first and foremost a vital problem, and also a cultural one. Behind the problem of the excluded middle is the public thinking of the average Western man who rejects a contemplative intelligence and adheres to a practical one, as Scheler would say. And there is the need for action—the voluntarism of a progressive middle class. If the average urban dweller were to accept the possibility of an object of stone that is also a grandfather, he would lose his objectivity, and with it the sense of freedom, located so emphatically in external objects. And he would feel subjected to a community excessively ruled by ceremony. But even further, the true face of his existence would acquire public status, that of not always excluding the third term, and accepting it in daily life, in that region where, in Buenos Aires, opinion, home, love, *lunfardo*, tango, or daily mythology operate.[7] Is it that América is constituted on the principle of the third possibility? This is adumbrated in Guaman Poma, that is, since the first years of the conquest, even when the motives are different from those of the contemporary urbanite.

Guaman Poma had been an official in the Spanish administration of Perú. His parents were probably indigenous and still lived in the environment of their pre-Columbian ancestors, even though it had been damaged. He tells us that he wrote his chronicle to exhibit the history of his people and to denounce the abuses of the conquistadors. But because he did not have access to anything but the argumentation traditional to his land, he exhibits a remarkable hybridity. He cannot keep his indigenous thinking from being evident throughout the whole of his writing.

A proof of this can be found in the progressive sense he impresses on his legend of the four ages. We have already seen in the more primitive stories, especially those of Meso-América, that the legend is never conceived as a progressive evolution of humanity, but rather as the creation of four humanities that are destroyed for religious reasons.

The word in the primitive world is a magic fluid which is charged with *mana*. It presupposes wisdom. Among the Aztecs the word was represented by a smoke spiral to note the sacred speech of a person of rank. Guaman Poma himself draws the Catholic prayer of some of the personages in his chronicle as a spiral.

Furthermore, the fifth humanity does not exhibit in myth a technical perfection when compared with the prior four. Rather, it shows a greater degree of integration and wisdom that likens them more to the deity, and thus the episode according to which the deity had to blind them so that they would not see too much.

Huarachi, in telling me the creation of the world according to the Chipayas, did not distinguish between the first generation of the *Chullpas* and the second generation of Chipayas. It was simply baptism that mediated between them. Thus, there was no progress made from one age to the next, but rather simply greater wisdom.

Then from where comes the concept of progress used by Guaman

21   The creation of the world, according to Guaman Poma.

Poma? It must be due to that "incipient rationalism" attributed by Imbelloni to the conquistadors of the 1600, influenced by the Renaissance
that had invaded Spain. This leads to the ensuing *euhemerism*, according
to which historical facts are interpreted in light of consciousness and all
irrational or mythic explanation is thus discarded.[8] Montesinos, the Spanish chronicler, turns Manco Capac into an evil leader who plots his politics
with enviable rationalism, as could only be done by a Frenchman of the
time of Richelieu.

On the other hand, the concept of progress responds to an elemental
schematism. It is limited to taking into account the quantitative accumulation of objects. This serves as a guide for a conception of history according
to which the past consisted in the absence of those objects, and the future
consists in their increase. It is this schematism that permits an undeveloped
mind such as Guaman Poma's to wield it. Only because of this are the four
ages conceived as progress in the sense of the French Enlightenment.

But his thinking continues to be profoundly indigenous. He meticulously observes all of the knowledge introduced by the conquistadors. He cites the Bible, speaks of the roundness of the earth, pretends to be a good Catholic, and speaks badly of the idols through which the devil spoke. But when he draws the Catholic God, he represents him as a bearded old man who lifts his arms and from whose hands arise the sun and the moon. Is it that the god is generating the opposites? At the base of the drawing, he adds four small animals that walk from right to left (figure 21). Is this reminiscent of the Aymara *amutaña* with the four petals of the cosmic flower?[9]

When he makes a map of Perú, he draws a large oval in which he distributes the geographical details just as was the custom with the European maps of the time. But in the center he places four couples oriented toward the four cardinal points. When at the beginning of his chronicle he represents the Holy Trinity, he adds the Virgin Mary in the lower part, as if he were segregating the earth. He also places the Father to the right, Christ to the left, and the dove above. Could this not be a three-plus-one four-part schema like the one used by Apaza Rimachi?[10] In the drawing of the city of Potosí he places the city emblem above, held by four personages.[11] Also curious are the rhythmic series he uses as a principle of organization to report, among other things, the ways of burying the dead in Perú. They are curious because he cannot avoid the Inca division into four zones. But the indigenous flavor is also found in the lack of both clarity and syntactical coordination of the text. It is natural, then, that a great researcher such as Ramiro Condarco would peremptorily dismiss Guaman Poma as "not having had the possibility of training his discursive faculties even moderately."[12]

Condarco is right, but his point of view is Western. Guaman Poma suffers from the limitation of lack of objectivity, and this is the main cause of the strange nature of his manuscript. But could this incapacity not result from a deep difference in the quality of his thinking? Could it be that we also suffer from a limitation—the inverse—that of objectivity? That is, we always require a chronicle be installed as a discursive and spoken object?

Between us and Guaman Poma lies a different conception of the word. Ours is informative and impersonal, and it encloses everything that it wants to say. It is, in sum, a word-object. But Guaman Poma's is drawn like a smoke spiral because it moves over the rent opposition between un-nameable divinities as is shown by the messianic quality that breathes throughout the chronicle. One could say that his indigenous thinking did not require a chronicle. It would have been enough with the drawings or with an action like Túpac Amaru's.

It seems that the difference between Guaman Poma and a Spanish chronicler such as Montesinos can be seen in two ways. Either Guaman Poma is inferior to Montesinos or each utilizes a distinct style of thinking. Guaman Poma, because he overly imitates the conquistadors, does not get to offer us the best of indigenous thinking. If this is true, one can point to two different lines of thinking in South América, one that goes from Guaman Poma to Apaza Rimachi and includes Huarachi, and which we have analyzed in the preceding chapters. The other line of thinking fills América from the time of the conquest through to today and has its strongest bastion in the city. The latter follows the law of the excluded middle; the former includes that third term.

Taking into account a split in ways of thinking should not surprise us. In the end it is the same phenomenon as when Jung distinguishes between introverted and extroverted people, and reports that Western life stands on an extroverted ideal, while the introverted is considered negative as antisocial.[13]

Ibarra Grasso similarly offers a new classification of races in two categories, H and F. In an interesting passage, he points out that anthropologists are always of type H; thus, all the examples in their photographs and published articles are always of the same type, but that does not mean that one cannot also speak of the existence of a type F.

Thus, if we distinguish two styles of thinking, it is not merely a question of a facile dichotomy, but of the probable exclusion of one of them, relegated to ineptitude by our culture. This style may be excluded because it undermines the necessary activities of urban life.

Let us accept the hypothesis, then, without making correlations with the above-cited classifications, that placed face-to-face with our way of thinking is an indigenous way of thinking. They coexist in South América. Moreover, the assumed naïveté and primitivism we attribute to Guaman Poma is due to our deep rejection of that type of thinking. To what extent does this way of thinking continue in our people? What is its true nature?

We have been treating the indigenous question as one of styles of thinking, which in América has two facets. On the one hand, indigenous people can be thought of as an ethnic group—the population of seven million indigenous people, given Rosenblat's statistics.[1] On the other hand, we could take into account the *criollo* population, linked in some way or another through physical characteristics or way of life to the indigenous people.[2] The *criollo* population is of course much larger than the seven million indigenous inhabitants, and it reaches to the very center of the large city. Those who are called *cabecita negra* in Argentina, *roto* in Chile, or *cholo* in Bolivia and Perú do not have a direct link to the indigenous world. Nevertheless, they have characteristics that they have carried with them from a distant past. In certain moments, these characteristics give political, social, and cultural cohesion to this mass of people to express open opposition to things that are specifically Western.

It is a population described, for example, by Oscar Lewis, in *The Children of Sánchez*, as politically, socially, and economically available, segregated from a middle-class lifestyle.[3] It is also the population considered by Argentinean sociology to be the result of an internal migration that at times became incorporated into the city and came together, for example, within Peronism and gives signs of strong internal coherence.[4] In taking this

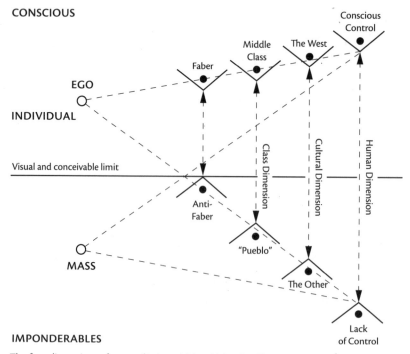

22   The four dimensions of contradiction within which scientific statements move, particularly those from sociology.

population into account, the indigenous is clearly transcended, and one moves to consider the characteristics of the so-called Américan *pueblo*.

What can we say of this Américan *pueblo*? Is their way of thinking similar to the indigenous? Specifically, can we use what we have observed up to now to understand it? I will analyze an exchange I recorded two years ago on the outskirts of Buenos Aires. Two *criollos* are speaking to each other. One is a folklorist from the northern province of Jujuy, and the other is a seventy-seven-year-old peasant from the Province of Entre Ríos. Alcohol acted to emphasize a way of thinking grounded in an affective tonality, and it implicated the interlocutors in the conversation to a greater extent than usual, especially regarding certain topics. Uneasiness floated into the dialogue, noticeably in such phrases as "We are a great family"; "We make up a *criollo* family"; "We are all speaking in a friendly way"; or "we are all brothers." Nevertheless, a certain analytical disposition imposed by the life they had both lived in the city destroyed the possibility of affirming a concept of unity. Thus, they said, "You can ask me what Jujuy is like or what Salta is like. My friend here can speak about Entre Ríos. This gentleman, who was born in Buenos Aires, can tell us about Buenos Aires." And he added: "This gentleman is the son of a *criollo*. I'm the son of someone who emigrated from Galicia; I'm also a good *criollo*." But this analytical attitude did not calm the uneasiness. Harsh references to the city would show up: "How can someone who is from the city get along with peasants like us?" Or, "When I came from Entre Ríos I did not know which way was up." This man would occasionally add, "When I befriend someone, we do not seem different to me."

Despite their zeal, they were unable to achieve a unity translated into "community" that would provide some rescue or salvation. It was useless to say, "Our Argentinean family is unified, we must realize we are all protected under the white and blue," "There are good foreigners who have come to live here with us," "We have one heart, not two," or "Our nation was made great by the greatness of our forefathers." The original uneasiness led to the feeling of a total absence of community. It was useless to invoke the "great forefathers" or "the blue and white." Do the national colors express community? Or do they, as a symbolic object, in fact obligate us to repress an emotional thinking entangled with a patriotic figure that mobilized the possibility of thoughts and attitudes hostile to *criollos*? If this were so, what were the *criollos* thinking? Evidently, the community sought must be framed in terms that no analysis or concrete symbol could fulfill. Put differently, could it be that the community could not be expressed in visual terms, in terms of an *outward direction*, but in interior terms, of an *inward direction*? Were they slyly looking for a unity that would save them, fundamentally rejecting the backdrop of solutions offered by the city? Beyond doubt, in them breathed a zeal for salvation at the level of the everyday, in that minor plane of being exposed to suffering and pleasure, where fear shows itself or where one must be courageous in order not to be defeated. They were, in sum, at the edge of the *así* of reality, what Choque would call the *ucamawa*, and with the same openness to the unnameable extremes. It is curious how they accepted their defeat with resignation. One could say that they knew it was useless to make an awkward gesture toward searching for understanding at the margins of a salvation, that the environment and the official culture, or more precisely the nation, could at no point offer them. Did they have a style of thinking opposed to that of the urban dweller, or did they maintain themselves in a backwardness both simple and obvious?

To understand this it is important to clear away the prejudice coined by the so-called scientific attitude, which tends not to see the problem as we have been presenting it up until now. The prejudice becomes evident in sociology, as when, for example, our sociologists insist on showing that there is a "transition" from a traditional society to an industrial society. The industrial society, according to them, wields rationality; the traditional society wields affectivity. In that rationality one finds a science with abstract concepts that can be used by everyone—a freedom or a deliberative decision, in the sense of being able to choose one's destiny. This turns into a magnification of the concept of volition.[5] Volition—everyday personal effort—is what will resolve all problems. One knows what one wants, what one is deciding; one is inserted in the general will; and even if one is not today, then one can in principle be part of it tomorrow. This is mediated by the idea of a humanity that progresses in a cumulative sense, multiplying freedoms and objects, and always polishing the rational attitudes. Faced with this, it is natural that two *criollos* such as the ones mentioned above become passive, since they do not exercise their volition in bettering their life circumstances, and instead of using abstractions and adopting impersonal attitudes, they get embroiled in a reality taken simply as *así*, and thus lack "deliberative decisions," or they access *"prescribed decisions"* and are immersed in a great uneasiness that leads them not to participate in progress. Gino Germani warns that an industrial society demands an increasing capacity of "self-determination" and "the elevation of the power of reason before the unreflective acceptance of the dictates of tradition and of the past."[6] But this is yet too simplistic.

The sociologist's attitude moves over four large planes of contradiction. The first results from acknowledging a transition from a traditional society to an industrial society. In order to acknowledge the transition one needs to measure it in terms of utility, which, together with statistics, tends to level the depth of the inhabitants' contribution to gauging the life of their society. The sociologist must also level all contradictions existing in the society he is studying. Sociologists simplify reality. Nevertheless, their work clearly fits with the middle-class common sense, the class to which the sociologist belongs. This tendency, elevated to a scientific criterion, implies discarding all manner of imponderables; it also requires acquiring

evidence at the cost of displacing contradictory elements to a secondary plane.

It could not be any other way. Rational method and rigor have to be
grounded on what is grasped in the full light of consciousness, so that it
follows that the scientific attitude applied to society makes any contradiction disappear. But a scientific criterion used in this manner is only useful
for a sociological analysis of class. Obsessed with the idea of the future of
the world, a future which ends up looking suspiciously like the United
States, the sociologist assumes the diagnosis must relate to the absolute
rationality of an industrial society.

The second contradiction is a consequence of the first. The sociologist,
insofar as he is a member of the middle class, faces Peronism in the case of
Argentina. Thus, he is segregated from his habitat and opposed to the
Américan *pueblo*. This can be seen in the class ideal summed up by
Graciarena: the frugal use of income, savings, the search for material
advantages, innovation, rationalization, and development.[7] The creed belongs to a cultural structure that appears impermeable and whose origins
date from the beginning of the contemporary age. Since then it has exer-
cised power directly or indirectly in a certain part of the world, in such a
way that more than a class, it seems to be a city culture, as I termed it in
América profunda, following Mumford. The middle class emerged as part
of the cultural structure at the end of the European Middle Ages. It is
different from the preceding ones to the same extent that bushmen differ
from pygmies. In fact, as Graciarena puts it, it achieves a notable rigidity
with respect to other classes, particularly the "Américan *pueblo*."

This contradiction is why sociology cannot take into account the real
contradiction lived by a middle class in South America. For example, it
cannot account for the manner in which the middle class collides with the
heavy biological structure of Peronism. It is useless to describe Peronists
as simply "available labor power" or a "rural proletariat" that migrates to
the city, or to try to explain why after 1930, precisely because of the
government prior to the massive immigration, it coalesced in a short time
around a charismatic figure. The Peronist "will to act," for example, arises
from a political disposition, but it is understandable that it is read as an
apparently "paradoxical" phenomenon by someone like Gino Germani.
The phenomenon is not sufficiently "explained" from the scientific angle,
except in terms of a simple description. This is the natural contradiction

into which our South American scientists fall insofar as they use a science which has not arisen from the same reality that surrounds them.[8]

The third contradiction is due to the deep middle-class identification with "Western culture," insofar as the middle class proclaims Western culture a universal form of life, with its main seat in Europe, and whose most extreme expression is the United States. All of humanity is now dealing with the consequences generated by the contradictions generated by virtue of the impermeability of the middle class. It has taken, for example in the case of Vietnam, an evident split: in the North a Leftist middle class and in the South a right-wing one, two parts of one-and-the-same culture based on objects, able to be easily assimilated by traditionally non-Western countries.[9]

The fourth contradiction is the most dramatic one. It lies mainly in the pretensions of "science" through which the ideology of the middle class is expressed. It is due to a great extent to the visual margin within which functions the Western man, whose cultural task and lifestyle demand the exaltation of consciousness because of the liberal structure from which it has sprung. Liberal individualism, born in the great European cities, has a concept of freedom that lies mainly in the free disposition of property. It emphasizes a conscious culture that rejects the domains of nonlucidity at its margins, particularly if these domains question the possession of property. One does not understand the historical experience of the West unless one takes into account this monopoly over consciousness on which it had based its Industrial Revolution. Marxism is important in the sense of modifying that state of affairs, but only at the level of strict consciousness. This is why it lost its true revolutionary transcendence; it goes no further than being an ideology for a disaffected middle class. In this way Marxism fits within the "bourgeois" pride of someone like Neumann, who speaks of the consciousness acquired by humanity in the last five thousand years of history but maintained by the concept of freedom at the level of property created by the West.

The four contradictions—the technical attitude, social class, the West, and rationality—stabilize the middle class in its segregation from the rest of América. It is useless for middle-class sociologists to try to overcome the problem of the Messiah of Development. The middle class always views the Américan *pueblo* as relaxing the ideals expressed above by Graciarena. But the segregated state requires the middle class to maintain a parasitic attitude on other sectors of the society as well. Even when it adopts attitudes opposed to the elite, in actuality it has a constant need for the elite to create certain sources of work. It also needs the elite to sustain a cultural parasitism when it imitates and keeps alive, through the professoriate, important and illustrious figures who have nothing to do with the middle class. The middle class is sterile. Because of that sterility, it exerts over the rest of América, on both the Left and the Right, a cultural and economic imperialism insofar as it attempts to convert the continent to what Graciarena calls the pedagogical creed, consisting of cleanliness, achievement, efficiency, and rationality. Its being segregated, its impermeability, and its culture of objects was what led Che Guevara to fail in Bolivia, and what has led to the constant displacement of the Radical Civic Union from power. Another step and we could speak of a crisis of a way of life. Is it the same crisis as when the *criollo* said that he did not know "what way was up"? In what sense did his companion remark laconically, "We are all a great family"? Or, better, why did he not really seem to believe in a "great family"? The impermeability of the middle class vis-à-vis the Américan *pueblo* can be seen in its essence in the judgment each member of the middle class makes of the *pueblo*.

Historically, one can track the border where these two styles of life grate against each other, the *pueblo* on one side and the middle class on the other, not only as different economic levels, but as distinct styles of thinking. This can be seen, for example, in that historical and controversial abruptness that was Rosas, who found his ultimate expression in the signing of documents of state, with phrases such as "Long live the Blessed Federation and Death to the savage and filthy Unitarians!" It was a coarse statement that clearly crashed against Urquiza's contemporaneous belief in "the absence of legal habits in the *pueblo*."

But Rosas's phrase channeled that margin of *outward direction* of the *pueblo* that backed him up. This was because he was a charismatic leader who in some way became intertwined with the reality lived by the *pueblo*, to the extent that they require daily protection and need to feel accompanied at the point where salvation is more important than solution. The phrase answered to a climate lived by the *pueblo* where the solution was paired to a salvation in terms of "dwelling" before a natural opening to fear in confronting the unnameable. That was a position contrary to that of the Unitarians. Their attitude was not emotional but one of hiding. They held onto a world of abstractions and available receptive intelligence. The intelligence judged the need for a conscious world and the consequent overcoming of a minor daily to-and-fro, from the auspicious to the inauspicious. Looking to good and bad omens tended to be "in bad taste," Mitre would advise, under the influence of the French.

It is curious that Unitarians and Federalists both dislocate the biological unity of the Argentinean psyche. The Unitarians do this because they are in a hurry, the Federalists because they are reactionary. They created the state of affairs which culminates in the dialogue between the *criollos* that I discussed at the beginning of this chapter. The *criollos* were evidently victims of a society of excessive urgency, affected by an alleged transition to an industrial society, which in the end was paid for with an emotional deficit. Urgency multiplies abstractions, impersonal structures that cannot be faced by the psyche and that lead consequently to the criminality of both the *Mazorca* and the first Argentinean presidential administrations, when the gradual genocide of the gauchos began. It is the consequence of a biological excision which is also an excision of symbols. Behind and implicit in these struggles the actors see unnameable gods.

When not long ago some sought the canonization of Eva Perón, one could see an abrupt turn of affairs, similar to what happened in Rosas's case. Even though the canonization was dictated from above, the truth is that it was received from below as something charismatic, as one could see in the altars propped up in her honor at every corner of a highly industrialized Buenos Aires. Eva Perón was not only a simple benefactor who was in the government, but also the one who took care of the *así* of reality which hounded everyone in the heart of the city, because she was "the one who has taken care of *me, here and now* in my life." Naturally, in that capacity she must be canonized. Eva Perón crystallized a symbol that took care of the uneasiness latent in the city, maintained by a recently urbanized rural population. That unease required the placement before the presence, the *así* or *ucamawa*, of everyday happenings which oscillate between good and ill omens, eating and not eating, pain and pleasure. Thus, it needs to place unity where it can reconcile this to-and-fro, whether one simply calls it fetish, sacred place, temple, Manco Capac, or, in this case, Eva Perón. There, in that symbol, what is channeled flows through paths through which it turns into faith, and the *pueblo* achieves lucidity in the face of the tearing of the original cosmos.

But all of this took place within the domain ruled by a middle class that had substituted for the unnameable gods a nameable and concrete desire for power. Thus, the canonization could not take place. The middle class does not believe in miracles and reacts within the parameters of its disapproval of such phenomena. In defense of its status, it pretends to reject the concept of the *así* of reality. Because the *así* appears excessively passive to the middle class, the middle class cannot be ingenuous when it encounters the *así*; that is why it cannot use the *así* to solve its problems. It turns to objects because they are products of Western culture. From that point of view, Eva Perón, the object, was no more than a corpse. The pathology was on both sides, like two sick parts of the country. But with a difference: *criollo pueblo* has great potential, while the middle class is impotent.

Can a culture be upheld merely as a system of abstractions and a knowledge of all causes, all manner of solutions for all of its problems? Or must it also maintain a seminal fountain arising from a world seen *así*, in the manner of presence, in the indigenous way, and in this way creating an opening toward other aspects? In sum, is it enough for man to live daily a system of solutions, or does he also ask for a system of salvation? Although he uses a different vocabulary, Stern answers: "Purely rational thinking carries with it the danger of depersonalization. The individual has to combat against that constantly by turning to the personal backdrop of thinking."[10] If this is true, maybe the urban dweller does have the means to incorporate the personal backdrop of his thinking. More accurately, perhaps the urban dweller is capable of carrying to consciousness what is segregated from him in his daily life? This leads us to state clearly the opposition between the two styles of thinking, but in a sphere that transcends the Américan problem, and which becomes the Western cultural task. In other words, indigenous thinking is not peculiar to the Indian, but is instead the patrimony of man in general. So, could it provide us the clue to the crisis of Western thinking? It would not be difficult to determine whether it does provide the clue, since in the end we are in América, that is, in a liminal zone of the West, at a point where ancient thinking in the indigenous style meets an extremely fractured Western thinking. The rabid orthodoxy used to perpetuate Western thinking in América leads, as is natural, to the loss of all of its efficiency. That is why it is urgent to clarify the extent to which our thinking is affected by an extreme form of thinking uncovered in the indigenous people.

The distinction between thinking in terms of causes—a causal thinking—and another which is not causal must be linked to the similar polarity between intelligence and affectivity in consciousness as put forth by traditional psychology. According to traditional psychology, every subject *sees* a world and delimits it in detail in order to confront it with efficiency. At the other pole, the subject *feels* the favorable or unfavorable aspects of that same world. At one pole the subject asks *why*; at the other, *how*. The *how* refers to modality, to the hues of emotional aversion and adhesion things seem to bring with them. The *why* refers to a constellation of causes and explanations given in a lucid world and accepted as such in full consciousness.

Insofar as there is a *how*, there must also be an organic vision of reality uniformly tinted by sentiment. Thus, "every object continues to be *inside* the totality of the world and to participate with all others with maximum intimacy," Stern writes. On the other hand, the *why* is apparent in an analysis of the same reality articulated through divisions, but with a particular tendency to see those divisions as independent of the totality. In this case, according to Stern, the object *goes out of* the world's totality and becomes independent. Consequently, affectivity fits a global vision of the world and intelligence fits an analytical vision of the world. The opposition corresponds to an active and a passive way of confronting the world.[1]

The predominance of an affective function or an intellectual function or, in Stern's terms, of a *saliente* or an *entrante* attitude, must coincide with specific cultural styles. Only in this way could we explain the opposition in South América between indigenous and popular culture, on the one hand, and urban culture, on the other, and their mutual impermeability.

Indigenous thinking and urban thinking answer to two styles of comportment and appreciation based on certain aspects of the psyche. Germani also seems to suspect this when he remarks that, from the angle of sociology, one can see that the emotional aspects are attenuated at a certain stage of evolution, and a "sublimation of affectivity is produced which must be channeled through reflective and deliberative forms."[2] He holds that a traditional society maintains affect as a characteristic of its social relation as opposed to the neutrality of affect proper to industrial society. Germani's distinction is a holdover from the old Marxist prejudice that opposes feudal to bourgeois society. Thus, it is not wholly congruent with the opposition we draw between the indigenous and the urban in South América. Nevertheless, it suggests the opposition between psychic structures present in an industrial society and not present in indigenous or popular social organization.

The public or official form of thinking in the city, whether in the university classroom, on the editorial pages of a newspaper, or in certain aspects of daily life, seems to be ruled by a *principle of causality*, appearing naturally as a *petitio principii* even though it may not be made explicit in all its orthodoxy. For example, when a person tells another that someone has died, the pained *why* of the other person can be heard immediately. In reality, theirs is not a question about the cause of death. Deep down, rather, the question hides the insistence that everything is explicable and that nothing can happen outside of consciousness.

In opposition, indigenous thinking takes place outside of causes, in a less conscious plane, where one tackles fear in the face of disintegration. That is why it resorts to fixed models, schemas, and rituals with which consciousness is restored. Thus, Guaman Poma resorts to the myth of the four ages to critique the attitude of the conquistadors; Apaza Rimachi uses a contradictory trinity to explain his world; or a sorcerer sets up the *nayrajja* to organize and socialize the space where he will operate; or on a plane of greater evolution, this is also present in Tiahuanacotan thinking, which is in terms of fish, condors, and felines that reconcile opposites.[3]

It is natural that a culture based on a causal thinking avoids the indigenous opposition between good and bad omens, between pleasure and pain. It does this through emphasizing and magnifying a domain that responds to the conscious plane in which it has placed itself. That domain is one of objects. It requires an *outward direction* of the personality. Any opposition or contradiction is overcome among things. That leads in turn to the exercise of volition, which succeeds in negotiating the objective world and feeding a cosmos based on intellection. Objects, inherent in that world because they are *seen*, serve as a guarantee for consciousness. A car is based on a way of thinking that is causal, analytic, *outward*, and characterized by rigorous generalization and abstraction.

But as intellection takes reality apart in order to appreciate its components and immediately afterward proceeds to put right whatever is not found in its proper place, causal thinking does not require salvation but solution. That is why an intellectual and active solutionism is opposed to an emotional and passive salvationism present in the indigenous attitude. The present style of life in the South Américan city, one associated specifically with the twentieth century, is reduced to a rigorous solutionism consisting in a creed of the modification of the parts, ruled by an analytic, quantitative, and causal criterion, backed by the urgency of constant chores.

It is in the end the thinking of the bourgeoisie which, at the close of the Middle Ages, faces traditional European bourgeois society. Only through an opening to a lucid world of causes, at the level of pure consciousness, can one understand the blooming of Western industrial evolution, which crystallizes in the Reformation and is later promoted by the Anglo-Saxon world, transported by Puritanism to the United States where it extends to the South Américan citizenry. When Sarmiento and Mitre organize Argentina, they do it with this criterion, imposing tasks, and establishing an education based on the exaltation of a causalist intelligence.

Thus, in South América there is, on the one hand, an indigenous cultural structure mounted on a thinking through *inward directedness* which personalizes the world; it emphasizes its globality because it faces the original tearing between the favorable and the unfavorable; it obsessively requires unity moved by a zeal for salvation, and it is explicit both in the *chiuchis* and in its organized religious form. On the other hand, there is an urban cultural structure based in a causalist thinking, limited to intellection, volition, the depersonalization of science, and the myth of the solution.

But political forms also accompany this structure. On the one hand, the indigenous cultural structure resolves the problem of government through theocracy, as in the case of the *chamakanis*, the "owners of darkness," the kings of the Aymara world. They have a vertical rule, an organized distribution of food, and the community predominates. On the other hand, the urban cultural structure adopts democracy, individualism, society, the magnification of science, economics instead of food, politics, and tasks.

One culture seems irreversibly opposed to the other. If an urban Bolivian wants to organize a business enterprise, he would not call a witch doctor like Apaza Rimachi; but neither would Rimachi call a Bolivian urbanite to resolve the problem of his ritual either. They each seem to find satisfaction in the fulfillment of their particular activities.

Though the cultures are opposed, the thinking is not. There must be a thinking as such which constitutes the reason for the other two, independent of any conditioning by culture. If so, there must be a way of crossing the limit from one thinking to the other. Let us see.

At a talk that I gave on psychology at a military post in the highlands, an officer asked me how courage should be faced, surely with a view toward a better understanding of his Indian subordinates. I answered that courage comes with fear and the latter is indispensable to understanding the former. He did not understand me. The military man is tangled up in pure tasks, in a pure *why*, without a *how*, and that causalist attitude leads him to use only part of man. Man, in light of causal thinking, is reduced simply to a mechanism in such a way that he can resolve the question of courage and leave behind fear without further ado. But this in turn, as I came to suspect, aided the military man in emphasizing the *white* and segregating the *Indian*. It seems as if in South América a causal and conscious thinking is sustained for caste reasons. This does not imply that the two forms of thinking can be paired within the officer or the Indian. How can the limit be crossed from one to the other? Or even better, in what way, especially in the urbanite, is another thinking, an indigenous thinking, found next to causal thinking? Let us see.

Above all the problem of thinking in itself cannot be reduced to establishing a "(conceptual) connection among representational contents," as Jung held.[4] Instead, the problem consists in, first and foremost, a total affirmation or negation that can succeed in providing a subject with an existential conformity so that he may increase his security before the world. With *yes* or *no* his consciousness becomes anchored and can decide on an attitude.

It is one thing to affirm "2 + 2 = 4," and another to say "Juan lives." In the first case one completely discards the possibility that the result could simultaneously be 5 or 6. Mathematics has a rigid logic according to which all contradictions or doubts can be discarded without further ado. Thinking in mathematics moreover goes from one affirmation to the next. Even when it denies that "2 + 2 = 6," it moves at a completely conscious level. We could affirm that consciousness in this case always constitutes itself. It is never necessary for it to restore itself.

If I affirm "Juan lives," things are different. Apparently this affirmation also discards the possibility of affirming simultaneously that "Juan does not live." Yet this does not take place in the same dimension as the mathematical judgment. To say "2 + 2 = 4" is to affirm something forever. But to say "Juan lives" is no more than a circumstantial affirmation which can turn into its contrary, "Juan does not live." "2 + 2 = 4" is a judgment that belongs to a reality in which the contradictory propositions exclude each other. "Juan does not live" seems to refer to another reality, where contradictory claims contaminate each other while each keeps its own force. The proof lies in that Juan's lack-of-life acquires an autonomous consistency insofar as it receives a name, death. I cannot conceive of life without referring to death. To say "Juan lives" is to emit a judgment fatally subject to change, where change implies that in the future the claim will contradict itself. Life and death compete with each other for Juan.

What happens with the subject who makes the judgment? When the subject says, "2 + 2 = 4," his consciousness keeps its integrity. But when he expresses, "Juan lives," that integrity is attenuated. It is no longer so easy to maintain the constitution of consciousness. It is necessary to restore it. Life and death, glimpsed as Juan's rending, cannot be resolved with a simple affirmation such as "2 + 2 = 4." What is missing is the existential reassurance, the security before the world which can only be reached with an affirmation on another plane, where the rending of the contradiction is eventually able to recover its unity.

When a person's throat becomes inflamed and the doctor says to the patient that he has laryngitis, he does not want to do anything besides reassure the patient with a simple word, and perhaps to make him notice that the sickness moves on a conscious plane. The reassurance rests on research that will discover the microbe that causes the sickness. In this case everything is kept on a plane of lucidity: from the name, through the conscious manipulation of research, to the backdrop, also conscious, in which causes dwell. Confronted with them, it is fitting to think of solutions.

But when instead of laryngitis, it is cancer, consciousness becomes uneasy. Here instead of a solution, what is required is salvation. Here a region opens up that is not frequented by causal thinking. Does it have something to do, then, with that domain where the divinity applied pressure and where the indigenous person operated through absence?

First of all, this is the domain of antinomies, before which the conscious "I" can do nothing except to have a premonition of the imminent proximity of its rending. Here conscious manipulation of solutions is not possible; all that is possible is locating where salvation lies. And this, in turn, cannot be achieved except through something that transcends the "I."

Transcendence is the necessary condition for the "I" to achieve again all of its existential reassurance and to restitute its lucidity. How is this achieved? It cannot be by finding a backdrop inhabited by conscious causes, because that would be to keep within the terms of the "$2 + 2 = 4$." It must be found, then, through a thinking which is opposed to the causal and which is, rather, *seminal*, in the Latin sense of *semen*, "seed, germ, origin, source." Seminal is that which one can see grow but does not know why, and because of that it seems transcendent, alien to the "I" and to everyday reality, and maybe superior to them, in the sense of *semel*, that which happens "only once," or "once and forever."

Only a seminal thinking can achieve the consolidation of an existential reassurance in the examples cited above. As a unity that transcends and which has germinated at the margin of the "I," it will serve as the salvation of the rending of seeing Juan torn between life and death, and it will also save the opposition within which Apaza Rimachi struggles, even in the case of a changeable and ambiguous trinity.

Seminal thinking consists, then, in finding a dialectical way to overcome an irremediable opposition, almost always through locating the conciliatory unity on a transcendent plane. Instead of moving over affirmations, as causal thinking does, seminal thinking confines itself to a negation of all that has been affirmed, whether life or death, and insofar as it is alien to any conscious maneuvering, it necessitates the germination of that transcendent affirmation.

This cannot be achieved without a change in general attitude. The necessity for a saving unity cannot be too far from an ascetic attitude. A seminal thinking cannot be achieved except in terms of contemplation and waiting, because it withdraws from a commitment to external reality understood as the "garden of objects." In this sense it distances itself from a causal thinking.

While a causal thinking is active, the seminal is passive. Causal thinking is open to the spectacle of the world in Whaelens's sense, insofar as it requires constant verification by consciousness. This verification is not achieved except on the dynamic basis of tasks executed in a domain populated by objects. Seminal thinking, on the other hand, turns its back on that world of objects because it requires the redemptive seed which is outside all tasks, in a sphere below consciousness.

But both are the extremes of a general thinking according to which any subject needs, on the one hand, the lucid connotation of the effect in order to find the cause, and on the other, when the contradiction turns into a rending force, the redemptive seed in transcendence. Both extremes are necessary in affirming the totality of existence.

Now it is fitting to ask, if a culture bases its thinking in terms of connotation and lucid causes, and not in a seminal thinking, is that due to a manifest superiority of it to all others, or is it because of a simple censure of all that is not conscious, a monotheism of consciousness? In other words, can one do without seminal thinking?

The criterion of causality used in everyday life consists in a piecemeal application of what each one believes is backed in a larger sense by science. But this is mere varnish, since, as we will see, a seminal thinking looms on all sides. Seminal thinking aims, if barely, to reconcile the torn extremes to which the experience of life is ultimately reduced. In the way in which one sustains one's family, talks of politics, or searches for that saving friendship, seminal thinking always inspires a requirement of salvation disguised as a fractured causality. And this is so because there are no public forms in the city for channeling seminal thinking.

The astrology column in the newspapers, the conviction before certain significant coincidences that happen to each one us and that we remark on with enthusiasm, or the fascination with hypnosis and telepathy serve as mediocre channels for seminal thinking. But they are always blocked by the halfhearted schematic jargon of a causal thinking.

In the philosophical plane the two ways of thinking are evident. This is clear in the different way in which Heidegger and Chardin refer to utensils. Heidegger reduces them to *something* which *shapes* the existence of a subject. This *something* is in turn *visible*, and thus its mathematical properties can be determined in terms of functional concepts.[5] He limits himself to a simple delimitation that connotes the functions utensils play in existence.

Chardin, in regard to the same problem, relates utensils to the concept of God and makes one dependent on the other.[6] God and objects are subjected to a teleological process whose ultimate goal must be what Chardin calls "Omega," a point of reconciliation of oppositions.

What is the difference between one thinker and the other? Chardin's thinking is seminal insofar as he makes contradictory qualities corporeal and assigns them a transcendental unity in the Omega, almost without noticing any methodological problems. It is a seminality that thinks through mutation. It is similar to the one espoused by Nagarjuna when he affirms that the negation of the *ens* and *non-ens* is the only path to reach supreme truth. It is also similar, in the end, to the one humbly espoused by Apaza Rimachi with his trinity.

Heidegger's thinking is, on the other hand, causal, because he does not abandon the aspects of reality that can be connoted and because he sets aside, in the same book, any concept which could promote a pure seminal thinking.[7] This can be shown when he rejects the term *life* because it cannot be connoted since the *being-there* "will never be defined ontologically if one begins by considering it as life."[8] He evidently rejects the term *life* in order to move onto a scaffold of definable and harmonized names without creating any real opening in the face of a requirement for salvation.

Chardin's tone is prophetic; Heidegger's is casuistic. One opens, the other closes. Chardin barely registers the conscious extremity of imponderable and unnameable concepts. Heidegger in contrast stays within strictly conscious terms. In virtue of their respective topics, both fascinate, but Heidegger less so because of the almost pedantic caution with which his thinking moves.

Heidegger furthermore plays with the possibility of a total consciousness in the sense of an absolute intellection. Chardin places that possibility at the end of a process which, he says, we do not yet understand. He reveals while Heidegger proves. Chardin places himself in a more open cosmos, while Heidegger encloses us in a cosmos where a conscious tyranny weighs us down. Chardin moves in the domain of unnameable things, and from there he handles the nameable ones. Heidegger does the opposite. Or, more accurately, he keeps within the nameable and leaves the rest to the grace of God. It is natural that through this path he declares "the evaporation of being."[9] In this sense he is evidently the thinker of a bourgeoisie whose liberálism has entered a crisis.

The opposition between these two thinkers is the same as that of the two chroniclers Guaman Poma and Montesinos, one indigenous, the other Spanish. This latter opposition is closer to our South América problematic and of lesser scale.

Guaman Poma's thinking oscillates between unnameable terms. From this comes the messianism which reaches at times an extraordinary lucidity, as when he accuses the Spanish and tells them, "You have idols in your house and silver all over the world." This transcends the limits of nameable things and leans only on the original tearing, where his thinking moves. That is why he does not achieve being as discursive as Condarco would like him to be. Guaman Poma tends toward revelation rather than discourse.

Montesinos's attitude is the contrary. He moves among things which are known and have names. His zeal for conscious thinking leads him even to euhemerism, through which he attributes to Manco Capac, as we have seen, political intentions that are overly lucid. Because of that he does not see heroes or gods. This had already happened to the European bourgeoisie of his time. They censured their seminal thinking when they were confronted with the Church. In fact, they barely succeeded in believing in monsters inhabiting the oceans, even though they tried to channel the myths of the City of Caesars, subordinating their own thinking to the fairly causal attitude of acquiring riches, understood in quantitative terms.

This leads us to another problem. When a causal thinking becomes extreme, does it eclipse a seminal thinking? In spite of Heidegger's casuistic attitude, it is worth noting that he is a great thinker because he does not lose altogether the seminal backdrop against which every man moves. This is why his account is fascinating; yet it is always within that corruption of conscience, in Herbert Read's sense, within which we who are in Western culture think.[10] This culture has been mounted on the exclusion of a seminal thinking of salvation. Can that be a consequence of the Industrial Revolution in which the required causal thinking has reached an extreme and has thereby created this violence of consciousness in our América cities?

If that is the case, then we can pose another question. If the complete understanding of everything that exists is not exhausted by a causal thinking, why is a seminal thinking necessary? It must definitely be because reality moves between two crisscrossing vectors: one is horizontal, so to speak, and moves among nameable things; the other is vertical and stretches between two unnameable poles. It is, in the end, what Hartmann proved when he distinguished between the "garden of objects," capable of being known, and a trans-intelligible domain knowledge will never reach.[11] Could it be that this trans-intelligible domain can only be reached by seminal thinking? That is why Heidegger does not reach this domain, while Chardin does. Chardin is speaking of the trans-intelligible when he refers to the Alpha and the Omega. Structurally, this conception is not far from what I wrote above of the Inca religion that leaves its trace in the *ceques*. The same polarity and the same tearing show up, both conditioned by a thinking in seminal terms. This offers, as much in Chardin's case as in the case of Inca religion, the possibility of speaking of the unnameable.

If we raise the need to exercise a comprehensive thinking, then no doubt both vectors must be taken into account. Only thus can a total understanding and a total reality be reached. Besides, as Hegel once remarked, a thinker cannot begin from any axiom other than common sense. If common sense is dual, then, and responds to certain problems in terms of causes and effects, and to others in seminal terms, which one would be a total thinking? Probably it would be the opposite of the one used publicly by the Américan city dweller even though it is one step from a total thinking. Science and rationality do not go further for him than being a simple causal thinking wielded to repressed seminal thinking.

On the other hand, as we have already seen, any so-called scientific formulation always takes place within a field full of contradictions. This itself relativizes the pretense to total truth of scientific knowledge, since, whether one likes it or not, it is always formulated at the margin of the contradiction within which the scientific subject moves.

Lévi-Strauss conceives synchronicity as a way of paying homage to a causal thinking because it takes into account progress across time. But its opposite, diachronism, is suspect. Structure seen without time's deformation of it is a form of accepting a seminal thinking, but by projecting it onto the primitive. Is it that he evacuates onto the object a salvation he does not achieve in his own domain? Is structuralism itself not a hidden form of naming a divine world that neither the French nor the Westerner takes into account except in purely causal terms? Here is the contradictory paradox of science that becomes even more pointed in América. Anthropology, philosophy, sociology are vehicles or methods to shift onto the object that which the subject doing science does not succeed in facing. But it is also true that doing the opposite, mobilizing a seminal thinking, will create a definite "dark period." Within such a period a causal thinking would be reduced to its natural size and scope. Let us see in the following pages how we can overcome this situation. For example, can one conceive of a seminal economy?

In América there seems to be an indigenous economy, on the one hand, and an urban one, on the other. One is conceived in seminal terms, and the conception of the other follows a connotative and causal thinking. Each conditions a distinct type of social relations. In indigenous society the individual cannot use his ego as a weapon, but rather allows himself to be led by custom, which in turn is regulated by the community. Furthermore, his regimen will also be irrational, and thus the individual will not quantify either his labor or his production. And as the individual does not constitute the economic unit, liberty as we know it does not exist. The custom of lending labor to the *mallku* predominates over the individual, who floats impersonally in the midst of communal decisions.

Our economy is instead conditioned by a society that accords autonomy to the ego, with the consequent capacity to dispose of money and to quantify in terms of a scientific economy certain types of relations, such as labor, commodity exchange, freedom of enterprise; in short, all that is expressed in terms of liberty, in terms of a scientific economy.

From this point of view there is no doubt that the distance between us and the indigenous world is enormous. But it is worth asking whether this is really true. In this sense we could sketch a paradox. When a subject among us wants to invest money, he consults the market. The market constitutes a symbolic place where economic relations are regulated. There all the contradictions are balanced, and supply and demand in particular are harmonized. The market is, in short, the point of greatest equilibrium within the problematic of the entirety of economics.

The indigenous market is far from ours not only in terms of the volume of operation, which is smaller, but also because the indigenous person does not use money, but rather lends services, always in accordance with revelation.

But our investor and the Indian coincide on a particular point. The investor goes to the market as a center, and the Indian does the same, with the difference that the investor's center is quantified and the Indian's is qualified. The modern market is the result of the mathematical and autonomous behavior of commodities. The indigenous market was, instead, at least until the sixteenth century, the place where goods were offered to charismatic people such as the *mallku* and the Inca. The modern market seems more intelligible, the indigenous more irrational; the former more conscious, the latter semiconscious. Besides, we decide about the market, while the Indian receives divine decisions in the market. We are free in the market only in terms of things, but subject to mathematical laws; the Indian is also free, but subject to religious norms. In both cases the activity revolves around a center which, in the case of the modern market, provides business ventures and regulates supply and demand. In the indigenous market this center provides the qualities which make labor sacred.

In short, the meaning is inverted. From a regime endured irrationally in ancient times, one moves at the end of 5,000 years of the evolution of consciousness to a visual process limited to money. Once the divinity disposed of man, now man disposes of divine forces, but with a difference; instead of grace coming from outside, it has turned into science and man disposes of it.

But is this a real distinction? Does an investor really look in a market for a relation among quantities, or is there also at play during the handling of commodities and bills of exchange a relation among qualities? The utility of a good maneuver in the market does not end with the amount of money gained; it also points to the very existence of the investor.

Economics could not be understood if it were taken only as handling goods in accordance with specifically economic criteria. It is worth asking, for example, what could be the most important and fundamental reason that leads the investor to the market. Is it just utility, or is it also something as far from economics as prestige?

It is evident that prestige is the psychological spring of the mechanism that regulates and lowers commodity prices. What is strange is that this happens in a society that has proclaimed its rationality and that has substituted regulations for religious norms, regulations each subject adopts in the name of reason. Prestige represents something residual that goes unmentioned because as a psychological factor it is assumed to have been overcome. There seems to be a strange relation between the numinous charisma of an indigenous economy and the charismatic halo of a subject who knows how to handle the risk of a price drop. Does this mean we maintain rationality at all costs, but with a snare in which its contrary, seminality, is hidden? Is it that the whole of the twentieth century mounts its rationality on the trap of the irrational?

Maybe it is not a trap, but rather that the two aspects comprise a human totality, part in the indigenous world and the other part among us, and in each but halfway. And since our humanity has not reached its complete development, a deficit or residue has been accumulating through time whose ultimate expression today is in Leftist parties. The Left poses again the problem of the qualification of the market. That is, they bring to the foreground what a business executive keeps in the background. The Left will not emphasize personal prestige, but in any case wants to qualify in some way the worker's labor, which the liberal world has quantified inhumanely.

But, of course, since the Left functions within a middle class (communism was segregated by the middle class and in no way by the workers), it falls into contradictions because it uses the same trap of the class which gave birth to it. The postulation of qualities such as "the worker's hunger" is not done to recover the plenitude of thinking. Rather, and this is what is deplorable, they do it to continue the pretension that everything can go on quantified, even though on a full stomach.

The truth of the matter is that behind the concept of the market breathes an evident seminality reduced to its minimal expression. This leads individual property owners, to the extent that they know how to hide their cheating in the buying and selling of goods, a step away from the limit situation. Behind the profit achieved in terms of causes is the seminality of prestige, and behind that their pure and naked life, the "nothing more than living" from which the question of salvation emerges. At that moment, nobody there knows the true reason why they are accumulating money and even less why they have to turn to a market. The investor functions, in the end, like the indigenous person, and like him he is subject to necessities by a universe torn between unnameable extremes, even though he does not know very much about it, nor does he have gods to comprehend these extremes.

At this point it is worth asking whether there is any real difference between a modern man and an indigenous man. The difference is evidently still large, but we have now found terms of comparison between them. The indigenous "I" is besieged by fixed models which dictate his conduct, while no such thing happens to modern man. The indigenous man *ascends* because when he becomes culturally mestizo, he exercises his freedom halfway in the mestizo *ayni*, as he maneuvers to recover what he invested in a festival. Modern man *descends* because behind the freedom he exercises through money, he is assaulted by the requirement of salvation, and he cannot speak about it since he lacks the revelation of a magical unity that can help him save himself. The indigenous person *ascends* from his salvation to the neutrality of money. The modern man *descends* from that neutrality until he grazes against salvation, though he is disadvantaged when compared to the Indian, since he ends up committing suicide when he loses everything he had in the market, because he lacks the unnameable gods.

Besides, there is no doubt that the concepts of modern or indigenous man are no more than abstractions, and thus, in the case of América, one should actually speak of someone real who is neither totally modern nor totally indigenous. This is what is vaguely called *pueblo*, but it alludes to an average type in which both the middle class and the peasant are present.

Now this *pueblo* moves between causal thinking and seminal behavior. This can be observed in people's conduct toward money. Money is a neutral element, useful to an abstract subject in economic transactions. Not just in Buenos Aires, but even more so in the Peruvian and Bolivian middle classes, one can observe that money is not a neutral element, but rather something that awakens a relation to one's fellow man that is deeply stirred by affective implications. A favor done in terms of money is understood as an affective assault, which in turn does not always remedy the economic situation, but rather traps the other person affectively through the loan. The loan is never returned because money has changed from pure economic value to a value of another order, loaded with salvation, a symbolic equivalent of "the golden flower" for the one who asks for the loan, a charismatic utensil administered by the neighbor. Thus, it is not a neutral element, but a vehicle that transcends symbolically its concrete reality. From an object of causal thinking, it has become an unacknowledged instrument of seminal thinking. Money and objects are moved, then, by a black mysticism according to which they are sanctified; but as this is absurd, since they are really neutral elements without remainder, the Américan ends up by casting them into hell with contempt, transferring to the *gringo* the ugly quality of asking for the return of the loan or else the noxious virtue of accumulating money.

The deep sense of underdevelopment must be evident in this zeal not to accept the objective and neutral value of money and things, or, better said, in having one eye on things and another on salvation. From this point of view, the French Revolution, an economic revolution in the end, which developed on the basis of a causal way of thinking, has not yet happened in South América. This leads us to consider two possibilities: one, to wait for something like the French Revolution; the other, to consider the possibility that in South América there will be an economy that does not have to go through that step. What is the difference between the two?

Barre defines economics as a relation between unlimited desires and scarcity. It is a Western definition typical of someone who uses a causal thinking promoted by a competitive society and does not have an idea of the totality of man. That is because he does not face his economy from that other thinking, the one that arises from a less conscious level and which can end in salvation. That is why he will not understand the primitive world, because in it revealed truth limits desire. In it one can surely love one's neighbor without asking for a loan, and can also rely on a law of satisfaction in the Inca style.

Mixing the two points of view would lead undoubtedly to chaos. But what is interesting is that beside a quantitative economy such as the one that moves a city, lies in an almost private plane a sort of seminal economy based on ancient structures. This can be seen at the domestic level or at the level of the neighborhood, in that psychological plane lived without conceptualization and without translation to a scientific plane.

It happens when one says, "I will always help when asked in a good way," or when in referring to someone, one claims, "I would give my shirt for him" or "my life for him." Does that "I will help" or "I would give" not reflect, perhaps, a request for a relational system in terms that are less quantitative and more seminal, pointing then to a qualitative economy, a *porteña maytha*? That this is an autonomous system becomes clear when the least suspicion of "being taken advantage of" is met with immediate censure. The subject stops his aid, and even turns what he was giving in terms of reciprocity into quantitative terms and demands money for his labor.

This happens in the depths of the city, in the marginal neighborhoods at the outskirts of the city. There one moves within the limits of a science of the "it seems to me," covered bashfully, almost as if it were a subversion, where neither boss nor authority enters. It is a marginal economy, fostered by an affective relation and limited to small jobs: someone building a dividing wall; or a woman sending her *empanadas* to the neighbor "for her to try"; or the man who lends money to his neighbor only because "in this world we all have to help each other." But it also happens subversively in the shop or the office when one wants a relation with one's boss in terms of an *inward direction*. It is, in short, a truncated sketch of what grounded reciprocity. It is also a nostalgic claim for that complete satisfaction found in the indigenous person.

It is most of all a reaction to a quantitative economy that places a price on bread, but does not succeed in tying the loose ends which these supposedly economic subjects drag through the depths of their neighborhoods in the form of black mystical beliefs. These beliefs find expression in the anti-economic attitude each person adopts in the face of money, or in the participation in an almost indigenous form of reciprocity. But in the end, since there is no real way out, they become explicit in the tango where the subject tries in vain to recover.

This is all part of that frightening *subjectivity* so feared in Western thinking, which takes the form of an immovable but suspicious firmness, not so much in the city as in the heart of the Andean highlands. That firmness is apparent when an Indian from Carangas does not want to sell his merchandise simply because "he does not feel like it." This is the anti-economic face of a world which one tries in vain to understand from an economic angle. But such a world, inevitably reduced to its simple causes because there is no available criterion to appreciate its seminal aspects, will never be redeemed unless these aspects are recovered.

Toynbee nevertheless notices seminality when he points out the importance of religion for the Quakers. They not only withdrew from letting the free-market forces of supply and demand fix their prices by imposing a very high price for their products; they also produced cacao drinks instead of alcoholic ones, not for convenience, but for seminal reasons—their religious principles. And what is remarkable is that they gained considerable wealth and entered the jumble of nascent capitalism of their time as a consequence.

Can one conclude from this that seeing reality from the angle of a seminal thinking is more primitive than thinking of the world in terms of solutions? Probably, but it is also true that man cannot live in a state of affairs without also finding meaning in that state. A seminal thinking humanizes the habitat in which one lives to such an extent that to take up a liberal or a communist position in South América is the same thing as lighting candles for the same saint but in a different guise. One is liberal or communist first to give meaning to reality, and only secondarily to put into practice the solutions proposed by one or the other. But further, the "modern" in its deepest sense, when placed before "primitive," is a term without meaning unless a new seminality is communicated to the current state of affairs. Only *outward direction* paints reality with new colors. To ask for new and modern things to solve problems is just to change colors. The problems are the same as of old. Between the stone ax and the atomic bomb lies the same unmeasured zeal for salvation, and a very small quantity of solution, hardly enough for two different densities of human population. Furthermore, to think that human historical movement will be made more understandable if causal thinking in terms of solutions is maximized, as Américan public education tries to do, is as monstrous as thinking that a headache could be cured by cutting off one's head.

This leads us to think that an in-depth understanding of what is happening in South América must undoubtedly include the possibility of doing science with antiscience, of conceiving, for example, of an economy of abstention based on that Indian who did not want to sell anything because he did not feel like it. In the end, he is not so different from the Quakers, but instead of answering to a religion, he does it in the equivalent terms of a simple affectivity.

A scientific knowledge is unnecessary to arrive at this understanding. Instead, what is required is an emblematic knowledge, and we are not ready for that. Once in Bolivia I proposed to a well-educated Marxist congressman the convenience of sacrificing the Aristotelian criterion of clear judgment in politics to take up instead, as an element in the struggle, the imponderables present among the *pueblo*. To find out about them he only needed to ask any *chola* in the market.

He answered me as one would have expected. It would be difficult for him to do that because one *chola* thinks one way and another differently, so which one of the two judgments would he keep? The answer was put in Aristotelian terms, and it revealed considerable mental laziness. It was actually quite difficult for him to suppose that the real issue lay behind the judgment, in the *chola*'s sheer giving of herself. This he was absolutely unable to notice and even less able to take up because he was a politician. He had adopted a magical criterion to arrive at a political action shining in its lucidity but lacking in content and completely inefficient. In a way, he was cutting off the head to cure the headache. Moreover, he did not understand what was happening with his *pueblo*. A Pumacahuan or a Willcan starts revolutions around imponderables. Not to understand this is to bow to criteria of a middle class that does not succeed in giving up the prejudice of lucidity, because to do so would result in a loss of status.

The same happens with food. When liberalism in the West raises the controversy over food, it does so after having arrived biologically to a causal thinking to be channeled by the modern economy. Thus, to turn food into merchandise was, for that culture, not something ominous, but it is unforgivable in América simply because the problem is still debated in sacred terms, and not just in the indigenous world, but also in the poor outskirts of large cities in the Américas.

In short, América suggests a hidden economy whose basis will have roots in certain colossal unpredictable imponderables; behind a coin used to pay for bread a chance for salvation slips in simply because it does not make sense to eat if one lacks a general framework that lends meaning to the act of eating. This is what translates in "not feeling like selling" even when one is pressed to by need, or in conceiving of man and food as irremediably linked by sacred ties.

This is all implicit in the sentiment of the Américan *pueblo*, not to mention of people anywhere in the world. No doubt any rationalization, translated exclusively into a science as understood nowadays, would be inefficient. To rationalize is nothing more than to infer a state of affairs

from another; that is, to conserve partially an earlier economy, as commu-
nists and liberals do. That cannot be. Something like the *pachacuti* is
missing which would really overturn the state of things, but the Western
world lacks the concepts to confront this need. In every case a really
Américan economy will clash with a deep incapacity to understand what
must be its true basis. But there are no pronouncements on whether the
tools available to conscious thinking on the issue are the right ones. Is it,
then, that in order to give birth to a new economy one must begin from
the irrational fact of mobilizing the Américan masses also in irrational
terms? In the matter of sciences for living, we are yet missing in América a
long Middle Age.

The problem of América is evidently not a problem of the Américan or of the *pueblo*, but largely of its intellectual middle class and the criteria used by it. Progress, causality, rationality, and science are the obsessions of a disoriented intelligence that does not manage to apprehend reality. This is alienation.

But this alienation is not the same as the one superficially wielded by the Left. The Left entangles alienation with economic motives, and it seeks help in a world conceived in terms of abstractions and thus cannot know with precision what it is that man alienates in América.

According to the Left, alienation is limited to the impossibility of achieving well-being—always within an elemental schema which likens man to animal—because economic exploitation as it really happens distributes profits differently from how it should. But even though this is the most important external aspect, alienation does not end here. It, rather, has deeper roots that go way beyond the origin of the Left into Hegelian metaphysics.

In any case, the true sense of alienation suffered by the average urbanite is revealed, particularly in Buenos Aires, when he winks to those present while he formulates the question "And how do you do this?" The *how* points to a knowledge of lucid causes, but it first of all implies a modality or a style of doing things conditioned by the community. Above all, it implies a deep fear of failure, since the latter would carry with it not just a lack of efficiency, something that does not matter to him, but ridicule and the ensuing affective depression.

The second term of the formula, expressed in the *doing*, is tightly conditioned by the *how*. No *doing* is unqualified; it is, rather, affectively sustained, understood almost as a collective conspiracy, that is, as if behind it breathed a fear of ridicule and a heavy obligation. Tasks, in short, are connected to norms that are emotionally sustained. It is common to say of a North Américan that he does not dwell on the *how*, but rather on the bare *doing*. That is what distances us from the way of life in the North.

But why is there such an absolute insecurity about how to *do* things? Could it be because tasks alienate the other extreme of the personality, *my* world, *here* and *now*, in short, the *así* of the world, which is not authorized by the pressing ideal of life of the company executive of the twentieth century, with its abstractions, its causes, and its solutions? Thus, when the average man faces the solution to things, he always seems to formulate in the depth of his being a certain zeal for salvation in terms of the aforementioned "*how* one is to do things."

The formula "And *how* do you do this?" betrays such a zeal. It leaves open the question of a certain interior way out which, naturally, eases the tension of the task.

But here again salvation is hindered. At no point can the average man open his eyes to the *así* of his true world, because he is psychologically besieged by the fear of *letting himself go*, moved, among other things, by the total conviction that finding solutions is always extremely urgent.

Therein lies the contradiction; and therein also lies the Argentinean peculiarity. On the one hand is the escape to a world of abstractions, causes, and solutions, and on the other the urgent need to find a point of repose within a world which is *así*. This same contradiction augments the tyranny of conscience. One does not, then, know how to think except in terms of violence.

I once gathered proof of this during a discussion I had with a Leftist intellectual on progress. He was scandalized by my casting doubt on the concept, and he replied rather severely, asking me who was going to make my clothes, how I would travel to my job. In short, he added, without progress there would be no city.

I was struck by the excessive anxiety accompanying his defense. The hurtful attitude, the quick and tense response, seemed to me symptoms that he had not accepted freely the idea of progress. It was, rather, entangled in anguished undertones which turned his defense into the symptom of a sickness that encompassed him as a subject. This was not the first time I observed a sickly defense on this topic.

I think that if we told Ceferino Choque that his *Gloria Misa* was useless, he would react in a similar fashion, but his attitude would be more peaceful because he would continue to believe his task to be more important than ours. What happened with my interlocutor, then? Is it that I was stealing from him a role he wanted ardently to live? Or is it that the slightest doubt about the importance of progress opened the door to an original tearing lived by him? Is it that my critique put him face-to-face with his immature fear that were he not to defend progress, he would be betraying his urge to *let himself go*, and thus lose his prestige as a civilized man? Or is it also that, in the end, the rational attitude is weak because the opposite way of thinking, the seminal, which moves between unnameable extremes and which was placed in the background, nevertheless continues to accompany very closely the most "rational" of assertions?

If a rationality moves against a background of anxiety, it is because something is missing. It is that solidity that every rational attitude believes achievable through the lucid manipulation of its instruments is not reached. What is more, the manipulation clashes with *paradoxes*. The paradoxes are the same ones Gino Germani pointed out in his historical analysis of the evolution of our Argentinean social structures, structures that do not fit the social statistics cited by him. The truth is that there was in my interlocutor, as well as in the sociologist, and one may add in the whole of the Argentinean middle class, a morbid urgency to participate in the structure of industrial society. This leads to a world of supposedly rational abstractions, but it creates a deep emotional deficit which I call infantile seminality.

Progress is an impersonal concept that can only be tolerated when one takes an active part in it as a sort of almost mystical ideal, never passively. Consider the exemplary iconography which usually accompanies the concept of progress when it is said to have "cost the lives" of many men. Our pedagogy is very partial to this ideal when it demonstrates the importance of a Pasteur or a Madame Curie. This is an ideal frequently wielded by journalists. A "progress" such as this cannot be tolerated passively, because tomorrow it may challenge one's existence. Could it not be that the interlocutor became angry because I had stolen from him the chance to defend something that he could not tolerate passively?

But what gives rise to the transference of salvation onto progress? It must be because handling a causalist conception of the world, which seems to be distinctive in every citizen, is not carried through comfortably, but is instead limited to populating the world with causes and names. Causality is fascinating because of the lucid and conscious operation of exchanging quantities in such a way that the cause seems equal to the effect. But causes are not used except to exercise the violence of consciousness, necessary to confront the impersonal and terrible face of a city based on abstractions. Education consists, above all, in being up-to-date on everything said about causes all over the world, except in South América. There is a colonialism of causes, just as there is an economic colonialism.

Only the weaknesses of the causalist conception of the world can account for the arbitrariness of government, the sudden plans, the surprising rationalizations, the ordinances which seem either invented or borrowed from the system of causes of the Western world, whether European or North Américan, in the name of a universality that harbors both an ardently zealous conscience and a panic of falling into the contrary. And since it is not natural to acknowledge all the causes that have been thought of, it is only cultural novelty that interests people. The way to find out about causes usually, then, becomes linked to the "seriousness" of the author found in a bookstore. The "seriousness" of the text is worth more than the causes themselves, particularly if there is a statistical consensus that "everyone" is studying the same thing. We are the Pharisees of culture.

Managing causes seems, then, to be more formal or ritualistic than rational. Is it that the urban Argentinean functions mentally in the same way as Apaza, the witch? Or worse, does he think like Apaza but just disguised in causal terms? It is curious that in the city to be communist or Catholic always means to "save" the world, just as engineers, physicians, structuralists, or psychoanalysts all tend to have messianic sides. But this also means that the other side, that aspect of the urban person reaching into his deeper regions, his witch side, remains in an infantile state. It remains at the level of the "it seems to me" or the more colloquial "for me," as I explained in another book, *De la mala vida porteña*. It is reflected in a niggardly way in the petit bourgeoisie of the large Latin Américan city, in the idolatry of the small kingdom of the home, where one raises children and kind things live. Only there is faith channeled, even if subversively.[1] This is the seminal buttress against the rest, the street and even the government, all of which belong to the opposed world of a causal and rational thinking that always has a cost.

There, in that place of the "for me," where each one of us withdraws in order to be able to face a city that is causally organized, seminality operates at the level of a guarded uneasiness open also to unnameables, but without any religion that expresses them. It has lost its full dimension and has found itself performing minor tasks, within "progress," "humanity," and all of that which deep down does not matter at all. What does one do, then, with one's own seminal thinking? One has no choice but to play out one's seminality among the unnameables, but in accordance with the urban folklore. In the city one can also find something like the theory of the indigenous overturn, according to which government is a minor equivalent of the Teacher of the *pacha*, and the thief is the one who provokes the overturn, and a military dictatorship is the equivalent of the Inca Yupanqui Pachacuti.

Real salvation is thus subverted by the solution, because one lives blocked by the demand for lucidity, and there is no knowledge of whatever is not lucid. Behind all the financial deals hides an insoluble salvation floating as a nonlucid instance over the business of the city.

The knowledge of fixed models that belongs to seminal thinking demands its rights. It turns the city from being the peak of rational endeavor into a large garbage dump of those same models used subversively, even though toned down from their use by the Indian and prehistoric man. This is because the city is the specific habitat of what is captured by the concept of the *bourgeois*, taken as a style of life, one characterized by a causal and purposeful way of thinking which no flesh and blood person can easily endure. And since this is a fiction, everything that man would want to play out seminally survives, though in a vacuum, as a requirement of a plenitude never to be achieved. In that case it will not be death or transfiguration in the great ritual, but simply its leftovers in a movie thriller; thus the censuring of consciousness. Hunches, doubts, boldness are big business for the schema of death and transfiguration, but they are hidden under the causal and conscious cloak of convenience, interest, profit, and economics.

And the only way to resolve this internal contradiction that permeates the whole of South América lies in the exaltation of effort and in turning to the world of objects. Whether there is an infantilism from the seminal point of view, whether there is an ability to handle the abstract world of causes, any contradiction is remedied through the lucid, clear, hard, and perfectly real world of the machine, the car, the house, or a city of cement and stone. It is from there that strength is gathered to simulate rationality, and any character who is emotionally immature finds his social justification in an IBM machine.

What is more, behind the obsession with industry, commerce, economics, or science, the middle class of Buenos Aires, for example, seeks only an easy justification not to confront its own immaturity. Causes scientifically isolated, known, and traditional are useful to channel a real urgency of location that the exterior world does not seem to offer at all. That is why the proof of the real inferiority of the Américan man, maybe even the true dimension of his drama, lies in a great uneasiness tied to his presumption of being civilized, of believing in development and progress. And that is why that eagerness for civilization finds shelter in the desire to plunder immorally what the twentieth century offers him, without the slightest commitment to any of it.

And it is natural that from that "for me" one notices the mutation implied in becoming an urbanite, because in reality a person does not know why he must be an individual, lack a home in the world, and always ask about causes. The urgency to take this on is so pressing that there is no time to arrive at seminal growth up to that point. Maybe that is why a stigma floats around in popular culture that one is an individual only through possessing something, that solitude amounts to an affective suppression, and that causality is a hidden way of asking for noncausal things. Together with individuality, society, and the individual, one lives longing for community and minor gods. But with a difference: while the *pueblo* is capable of canonizing Eva Perón, the middle class cannot convince itself that Che Guevara is its hero and readily separates itself from him.[2] This is its intimate contradiction, but one that nevertheless does not fail to show a certain degree of authenticity. The middle class knows that, in the end, it performs the same manipulations of concepts that Apaza performs, or that it would like to recover the ingenuousness of Guaman Poma to initiate the great heroic phase with the *así* of the surrounding world. But in order to do that it is necessary for it to lose its fascination before the nameables and to venture an investigation of the unnameables.

I remember the expression of terror of that interlocutor when I denied him the validity of progress. It was the expression of a believer that really sees the unnameable. Progress seemed to him to be the myth of the city, like a living paradise engaged at the level of a clear and distinct truth, carried out intellectually and scientifically, even though with the burden of being, deep down, a sort of fallen religion with a strong salvationist side. Progress saves and remedies the situation in the city. This role used to be transferred to the gods but today depends on the effort of each person, in such a way that any mediocre person can evade understanding his own situation in the world merely through wanting to improve his city. But there is no doubt that progress, endured in this manner, is a hybrid concept, with the added difficulty that progress does not get into the problems of the real dimension of one's life. In this sense, there is no escape through the external world since this world disconnects man from his internal tension which, in the end, is the only thing that can provide his salvation. He is missing the *así* of reality. But then, in what does the *así* consist?

In América there is, on the one hand, a thinking that operates in terms of fish and condors and, on the other, one that thinks at the level of atomic plants. This is the same opposition as that between the ancient Tiahuanacotan culture and modern cities like Buenos Aires, Rio de Janeiro, or Santiago de Chile.

And there are two cultures. One follows the line of fear and searches for seminal wellsprings through an ascetic attitude, which evokes *uk'u* as body and affectivity.[1] The other embeds itself in the periphery of the continent, turns to tasks supported by an intelligence that wants to overcome the fear and that hypostatizes science and reason. Both in turn seem to have their own political organizations, one theocratic, the *chamakanis*, or Aymara kings, and the other industry, commerce, and the twentieth century. We have already seen this. But América does not consist in a contradiction, but rather in something that overcomes it.

The true development of South América does not lie in the new structures; they have not been able to condition the conception, creation, or even with the aid of foreign capital, the simple installation of atomic plants. That is because there has not been a real capacity to rise above thinking in terms of fish and condors, or even less of maintaining itself publicly at the level of this way of thinking, developing it beyond where the

Aymaras took it, since no feline seems to reconcile the contradiction that lies inside the urban dweller.

To see the contradiction formulated in these terms means to abandon oneself to a causal, connotative thinking that eludes its own contradiction, because as it lingers in the antinomies, it lacks commitment. Instead, thinking in terms of seminality implies having faith. But here again the other problem presents itself: knowing what to do in order to believe. It is impossible to mobilize faith mechanically. Through the *how* to believe, the *what for* and *why* believe, one returns to the antinomy again and ends biting one's own tail like the snake. What to do then?

Maybe everything lies in reassuming a prior attitude, prior even to thinking, and claiming what I am calling the *así* of reality. This is to return to the problem of the Chipayan hut. The question posed by the hut was not one of populating the world with causes, but simply of accepting the presence of the hut's roundness and its inhabitants, the Chipaya.

To reach the *así*, it is necessary to *see*. There are two ways of *seeing*. One can see merely to connote an object so as to situate it or to note whether it is well or poorly placed. This way of *seeing* only aims at connoting reality in order to use it, which remains a primary form of staying inside oneself, entangled in the necessities dictated by one's biology.

When one reaches out to take the bread and brings it into one's mouth to eat it, one goes out of oneself in order to return so as to remain within the domain of one's own subjectivity, proximate to the bread, sincerely ready to feed oneself. In this case, the bread did not stop in front of the senses. It instead slid before them, almost becoming not so much an object as *something* nutritious.

But really to *see* reality must be something quite different. This involves entering into the mystery of the *así* of reality, which could be found, for example, in the way of making bread or in the peculiar beauty or ugliness of it, or in thinking of the one who kneaded it, of how that was done and how much they were paid, or, going even further, thinking of the long history during which bread has fed man, and, in short, ending up in the mystery that bread exists. But here bread is no longer an object. It becomes something sacred. The *así* of the bread is recovered, its simple, though tremendous, presence. At this point it is difficult to eat it without further ado, since one may look at it or worship it because it is now a lot more than a solution to hunger, and in a way, it moves into the domain of salvation. There, in the case of eating it, one transcends simple nutrition and one feeds on the true dimension of the food.

That is why to *see* the *así* of bread is terrifying. It is not because of the bread itself, but because of the mental inclination of the average man of the big city, protected by a secondhand science, thinking in terms of utility, believing that the issue has been treated with sufficient seriousness. Because of all of that, the surprising dimension of bread must appear monstrous to him. It is the monstrosity that peeks out in the *presence* of things, when they are not alone in an empty space, but rather are tainted by a numinous background which provides them with a raison d'être that transcends their mere utility. It is then that they achieve being *present*, charged with the mystery of the pure *así* at the level of the indigenous *guauque*. It is there that the lucid and horizontal vision of causes intersects the vertical play of the unnameable extremes and the deep tearing that separates them.

But this has nothing to do with the folkloric fact called "América." We could be speaking of Africa or Europe; it would be the same. It is a question of the *así*, which imprisons man in his totality and implicates him completely. This cannot be provided to him by the folklore of América, but rather, and above all, by the vision of the presence of América in its full existential dimension.

What I am saying does not enter into the anti-folklore urge of the ruling classes. This urge and the pro-folklore tendency of some other sectors coincide at some points. The one group depopulates the world of its habitat and repopulates it with causes. The other sees folklore as an object, with the purpose of investigating causes. The two are equally inauthentic postures. They denote, in short, the attitude of an urban person, someone who does not want to lose the validity of his style of thinking. The *así* of América has nothing to do with either a pro or contra attitude toward folklore.

This is why history is not useful either, because the *así* of reality has never been *seen* along its trajectory, except indirectly. We can see this reflected in some testimonials. In a letter written just after 1800 by Manuel Carrillo de Albornoz to Cisneros, he warns Cisneros that América could be lost if the leaders continue their complaisance toward the "effeminacy caused by these countries."[2]

In another letter, dated 1812, Belgrano expresses "the firm *resolution* we have reached sustaining the *Américan independence*."[3] During the same period, for example, the national government orders that a philosophical history be written "to perpetuate the memory of the heroes, the virtues of the *sons* of South América."[4] The enthusiasm for things Américan acquires a personalized, even maternal, dimension, when in a letter from San Martín, cited by Bolívar, San Martín remarks that "*América will not forget when we embrace*."[5]

But the quality and the pride of feeling oneself a *son* tend to disappear when the extreme is posed: the proclamation of the necessity of an Inca monarchy for the new nations. From that moment on América became merely a geographical base, and, especially in the Argentinean case, the official language substitutes the term *Patria* for América.

San Martín had already written in 1814 "the *Patria* will not carve a path through this side of the (Argentinean) North."[6] And in 1858, Sarmiento, in his prologue to Mitre's history of Belgrano, writes, "With this minute and heterogeneous population the revolution of Argentinean independence was begun, a revolution which founded six republics in the South Américan continent."[7] When Tejedor writes to the governor about Lopez of Paraguay, he mentions the "future of América," but also that "impartiality and disinterest are *rare* in the annals of América."[8] Finally, San Martín notes in his old age that in América there could be either legal governments or de facto governments and that some governments are representative and others are absolutist, but that "the governments of América *lack*" both guarantees.[9]

Praxis turns into the monopoly of the ascending industrious class and the Américan fades away and with it the possibility of apprehending its *así*. On the one hand, there is an attitude that is expressed in universal terms, terms evacuated of the entirety of the geographic continent; and on the other, an América is segregated that is black, passive, and retrograde, a fountain from which spring tyrants and undesirable populations. What is more, at the end of a short lapse of time from independence until the organization of the country, there is a return to Carrillo de Albornoz's opinion of the "effeminacy caused by these countries." Even Mitre thinks that to be civilized is a question of virility.

Today the Left maintains the same thinking, though in terms of progress. The daughter of Mitreism in History, it adopts an activist attitude before América which borders on a certain proclamation of virility. The anticommunists say exactly the same thing when they fight for their interests. América seems to be, in short, at the end of the 150-year struggle, a place where a North Américan or an immigrant can *"make it* in América." She is no more than a tabula rasa, the stage on which objects move.

It is evident that the Spaniard Carrillo de Albornoz was not mistaken. Behind the term *effeminacy* and the expressions used in the aforementioned letters, one can notice that América exercises an ill effect on European ways of thinking. Beyond being a simple geographical support, América seems to provoke a certain uneasiness, and as the illustrious men were keen on stabilizing its existence in terms of *homo faber,* they threw everything other, everything they could not resolve, into the dung heap of the *effeminacy* of a black América. They themselves did not succeed in confronting the *así.*

Is it that they knew that the *así* of América would block the *homo faber?* Here there are two possibilities: either América is the hole where a humanity limited to *homo faber* is to be buried, or *homo faber* covers only one aspect of the totality of man. In the latter case, it is possible to think that the blockage is due to the fact that in América residual aspects of man accumulate, those aspects that were not predicted by Western thinking. The first conception seems too schematic; and with respect to the second possibility, it is necessary to investigate the true meaning of the blockage. Could the blockage be due to a dialectical moment pointing to the rescue of the missing part of the mutilated conception of modern man? Not to accept this would be to suppress the so-called Américan *pueblo* so that a small executive bourgeoisie may fulfill its programs of development, and this is impossible. Sarmiento's and Alberdi's naïve attempt to substitute Anglo-Saxons for the *criollo* population in order to incorporate the flourishing and recently organized republic into the Western community did not seem to have much effect, even though a corporate elite continues to contemplate such a plan.

The *así* of América begins to show at the moment when there is no more enterprise. It manifests itself at the end of an action, when the average man wants to set up an industry and thinks about future buyers, or when someone writes a book and reflects on the editor, the reader, bookstores, the empty space between one city and another, or when someone finishes a science degree and thinks about the future customers.

In that moment the geographic habitat appears, burdened with uneasiness, almost like an irremediable residence, where one will have to devote oneself to one's professional activity in the midst of a reality which is *así* and not as one imagined it when one was a student. It is there that what is "Américan" reveals itself to the middle class as something passive, as adopting bad habits, "allowing oneself to rot," which is not remedied by all the usefulness accumulated by studying. América at that point seems to mean "anything goes," because each person *falls* as his illusions crumble, smashed against the question *to what end?*; a question that lacks an answer either because there are no more Indians or simply because the telephones never work "in this country." There lies the disappointment of having been born here, and that lead Martínez Estrada to concoct pompously the concept of the seventh solitude, and others to proclaim unspeakable heresies under the guise of consenting to assumed original sins. It is, in sum, the same as the "feminization" of which the Spaniard spoke. We are in the same situation.

It is the question of the monstrosity of the *así*, which in the case of bread means becoming responsible for the full dimension that bread qua object carries with it until it sets up the necessity of salvation prior to nutrition or on par with it. In this sense, the *así* of América is frightening. It proposes not the monstrosity of América, but rather of man himself. To tolerate the presence, the *así* of something like bread or of América itself presupposes the acceptance of the deep contradiction between unnameable terms within which one has always struggled. The *así* creates the irremediable opening toward the totality of what is given *así*, that which is not altogether conscious, which one has cancelled out because of negligence or comfort, where the reality and darkness of oneself are fused in the domain of that which is not useful. It is the residue, the margin each one of us has left in his journey and which turned into something dirty. Any *why* or *what for* crashes against that residue since a negative perspective opens where the natural vision of things is inverted, one's dispossession is measured, the degree of one's own ugliness, in symmetrical and inverse proportion to reality. It is the irruption of the unnameable into the domain of the nameable. What is important is turned into something residual because the military uniform that one put on to augment one's stature is invalidated, as are all the subjects studied by the university student, the brilliant lecture delivered in some university, or being a communist, a nationalist, a centralist, or a federalist, or the stingily written history that demonstrates a lucid will toward a democracy which Peronism co-opts so easily. Why? Because in the face of the absence of a meaningful content one is presented with the empty schema of a sort of original fall. And faced with that, thinking in terms of atomic plants has no validity, but it does make sense to think simply in terms of redemptive fish, condors, and felines so as to see what the fall consists in. This, and no other, is the consequence of recovering seminality so as to overcome its infantilism.

But all this leads us to ask: to what is existence then reduced? That is, within which philosophical schema is it fitting to connote our existence so as to take into account everything that happens with man? At this point, there is a community of destiny in América in which all social spheres fit. The Américan lifestyle is constituted by it. Can we, then, frame it with a philosophical term that is its own? Let us see.

It is odd that the marginal Spanish spoken in South América, particularly when one wants to speak properly, becomes excessively and suspiciously qualified, to the point that it becomes very cumbersome. For example, though an expression such as *I am* is always accompanied by a certain effort, so that what one *is* is glued to the subject and emphatically affirmed, one never *is* totally what the predicate expresses. One *is* never totally a physician. When one says *I am a physician*, one always adds a *but* which rescues what is omitted in the claim.

It is also interesting that the verb *estar* is present in a large number of expressions, such as when one says *estoy escribiendo* (I am writing) instead of *yo escribo* (I write), *estoy trabajando* (I am working) instead of *yo trabajo* (I work), or *estoy creyendo* (I am believing) instead of *yo creo* (I believe).[1] As the verb *estar* is placed between the subject *yo* (I) and the verb, a distancing is produced; the self is separated from that which is connoted and becomes alien to it.[2] Is this use of *estar* a way of showing a lack of trust in the act of connotation itself? Is this the result of the subject's keeping itself within a passive plane, as if it were adopting a contemplative attitude because everything comes to be seen merely as circumstance?

This coincides with the Argentinean and, even more widely, Américan characteristic, which seems to consist in submerging everything stable within circumstance, as if whatever one is doing were the momentary product of a great instability which hovers in an unseen background. A recently established government is always unstable, what one owns is also unstable, and one even excuses one's opinion by accompanying it with *it seems to me.*

Generally, the stable is submerged in the unstable, that is, the world is populated by circumstances, and what *is* is reduced to what *está.* That which *is*, for example, Pedro's goodness, *is* not really, but rather *está.* His goodness is just a ghost. When one says *I am good* (*soy bueno*), one thinks that within the contrary formula "*estoy* en el *ser bueno*" (*estoy* in the state of *being good*). One adds, in other words, the subversive conviction that there is no *being good* as such, since one *will* not *be* good if the circumstances do not allow it.

The formulation of what *is* leads us immediately to the possibility of a *not being* any more. In a way, being is reduced to circumstance; it is made to dwell within circumstance, as if nothing that happens could move beyond just *estar.* And insofar as the *is* is substituted by *estar in the being,* the world is populated by a dramatic instability.[3]

As I already remarked in another work, the verb *estar* appears in Spanish, but not, oddly, in other languages. Spanish grammar indicates that *estar* be utilized in the case of circumstance, while the verb *ser* (to be) is used to designate permanent states.

Slaby and Grossman note, for example, that the verb *estar* indicates place ("estar en casa" [*está* at home]); mood ("estar alegre" [*estar* happy]); congruity or fitness ("está bien" [*está* fine]; "el traje está bien" [the suit *está* fine]); understanding ("ya está" [*está* done]); duration ("estar escribiendo" [*estar* writing]); accessibility or purpose ("estar de paso" [*estar* on one's way]; "estar por decir" [*estar* on the brink of saying]; "estar para eso" [*estar* there for that purpose]). In every case the verb seems to function to point, but since it does not commit the subject, the verb says nothing about the subject. The subject appears entangled in the attribute transitorily in such a way that the attribute, due to the nature of the verb *estar*, says nothing about the subject. This is because the verb points directly to the world without the intervention of an unqualified anonymous subject. Is this the consequence of seeing the *así* of reality?

Undoubtedly, the speakers who created the language must have had an implicit conceptualization that excised one domain of existence, ruled by the verb *estar*, from another, ruled by the verb *ser*, in such a way that they divided the world between the definable and the indefinable. *Estar* implies lack of essences and leads in effect to the temporary fall of the subject to the level of circumstance.

Clearly, this verb appears not just because of a desire to connote another sphere of reality, but also because the accident has been segregated, or at least delimited to a non-essential reality. It creates the possibility of connoting a world without definitions, a world where only circumstance abounds. However, circumstance was precisely that which according to Aristotle was not the object of philosophy; it was merely the starting point to be overcome in order to arrive at the domain of being and thus enter the domain of definition.

As *estar* corresponds to the domain of anti-definition, it becomes segregated and it thus acquires an honorable autonomy that legalizes and stabilizes its regime. Not everything linked to *estar* is pejorative, but rather responds to a way of thinking implicit in the cultural body that created it.

From this perspective, the verb *estar* provides a concept of surprising richness. We know that *estar* comes from the Latin *stare*, "to stand up," which implies restlessness. *Ser*, on the other hand, comes from *sedere*, "to be sitting down," which connotes a foundation from which springs the possibility of definition. A definable world is a world without fear, while a world that instead surrenders to the fluctuations of circumstance is to be feared. The opposition between *estar en pie* (to stand) and *estar sentado* (to sit down) implies an opposition between *restlessness* and *repose*. But in what does the restlessness of a mere *estar* consist? Could it be that it is comprised of that order of life where lucid and causal thinking intersects with another thinking that is neither lucid nor causal, a seminal thinking, a thinking that lacks definition, a thinking in which the unnameable erupts through when faced with the vision of the *así* of reality? The choice of the verb *estar* in the everyday speech of América is a choice over a verb that commits the subject to a greater degree. Is this choice due to an appeal to a truth—a truth that inquires into the unnameable, as if one were searching for another way of *being* (*ser*) or *sitting down* (*estar sentado*)?

There is something of this in Don Quixote and also in Sancho Panza. Don Quixote does not notice the *estar*, or the mere givenness, of a world where the cavalry does not ride in. Sancho Panza, in contrast, is *too* immersed within it. Nevertheless, Sancho Panza represents the *pueblo* as conceived of by an intellectual like Cervantes: very idealized, almost as if he were the crystallization of a longing. Quixote represents the tearing apart of a desire to *be* (*ser*), but ends up in a lamentable and mere *estar*. His drama is drawn from his not having been able to choose a being adequate to his *estar*. Thus, he remains vulnerable to such deplorable circumstances as when the wind mills toss him up in the air.

Cervantes's work fascinates us because like Quixote we are caught in circumstance, with the same schema of the fall. Though it is not proper to proclaim this publicly, we, who cannot even believe in a cavalry, simulate *being* (*ser*). Thus formulated, the problem is not one for Quixote, nor of the people of the Américas, but of man in the twentieth century.

This is what Heidegger says in *Being and Time*. The great majority of his work reflects a philosophy of *estar*. But as this *estar* is understood as "existence," that is, as *estar afuera del ser* (*estar* outside of being), Heidegger points to what happens with *being* (*ser*) and not with *estar*. Now Heidegger develops the conventional sequence that goes from existence to *being*. This is natural because it is what is traditional. But the theme of *being*, such an obsession for the Europeans, is nothing more than a Greek inheritance, coined philosophically by Western thinking, and because of that it reaches us in the twentieth century as something absolutely empty, as Heidegger shows. Thus his move to a philosophy of time. It was natural to arrive at this point at the conclusion of a way of thinking drained by the Industrial Revolution. This way of thinking, which sees only in terms of causes, cannot countenance the simple *estar*, since *estar* lacks connotations. Without a doubt, this is why behind his philosophy of time Heidegger reveals an obsession with activity, with enterprise, as an inalienably pressing demand of the German bourgeoisie.

But Latin América is fortunately a world without an Industrial Revolution, situated at the margin of history and at the "limits of the West." Enterprise is, then, the obsession of a minority. This explains the divorce between *enterprise* and that mere *estar* in which all that is ours moves.

Enterprise is understood in América as making *something* (*qué*) with the aim of simply *estar bien* or *mejor* ("*estar* well" or "*estar* better"), as if enterprise were merely a way of making the *estar* ready for use. The question is one of working all day to achieve comfort, attained by buying the *qué*, or things. One readies oneself. One becomes motivated to *make* when one wants to *estar bien* (*estar* well), and one *está bien* (*está* well) insofar as one *has*. A priest in La Paz remarked to me that behind North Américan enterprise is a philosophy of *having* that goes beyond enterprise itself. Naturally, this leads to *estar bien* (*estar* well) in visual terms, but without transcendence.

Estar bien (*estar* well) among objects acquired through enterprise is evidently an excessively visual and easy way of achieving plenitude. It is already to have fallen to the world of things. It is, to some extent, a loss of freedom. Each and every middle class, and thus all elements of the Left as well, longs for such a fall.

Verstraeten, for example, critiques Lévi-Strauss in the name of Marxism because he fears that Lévi-Strauss might be deprecating enterprising ac-tivity. He suggests that the Bororo "tend toward nothingness" because they live from ritual.[4] But could it not be that Verstraeten has posed the problem in terms of a being that is excessively visual and bureaucratized? Like the good Westerner he is, he has lost the original question of his *estar*. In the end, a ritual, no matter how primitive, is not far from Verstraeten's own act of writing a book. This is what a certain type of naïve Marxist does not understand.

For the Américan, enterprise is something placed outside and lacking in consistency. One cannot say to him even what the common man of Buenos Aires says—"Well, this really is"—since that points to something outside the subject, entangled in objects, and places everything that *is* in the effort necessary to achieve it. It does not respond to what the search is really about, the necessity of finding a true plenitude. Enterprise is a departure from mere *estar* to the domain of objects that can be *possessed*. Since *possession* takes place in a visual domain, it contradicts that which is deep in the conscience of *estar*—that zeal for plenitude implicit in *estar*. That is why when one says, "I am working [*estoy trabajando*]," one actually wants to avoid work, because work, due to its visual nature, says nothing of plenitude. That is why *possession* provokes a withdrawal from the old basis of a simple *estar*, in order to avoid intolerable alienation. And this is also why having things is never completely satisfying; because to achieve truth, it is necessary to *estar* even if *estar* "calm," "far away," or "alone." It is well known that if one does not do so, mere *having* leads to the novelty of having more and more things. But as popular wisdom astutely puts it, "This leads nowhere." Besides, one does not understand life itself without the possibility of facing one's own plenitude.

And this happens because *estar* has been reduced to each one feeling oneself within that limit of being only *something* that *está* and which one could call man. It is not the man created by the European bourgeoisie, but rather that other man, besieged by the police and the military, susceptible to being counted statistically, obliged to vote, someone to whom opinions are attributed, opinions not heeded by anyone, and to whom a monthly salary is assigned. And all of this is done to certify convincingly his heroic humanity, which, at base, everyone doubts.

Estar so conceived constitutes the true point of departure for any analysis of existence. It is, in the end, an *estar* reduced to *inhabitation*, to *here* and *now* and materialized nebulously as something around which everything turns. This is what one reflects on when the *así* of reality is recognized, when one is touched by its presence. *Estar* thus conceived requires a plenitude because, just as with the indigenous *pacha*, this thinking opens the world of the unnameables. The *estar* and the *pacha* seem to be the same thing.

The *así* is conceptually concretized in *estar*, with its simple possibilities of "what my life can be," that is, of "just living." This leads one to the rupture, the rending. But within that state, one feels one just *está* (is); one also feels *badly*, because neither the Américan city nor the modern world provides a public path to channel that *está*.

As there is no public path for *estar*, *estar* turns the subject into something prior to being named a property owner and, worse yet, into something prior to being considered a divine creation. Lacking a public path, *estar* turns the subject into a biological unit that barely possesses the rudimentary tools necessary to confront his environment. Thus, for the urban dweller or for the indigenous person, the theme of *estar* does not revolve around civilization or progress, but around "just living." One can see this, for example, when a person manifests the primary wonderment of surprise at being an engineer in a large firm, and when he sees this as a miracle. It is the sensation of dispossession that accompanies the supposed potential wealth of our América. It is that sensation to which we feel reduced, even when we are executives.

Concretely, we can say that *estar* implies an attitude that avoids definition by means of, for example, formulations such as *estar trabajando* (*estar working*), with which it points to a decided preference for circumstance. In turn, there is no public way to understand this circumstance. Instead, one is left with a mere *it seems to me*, that is, circumstance understood in terms of a seminal thinking, but reduced to an infantile stage.

Nevertheless, this does not exclude that circumstance itself—or the deep sensation of an unstable world, in which everything *is done*, including glory and honor—provokes in the *estar* the necessity of an *estar con* (*estar* with), which is a requirement of community. This is what Felix Schwartzmann says masterfully when he analyzes the feeling of the human in América. In turn, this requirement implies a form of dwelling in the world.

All of this constitutes the *estar* as effectual, a real manifestation of it as a style of seeing things, almost as a conception of the world. Does this not link with dwelling, seminality, and community associated with the *utcatha* of the Aymara? If so, the similarity with the indigenous conception does not constitute a disadvantage. It instead provides the benefit of recovering both a style of life that moves along a perceptive and visual horizon of friendly things, as well as the vertical line of a great mystery. The real mystery of man begins to manifest itself here insofar as man is pressed by unnameable opposites. *Estar* is, in sum, a placing of oneself at the intersection which opens in the *así*, where an authentic vision of man appears. From there it makes sense to think of the attitude the people of the Américas must adopt when faced with enterprise. It is the advantage of being underdeveloped. On this side we can play out the game of chance that is our own history.

When Lévi-Strauss describes the social organization of the Bororo, he mentions three structures: a diametrical one that divides the community in two halves; a concentric one that places the sacred in the center and the profane at the periphery; and a third, triadic one, according to which each of the eight clans of the village are subdivided into three parcels of land, upper, middle, and lower. According to Lévi-Strauss, this leads to what appears to be an exogamy ordered by the two halves, and a real endogamy in accordance to the triadic scheme.[1]

But these structures are not completely decisive for an indigenous person. They only constitute one element that can be connoted for our Western way of thinking as we satisfy our urge for awareness. One *sees* what happens in the village of the Bororo, but one does not understand their lives. Structures are only an aspect of this life, but not life itself. What is missing to gain greater understanding?

We have seen that the concept *estar* seems to encompass the "just living" of man. But something must be lacking. To say *estar* is, in the end, no more than to connote with a term what takes place. But how to go beyond that to understand the solidity the mere *estar* has for an indigenous person? I believe one does not understand the mere *estar* unless one also attributes to it a certain demand made by the *absolute*, but which is kept implicit. *Estar,* to the extent that it is a settling of oneself within reality, or a taking root in it, transcends circumstance: what *estar alive* and *estar dead* have in common cannot be accounted for except insofar as the *estar* in both cases participates in the *absolute.* If Juan enters a gathering of friends, he does so in absolute terms. The urge for totality implicit in Juan will lead him to command respect in the gathering or to hate those present because of his own shyness. If the former, he exercises the absolute positively; if the latter he does so negatively, as withdrawal. In both cases he will do so in terms of a simple *just because,* proper to seminal thinking.

The structures to which the Bororo turn are only an aspect of the demand of the absolute, the aspect which can be visualized, conceived in terms of causes and connotation. This is the aspect the Westerner can apprehend easily.

What would happen if we were to compare the Bororo's absolute with Lévi-Strauss's? It is not difficult to establish that the tendency to think in terms of connotation and the zeal for conscious awareness lead naturally to a systematic labeling of the absolute and, in the end, to a displacement of the absolute to the indigenous world. Similarly, we can ask further whether the theory of the logical importance of savage thinking is not another unsuccessful way of bringing a totality, one that had been relegated to the primitive during the last century by a positivist bourgeoisie, closer to the civilized frame of mind.[2] Is not the very concept of diachrony an attempt to abolish time, which is something the Bororo do constantly? Is it that the drama of modern Western thinking lies in not achieving the reestablishment of the absolute and in not knowing what to do with the requirement that demands its installation?

An obvious symptom of this can be found in Heidegger's theorization of "evaporation of being." The necessity of establishing the existence or nonexistence of being prompts Heidegger to conduct a phenomenological analysis of everyday life. But this approach is ultimately no more than the application of a connotative and causal way of thinking, almost like preparing a balance sheet or forecasting an already known result. He introduces the curious alternatives of an authentic and an inauthentic existence from motives that are not really philosophical; they do not seem to respond to anything other than a desire to segregate "inauthentic" existence conceptually, not just because of its fit with tools and with community, but, above all, because it demands the absolute.

The authentic, in turn, seems intertwined with a traditional European bourgeois attitude of obsessive confrontation with time. This obsession is motivated ultimately by a thinking that travels horizontally at the level of the world of things, in that constant zeal to search for clear causes. Heidegger's terminology confirms it. Being *evaporates* because at no time can it be given *to-hand* or *to-sight*, and there can be no faith in things that cannot be touched or seen, that is, in that which is not present to consciousness or has no cause. Existentialism is the thinking of enterprising people who grant absolute validity to enterprise. In other words, more than the "evaporation of being," it is a sublimation of being. The proof lies in that seminal thinking hides itself and enters another dimension, as we shall see.

Are not psychology and anthropology the sciences that take up this problem in an objective way? European science seems to have an existential strategy behind it: philosophy demonstrates the emptiness of being, while scientists—Jung, Leehardt, Eliade, Van der Leeuw, Gusdorf—devote themselves to a style of thinking opposed to their own, but toward which, in spite of themselves, they feel an obvious fascination.

At root, this is due to the trap into which the West has fallen as a consequence of the Industrial Revolution. Nevertheless, the fact that the profits provided by this revolution were acquired on the foundation of a man who did not cease to be "primitive" cannot be erased by the profits themselves. In short, the indigenous person and the Westerner must not be very different since they both require the absolute, but while the indigenous person makes the absolute concrete, the Westerner lives it negatively, in hiding, and always segregated from it, as if it were for the *masses*.

If Lévi-Strauss's and the Bororo's *estar* point to the absolute, then evidently they have *estar* in common. Mere *estar* as dispossession and nakedness would not be tolerable unless it were buttressed by a desire for the absolute. The absolute provides consistency to the *estar*, and it is what turns both indigenous life and the life of the anonymous inhabitant of a large city into a miracle. *Estar* is the settling into the real habitat of the home, the landscape, work, the city, and so on. But this habitat has two dimensions. It is lived as given, which implies a connotative, causal thinking. It also may be understood as a point of repose or fall in the long trajectory between unnameable opposites: life and death, good and bad omens, Pachayachachic or Guanacauri, or their modern version, macro-

and microphysics. The absolute, in turn, is seminal understanding, tensely arched over the tearing in which the cosmos always finds itself. It is only because of this absolute that it is possible to tolerate a simple *estar* when that *estar* reaches the state of dispossession.

The absolute appears in a major or minor dimension. One marks the signposts of its minor dimension in the simple magical ritual of the indigenous person, in the *I hope* with which the urban dweller tries to affect events, in the satisfaction he receives in having accomplished a day's labor, or in the good role he plays at a gathering.[3] But the absolute appears in its major dimension in the achievements of science or in the encounter with a divinity. These are the posts where seminal thinking stakes its reasons, so that the mere *estar* does not disintegrate, moved by an intuitive search to find, always in renewed form, something of which one could at least say, "Well, yes, this truly *is*."

This scale oscillates between the two extremes of the visual and the invisible. The visual order is connotational, *estar* at the level of reality, thinking in causal terms from which not even *ser* can escape. At this level, the order of things provides that which "is already known." But this does not reveal the truth of *my* life, *here* and *now*, before the *así* of my habitat. My habitat can only find its limit in an unnameable and invisible divinity.

And since the absolute arises from the opposition between fear and the desire to overcome it, the need for connotation presses upon one and with it the vital sense of the absolute is lost. This is the true difference between the indigenous person and the urban dweller: the indigenous person maintains his desire for the absolute in an unnameable plane; the urban dweller tends to connote it and converts it into a book. Whether religious or scientific, such books are no more than the visualization of the absolute, with the attendant bureaucratization of connoted knowledge. But such projects are undertaken to keep the absolute close to home and magically trapped. There the absolute is not so much lost as subverted.

Science and religion are visualized absolutes. They encompass the bureaucratization of faith and of intelligence. They are visual forms lived at the level of organization, but motivated by a very simple mechanism: to feel the world a little less unfavorably, a good world, institutionalized in the good church and in the good academy of science. We could say, then, contrary to Heidegger, that a hardening of forms has *evaporated* being.

This motivation is precisely what has provoked the deep crisis of Western man. An excessively visual world has hindered in him the possibility of feeling and of a seminal outpouring of his feeling of the absolute, undertaken in terms of his faith. No room can be found for that which "seems to me." True culture cannot be found either, unless the individual's contribution to culture—in other words, how he readies his seminality for use— correlates with the culture imposed. The crisis of the twentieth century rests in the failure to recognize that *I am the fountain of my possibilities*, the fountain that feeds everything else seminally, the cultural scaffolding that surrounds it all.

But whether there is a crisis or not, the topic of the *absolute*, insofar as I am the fountain of *my own* possibilities, gives continuity to the so-called mass, or *pueblo*, segregated as it is from the middle class. Because of it, the life of someone in a boarding house does not completely lack meaning, nor does the life of the provincial person awed by the city when he enters it in search of better luck. But it explains why one never integrates oneself totally into the business firm that gave one a job, nor identifies with the title received or the government job one holds. From the angle of pure *estar*, the absolute is to be found in something else.

The absolute is what sustains the children of Sánchez, who—available and biological—survive in Mexico without any direct inheritance from their peasant fathers, but who, nonetheless, have not committed suicide, despite not having achieved an urban role that would enable them to make an honorable living.[4] This is what also explains the ironic smile of the indigenous people of Southern Bolivia when, according to Ibarra Grasso, they see the gringo in his car but prefer their own old mule.

In sum, this is what turns the indigenous *pueblo* resistant to the catechesis of religious people and of the middle class, and confers the same strength onto a whole *pueblo* disseminated throughout the Américas. That is a why a worker of peasant origin, whether Indian or not, resists bourgeois democracy or incendiary Marxism. He resists them simply because they are too schematic, programmatic, and quantitative, and thus fail completely to capture his demand for the absolute, a demand very difficult to express. One can find traces of it in the commonplace expression, "I believe in God, but the one that is *everywhere* and not the God of the priests." People use this turn of phrase to translate the absolute into unnameable terms, almost as if the absolute required cosmic totalities equivalent to lightning and thunder, or totalities split between good and bad omens, or as if the absolute required one to believe one is living in the fifth age while being afraid that it may end at any instant.

The advantage of Peronism, which renders it profoundly Américan, lies in that, in spite of recent Marxist infiltration, it continues to be a party without a doctrine, bound to a charismatic personality, sustained by strictly emotional impulses. Its extraordinary coherence can only be explained when one understands that everything about it is invigorated by a deep demand of the absolute. Its tone does not strictly enter into the Westernized thinking of a middle class.

What is more, at base, the meaning of what is referred to as the inferiority complex of the South Américan man is nothing but a guilt-feeling for needing something absolute, mobilized by a deep seminal thinking. His demand for the absolute carries him to formulate it in unnameable terms when faced with a Western culture that names everything. Western culture arrives limited and impoverished to this liminal zone of the earth after having lost its universality. And because of that it exaggerates the importance of the schematized and visible aspects of life and segregates out important aspects of man. The pejorative ring that the words *mestizo* or *cholo* have in the mouths of the South Américan bourgeoisie is precisely due to the suspicion that the anti-Western behavior of the mestizos arouses in the bourgeoisie. But then the bourgeoisie do no more than defend a visualization of the absolute that the West does not succeed in providing. This is the reason for the failure of sociologists, economists, government planners, psychologists, or ultra-revolutionaries: they lack tools, in this sense. Before the Américan *pueblo* there is nothing to do but be Américan, and this means to recover the unpredictable springs only the *pueblo* can provide.

From the point of view of man, the old longing for achieving an absolute is in his very blood. It cannot be avoided simply because one deals with it in everyday life. A new refrigerator never completely closes the question of the absolute. The usefulness of the refrigerator never really provides the ultimate reason for why it was bought. It fascinates us as a piece of useful machinery in the lucid and conscious field of causes. It is in that field that quantities are exchanged in such a way that causes are the same as effects. Awareness is gained as they are made equal. But the refrigerator also *está ahí* (*está* there), in front of me, and there is no answer to this miraculous *estar* that is mine and is the refrigerator's.

This is what is enclosed within the *uca* or the *así* of the indigenous *ucamahua*: it takes up all of *my estar* and that of the object. But this does not mean that *my* self is made equal to the object. Rather, it is natural that from this point on one ends up thinking that the object is really only a circumstance, as the indigenous person might think. But it is a lesser circumstance than one's self, because at the very least one can bring to consciousness everything that man is, as a circumstance that is at once greater and more heroic, like an original fall. And with this one grazes the absolute.

And here we find again the opposition between the indigenous person and the urban dweller. Both reach the absolute made concrete like a parable of an original fall which needs to be remedied. The indigenous person fills it with a deep sense of his contradictions and his rituals; but the urban dweller does not know how to fill it, because the twentieth century does not offer him the seminal truths he needs to do it.

If the urban dweller were to ask himself at this point, "Who am I?" he would see himself reduced to a "just living," carrying his absolute on his back and a *who* that is lost in mystery. This nebulous *who* is the sum of what one achieves through this path. But it is a lot. Buddhism, for example, extracts from this experience the *Así-llegado* (arrived that way). *To arrive* in the Buddhist sense is to become completely aware of the heroic circum-stance—the *así* that a person is. But it is to become aware of the *así* that one is, in the way the indigenous person does when he thinks of man—*runa* or *haque*—as connected to the "score of the game." To say that of man is also to define him by his absence, and it is to achieve his true meaning since such absence scrapes against that region in which the unnameables are present and the gods exert pressure. It is the truth of the absolute reflected at the crossroads of the *así*.

The comparison with Buddhism ought not seem strange. Indigenous thinking and Buddhism start from the same point and move the same springs. They start, in short, from the only truly philosophical experience: the surprise of discovering the crossroads that obtain within mere *estar*, bearing the sense of the absolute, even if through negation. It is all that man, in the end, can think about himself. That is why it can also be found in the urban dweller. And that is why not to accept it is to fall into an infantile seminality. Whether we like or not, man is half filled with things and half filled with gods, even in the twentieth century, and especially in

América. This is the most fecund possibility provided to us by indigenous and popular thinking. Because, on this side, it is only recently that one finds the possibility of creating a world with atomic plants. These are nothing more than a circumstance of that absolute which is man, a detail in the great crossroads of his *así*.

NOTES

INTRODUCTION: IMMIGRANT CONSCIOUSNESS

1 Ocampo remained as director of the journal until 1971.

2 Gordon, *Existentia Africana*.

3 Du Bois, *The Souls of Black Folk*.

4 Anzaldúa, *Borderlands/La Frontera*.

5 Dussel, "Europe, Modernity, and Eurocentrism."

6 Mignolo, "Delinking: Don Quixote, Globalization and the Colonies."

7 See Maldonado-Torres, "On the Coloniality of Being."

8 It would be interesting to bring into the conversation the intervention of Afro-Caribbean intellectuals of the French- and British-speaking islands who were either contemporaries of Kusch or whose work overlapped, in the 1870s, with the publication of Kusch's later work.

9 Halperin Dongui, *Proyecto y construcción de una nación, Vida y muerte de la república verdadera*, and *La república imposible*.

10 Sarlo, *La batalla de las ideas*; Altamirano, *Bajo el signo de las masas*.

11 Teresa Gisbert de Mesa, "commentaire to 'La colonization des langages.'" A panel debate with the participation of Serge Gruzinski, Arthur G. Millar, William F. Hanks, and Walter Mignolo at the international conference, *Le nouveaus monde/mondes nouveaux. La experience américaine*. Edited by Serge Gruzinski and Nathan Wachtel. Paris: Ecole des hautes études en sciences sociales, 1996, 322–34.

12 The original reads, "Esta segunda edición responde a un motivo evidente. El año 1973 marca una etapa importante en el país. Argentina ha puesto en marcha la posibilidad de su autenticidad. Entre todas las propuestas económicas y sociales de todo cuño que suelen adoptar fácilmente como solución, surge una clara propuesta cultural brotada de las raíces más profundas del pueblo. Quisiera yo

que estas páginas sirvan para entender esa propuesta, a fin de que no sea malversada una vez más" (Kusch, *El pensamiento indígena Americano*, 2nd ed., 1).

13 Jauretche, *El medio pelo en la sociedad argentina*, 1957; Jorge Abelardo Ramos, "Entrevista," http://www.elhistoriador.com.ar/; Abelardo Ramos, *El Marxismo de Indias*, 1973; Hernández Arregui, *La formación de la conciencia nacional*, 1960.

14 Montenegro, *Nacionalismo y coloniaje*, 1943; Roberto Vila de Prado, "Popular Revolutionary Nationalism in Bolivia: Ideological Formations and Transformations (1930–1955)," trans. Jeremy Jorden, *Revista de humanidades y ciencias sociales* 2, no. 1–2 (2006): 1–32.

15 See Zavaleta Mercado, *El poder dual* and *La revolución Boliviana y la cuestión del poder*, 1967.

16 Kusch's awareness of the coloniality of being is analogous to the existential situation that prompted W. E. B Du Bois's conceptualization of "double conscioussness" and of Gloria Anzaldúa's "la conciencia de la mestiza."

17 See chapter 12, where Kusch reflects on a folklorist from Jujuy and a farmer from Entre Ríos.

18 Ricardo Guiraldes's *Don Segundo Sombra* (1927) remains the narrative that closes the cycle of the gaucho.

19 In the 1880s the elite of landowners and rulers of the country, in their triumphal march toward civilization, did a remarkable job in lambasting all sectors of the population that did not respond or correspond to their way of life and were not collaborating in their design to drive Argentina in the rout of France, England, and the United States (in that order). Eugenics offered them the terminology of "degeneration," which they applied to identify problems and problematic people that their civilizing mission had to face, as well as to the undesirable population. Eusebio Gómez, a well known criminologist, published a book titled *Mala vida en Buenos Aires* (1908).

20 The original reads, "Cuando alguien nos dice *rajá de ahí* suponemos que se nos está informando que nos vayamos. Estamos seguros de ello. Pero decir que una expresión sirve sólo para informar sería demasiado superficial. . . . Por que ese alguien que dice aquella frase no sólo nos informa de que nos vayamos, sino que también nos *borra del mapa*, como decimos. Y es que el lenguaje sirve para modificar mágicamente la realidad, suprimiendo en este caso lo que es molesto. . . . En resumen, las palabras primero nos informan, luego nos sirven de fluído mágico y finalmente denuncian nuestro verdadero y secreto pensamiento sobre la vida y el mundo" (Kusch, *De la mala vida porteña*, 1:323).

21 See also the observations about this scenario-anecdote in María Lugones and Joshua Price's "Translators' Introduction."

22 Kusch, *La negacción en el pensamiento popular*, 2:569.

23 A prisoner of Western patriarchal language, Kusch employs the word *hombre* to refer to "hu(wo)man being." This unawareness is more striking in his last two books, when he interviews elderly women, yet, regarding the philosophical dimension of their discourses, continues to reflect on "el hombre Americano."

24 Fanon, *Black Skin, White Masks*, 11. See also Wynter, "Towards the Sociogenic Principle."

25 The original reads, "En el fondo supone la búsqueda de un nuevo modo de pensamiento o de lógica, quizás una lógica de la negación, como dije en otros trabajos, que implica un redimensionamiento del hombre. . . .

"A la filosofía, al fin de cuentas, sólo le corresponde detectar el eje fundante o esencial en torno al cual tiende un margen de racionalidad, porque si se limita totalmente a lo racionalizable no comprende todo el fenómeno. Pero esto último ocurre siempre con un filosofar académica que, por ser colonial, no comprende un filosofar propio que debe ir de lo deformante hacia lo absoluto" (Kusch, *Esbozo de una antropología filosófica americana*, 3:256–57).

26 I use these three terms as equivalent as I refuse to obey to "disciplinary" definitions that respond to a set of arbitrary principles and to an order of knowledge that distinguishes between epistemology and explanation in sciences: hermeneutics and interpretation in the humanities, and "thinking" in a Heideggerian way. Delinking and epistemic disobedience, which Kusch in a way practiced relentlessly, is the first step in avoiding the trap of "territorial thinking," that is, thinking according to hegemonic (epistemic and hermeneutics) expectations of what thinking and rationality are.

27 Maldonado-Torres, "On the Coloniality of Being."

28 Armstrong, *Islam*, 142.

29 Abu-Lughod, *Before European Hegemony*.

30 By "epistemic de-linking" I refer to and start from Aníbal Quijano's basic formulation, which dates to the beginning of the 1990s. In a section titled "The Epistemic Re-constitution: De-colonization," Quijano calls for de-colonization, starting with a "desprendimiento" (de-linking; some times badly translated as "to extricate oneself"), in order to move toward "epistemic de-colonization": "First of all, epistemological decolonization is needed to clear the way for new intercultural communication, for an interchange of experiences and meanings, as the basis for another rationality which may legitimately pretend to some universality" (Quijano, "Coloniality and Modernity/Rationality," 168–78).

31 The original reads, "todo esto es implícito al sentir Americano, por no decir al de todo pueblo en cualquier parte del mundo y no cabe duda que cualquier racionalización, traducida exclusivamente a una ciencia tal como se la entiende hoy en día sería ineficaz."

32 I have dealt with this issue in detail, following the lead of Johannes Fabian's concept of the "denial of coevalness" in anthropological discourse, mainly in the nineteenth century. Mignolo, *The Darker Side of the Renaissance*.

33 I am aware that there is "diversity" and "heterogeneity" in Eurocentered history. While there may be many kinds of Christians, as well as different philosophical schools and scientific interpretations, they are all based on the assumed universality of Western Christianity and Western secular philosophy and sciences. The rest of the world is either absent, or behind in time, or someplace else waiting for the civilizers.

34 Bambach, *Heidegger's Roots*.

35 The original reads, "En material de filosofía tenemos en América por una parte

una manera oficial de tratarla y, por la otra, una forma, por decir así, privada de hacerlo. Por un lado está la que aprendemos en la universidad y que consiste en una problemática europea traducida a nivel filosófico y, por el otro, un pensar implícito vivido cotidianamente en la calle o en el campo."

36 See Rudolf A. Makkreel, *Dilthey: Philosopher of the Human Studies*, esp. "Anthropological Reflections and the Categories of Life (376–84) and "Style and the Conceptual Articulation of Historical Life" (385–422) (Princeton: Princeton University Press, 1992).

37 Laclau, *On Populist Reason*.

38 Mignolo, "Delinking: The Rhetoric of Modernity, the Logic of Coloniality and the Grammar of De-coloniality."

39 Laclau, *On Populist Reason*, chaps. 7 and 8.

40 The expression "re-existence" was coined and brilliantly elaborated by Adolfo Albán Achinte in his doctoral dissertation, "Tiempos de zango y de guampín: transformaciones gastronómicas, territorialidad re-existencia socio-cultural en comunidades Afro-descendientes de los valles interandinos del Patía (sur de Colombia) y Chota (norte del Ecuador), siglio XX" (Quito: Universidad Andina Simón Bolívar, 2007).

41 See the *Miami Herald*'s special series "AfroLatin: A Rising Voice," specifically the interactive map "Afro-descendants in Latin America" (http://www.miamiherald .com).

TRANSLATORS' INTRODUCTION

We thank Neal McTighe, our editor, for his intelligent attention to this project, the sophistication given to every detail of the editing process, and most of all for his patience with us and his savvy taking us by the hand through the editing.

Translators' note: Kusch read Jung, Rowe, Collingwood, Eliade, Heidegger, Jaspers, and others in Spanish. We decided not to use the English translations of those texts because Kusch's analysis and comments refer to the specific meanings of the words in the Spanish translation. Using the English translations distorts Kusch's meaning. Thus, we translated Heidegger from Spanish (the version that Kusch used) into English. The pages in the endnotes refer to the Spanish edition.

1 Palermo, "Inscripción de la crítica de género en procesos de descolonización."

2 See chapter 2 in this volume.

3 The masculine pronoun is used throughout by Kusch. The Andean construction of gender included females as knowing subjects and as experiencing the world in its *así*. The relation between males and females was characterized by opposition, inseparability, symmetry, and complementariness in the balancing of the cosmos. The precolonial Andean understanding of gender did not reduce the gendered subjects but included all of each person's strengths in the reproduction of life and culture. One's weaknesses were complemented by the other's strengths. The colonial understanding of gender performed a devastating reduction of everyone's possibilities. See

Horswell, *Decolonizing the Sodomite*; Silverblatt, *Moon, Sun, and Witches*; and Lugones, "Heterosexualism and the Colonial/Modern Gender System."

4 Conjugation of *estar*: *estoy* (first-person singular), *estás* (second), *está* (third), *estámos* (first-person plural), *están* (second and third).

5 Moraga, *The Hungry Woman*, 6–7.

6 Guerrero, "Encuentro internacional." Guerrero calls for "acorazonar de la epistemologia"—giving heart to epistemology, one knows with the *chuyma*.

7 Thanks to Pedro di Pietro for these ways of stating the issue of nonfractured space and the political question of lived spatiality.

8 The image of the fishbone comes from Laura Pérez's image of the Chicano/a, in "El Desorden, Nationalism, and Chicana/o Aesthetics."

PROLOGUE TO THE THIRD EDITION

1 The third ("present") edition of *El pensamiento indígena y popular en América* was originally published in 1977.

PROLOGUE TO THE FIRST EDITION

1 For a discussion of "América," and of the use of *criollo* in Argentina, please see the "Translators' Introduction."—Trans.

2 For a discussion of *pueblo*, please see the "Translators' Introduction." *Pueblo* is a crucial word in Kusch's text. When he later writes about popular thought, he has the thought of the pueblo in mind. He is distinguishing between that thought and the thought of the Westernized intellectual elites. The English term *people* does not capture that distinction, but rather collapses it.—Trans.

3 On sexist and nonsexist language, please see the "Translators' Introduction." In translating the masculine pronouns in the text, we could have used what has become the apparently nonsexist standard phrase of "he or she" to note that the author is thinking of both genders. We did not, however, follow that usage, because it tends to obscure rather than highlight gender issues. Kusch does not often think about the difference that gender makes, and one is often left, therefore, with questions about that difference. We will mark in our translation when he takes gender into consideration.—Trans.

ONE AMÉRICAN THINKING

1 Schwartzmann, *El sentimiento de lo humano en América*.

2 Tönnies described the change from a relatively homogeneous social body to a more complex one marked by increased specialization.—Trans.

3 Guaman Poma de Ayala, *Nueva crónica y buen gobierno* (*The First New Chronicle and Good Government*).

4 Bertonio, *Vocabulario de la lengua Aymara*. See "*Cancatha*: Being, and flow of events" and "*Cancaña*: Being or essence" (2:35).

5 "Estar" is a key concept for Kusch. For a discussion of his use of *estar* and *ser*, please see the "Translators' Introduction."—Trans.

6 Bertonio, *Vocabulario de la lengua Aymara*, 2:382.

7 Ibid., 2:382–83.

8 Franz Crahay, in his article "El 'despegue' conceptual," critiques Tempels's and Kagane's effort to elucidate a Bantú philosophy in Africa. He demands, for example, that they take into account "the innovations of contemporary philosophy and that which constitutes the originality of the great non-Western philosophical traditions," and he also mentions "procedures that can be universalized" and "the progress of philosophy" (57). Crahay's reaction is understandable, given that he is an academic. Personally, I believe that neither universality nor philosophy as it is understood in the West holds much interest in this recuperation of an autochthonous way of thinking. The latter for its part has a finality much more universal than a Westernized academician would suppose.

9 Bertonio, *Vocabulario de la lengua Aymara*, 2:311.

10 Ibid., 1:12. "To remember the forgotten: . . . amutaskhatha."

11 C. G. Jung notes that such a symbol means that "the center of gravity of personality is not the ego, which is just a center of consciousness, but a virtual point, so to speak, between the conscious and the unconscious, which might be called the self" (*El secreto de la flor de oro* [*The Secret of the Golden Flower*], 9). In another section of the same book, Jung adds: "In a sense it is the feeling of 'being replaced' but really without the addition of the 'being deposed.' It is really a 'detachment of consciousness' in virtue of which the subjective 'I live' becomes an objective 'it lives me'" (69).

12 "Indio astrólogo-poeta que save del vuelo del sol yde la luna, y clip y de estrellas y cometas—día domingo mes y año y de los cuatro vientos del mundo oro para sembrar la comida desde antiguo. Indios que los indios filósofos—astrólogos que saben las oras y domingos y días y meses año para sembrar y recoger las comidas de cada año" (Guaman Poma de Ayala, *Nueva Corónica y buen gobierno*, 883).

TWO UNDERSTANDING

1 *Challar* means "to make an offering," for example, to the Pachamama by pouring part of one's food or drink onto the ground. This is a common, everyday gesture. All manner of things can be the object of these ritual offerings.—Trans.

2 *Huilancha* comes from *huila*, "blood," in Aymara, and in general designates a blood sacrifice. Below we analyze this ritual as well as the *Gloria Misa*.

3 In the following, we translate *conocimiento* as "understanding" and *saber* as "knowledge."—Trans.

4 This classification belongs to "scientism," which became influential in the waning years of the nineteenth century and which today governs the thinking of the average urban dweller of América.

5 Bertonio, *Vocabulario de la lengua Aymara*: "Thing: cunasa" (Cosa: cunasa) (1:145); "Thing of Gods, of men, etc.: yaa" (Cosa de Dios, de hombres, etc.: yaa)

(1:146); "Cunasa, anything" (Cunasa, cualquier cosa) (2:59); "Yaa: thing, or business, or mystery, etc." (Yaa: cosa, o negocio, o misterio, etc.) (2:389).

6   In La Paz I gathered data which confirms that the Aymaras currently call *yaa* all the objects to be used by a wedding couple.

7   "The SAE microcosm has analyzed reality largely in terms of what it calls 'things' (bodies and quasi-bodies) plus modes of extensional but formless existence that it calls 'substances' or 'matter.' . . . The Hopi microcosm seems to have analyzed reality largely in terms of events (or better 'eventing')." B. L. Whorf arrives at this conclusion after analyzing both European languages and Hopi. Whorf, "The Relation of Habitual Thought and Behavior to Language," n.p.

8   Bertonio, *Vocabulario de la lengua Aymara*, Introduction, Part I.

9   José Imbelloni mentions a "classificatory device" that consists in "*Masculine-Feminine, Right-Left, Above-Below, White-Black* boxes, whose final and most consistent development is manifest and visible in the Taoist system, even though its initial elaborations were really as ancient as the first attempt at accumulation 'directed' at elemental wisdom, and valuations under the mantle of Vigor and Potency, Favor and Disfavor associated with them" ("El 'Génesis' de los pueblos protohistóricos de América," 349).

10 Bertonio, *Vocabulario de la lengua Aymara*, 2:374.

11 Ibid., 2:373.

12 Miguel León Portilla states in his book *La filosofía Nahuatl estudiada en sus fuentes*: "One can conclude . . . that *in ixtli, in yollotl* (face, heart) is a classic Nahuatl *masking* created to connote what is exclusive of man: a well-defined *self*, with peculiar features (*ixtli*: face) and with a dynamism (*yollotl*: heart) that makes one go after things, in search of something that fills one up, sometimes without direction (*ahuicpa*) and sometimes until one meets with 'the only real thing on earth, *poetry, flower and song*'" (202). He later quotes a Nahuatl text which reads: "Mature man: / a heart as firm as stone, / a wise face, / owner of a face, a heart, / capable and understanding" (240).

13 Gonçalez Holguín, *Vocabulario de la lengua general de todo el Perú llamada lengua Quichua o del Inca*. We read: "Rikcini. To know (*conocer*) another" and "Riccichacuni. To know (*conocer*) all those who are the subjects discussed, or to know (*conocer*) those of a house" (316).

THREE LIMIT

1   A number of important and relevant facts related to this and other topics are available in the *Curso de filosofía Indígena* (a xeroxed publication from the Universidad Técnica de Oruro and from the Town Council, Oruro, 1967). This material includes fieldwork reports by the students that took my seminar of the same name in August and September of 1967 at that University. The following pieces were included: Rodolfo Kusch, *Discurso Inaugural*; Hugo Salvatierra, *División Política Del Departamento De Oruro*; Antonio A. De La Quintana and David Segundo Gonzalez C., *El Ayni*; Eduardo Arce Duran, Arturo Alessandri, Guiller-

mina Camacho, and Carlota Bustos, *Toledo*; Hugo Salvatierra Oporto and Jaime Salvatierra O., *Breves Apuntes*; Aldina Fernandez Ch., Carlota Bustos, and Guillermina Camacho, *Fiestas y Vestimenta*; Flora Herbas De Verduguez and Olimpia Quiñonez, *Mitos, Supersticiones y Leyendas*; Lic. Macrina Quiroz S., *Medicina*; Adela A. De Vargas, Lic. Macrina Quiroz S., and Edith Loredo, *Medicina*; Juan Díaz Arreaño, *Medicina*; Marcelino Alconz Mendoza, *Costumbres y Ritos de las Diferentes Provincias al Oeste de Oruro*; Francisco Cruz R., *Fiesta y Música*; Martirian Ramirez, *Ayni y Ayllu*; Otto Saucedo, *Organización Política y Administrativa de la Comunidad de Toledo*; Freddy Espinosa T., *Datos Recogidos de las Poblaciones Más Antiguas de Oruro*; Luis Morales, *Economía e Industria Artesanal*.

2 That is, a table, the standard Spanish meaning of the term.—Trans.

3 Paredes, *La Paz y la Provincia El Cercado*.

4 *La pena* (trouble, grief, difficulty, sorrow), rendered *yaquí* in Aymara, is a fundamental concept in the indigenous worldview, as we will see later on.

5 Claude Lévi-Strauss says on this point: "The indigenous person is a logical hoarder: without pause he re-knots threads, folds untiringly all the aspects of the real onto itself, whether they be physical, social or mental" (*El pensamiento salvaje* [*The Savage Mind*], 386).

6 Bandelier, *The Islands of Titicaca and Koati*.

7 Paredes, *Mitos, superticiones y supervivencias populares de Bolivia*.

8 Tschopik, *The Aymara of Chucuito, Perú*, 174ff.

9 Max Scheler refers to a prejudice in the majority of modern thinkers according to which "all of our emotional life—and for the majority of philosophers this includes all our appetitive life—must be attributed to 'sensibility,' including love and hate. At the same time according to this division, *everything that is alogical* in the spirit—intuiting, feeling, tending, loving, hating—depends on the psychophysical organization" of man. His formation is a function of the real variation of the psycho-physical organization within the evolution of life and history, and it depends on the peculiarity of the context and its effects" (Scheler and Rodriguez Sanz, *Ética*, 2:24). Also see Gurvitch, *Las Tendencias actuales de la filosofía alemana*, 93ff. Gurvitch also evidences the same prejudice with utmost clarity when he takes up Scheler's position against Husserl. For Husserl, "essential intuition, the Wesenschau, consists in the act of perfect adaptation between a signification and its realization, between that to which one aims and that which is given. In spite of that, Scheler notes, one can observe cases in the pure flux of the lived, in which contents are present which do not have *direct significations* and which are nevertheless precise, clear and understandable intentional acts" (ibid., 89–90). Teodore Celms notes that "moments of evidence such as sensations and the sensible moments of feeling and will are called by Husserl sensual data or hyletic," which are opposed to the noetic, which understand the acts of signification, of realization, etc.; in sum, they refer strictly to consciousness, and that does not occur with the hyletic ones (*El idealismo fenomenológico de Husserl*, 80ff).

10 Heidegger, *El ser y el tiempo* (*Being and Time*). It is curious how Heidegger is always governed in his analysis by the somewhat intellectual criterion of con-

notation, as indicated by the expressions *at-hand* and *before-the-eyes*. The same is true when he affirms that "fear always reveals the *being-there*, more or less openly in the being of *its there*" (163). To take *being* and not *there* must be a definitive feature that distances an Américan vision of existence from a Western one. Sartre, returning to the topic of emotional life, says something similar to what Heidegger has said when he affirms that "l'emotion est une réalisation d'essence de la réalité-humaine en tant qu'elle est affection" (emotion is a realization of the essence of human reality inasmuch as it is affect) (*Esquisse d'une théorie des émotions* [*The Emotions*], 52).

11 Wolff, *Introducción a la psicología*: "Emotion is a lack of balance. . . . It seems to be due to the breakdown of a coherent situation" (146). The same is true of James Drever who in his *Diccionario de psicología* [*Dictionary of Psychology*] says about emotion, among other things, that it is "a complex state of the organism that encompasses a wide range of bodily changes . . . and in the mental plane a state of excitation or *perturbation*" (98). Jung says about affect that it is characterized "by a peculiar *perturbation* of the representative process" (*Tipos psicológicos* [*Psychological Types*], 2:196; my emphasis).

12 Sayres, "Status Transition and Magical Fright."

13 Valda de Jaimes Freyre, *Costumbres y curiosidades de los Aymaras*, 25ff.

14 Morote Best, *La vivienda campesina de Sallaq con un panorama de la cultura total*, 96ff.

15 Olano, *La medicina en el idioma incaico*, 16–18.

16 Gonçalez Holguín, *Vocabulario de la lengua general de todo el Perú llamada lengua Quichua o del Inca*, 350. It is curious that both words appear together, even at the cost of alphabetical order. Could it be they were used as opposites?

17 Bertonio, *Vocabulario de la lengua Aymara*: "*Alakha haque*: clear man who does not dissimulate, not bent" (2.2); "*Manqhue*: depth, or depth in water, earth and other things" (2.215).

18 Gonçalez Holguín, *Vocabulario de la lengua general de todo el Perú llamada lengua Quichua o del Inca*: "Vku. The body of the animal, or person"; "Vcupicak, or vcun. The thing inside" (349).

19 Stern, *Psicología general desde el punto de vista personalístico* (*General Psychology from the Personalistic Standpoint*): "The separation of the inward direction from the outward direction is possible only by virtue of an abstraction. . . . What is important are the tensions between inward direction and *saliencia*, that is, the dynamic relations of the sphere of emotion, with the intellect and will. But at the same time feeling . . . shows itself to be the *mediator*; particularly close to the unconscious regions of the person" (2:435).

20 Gonçalez Holguín, *Vocabulario de la lengua general de todo el Perú llamada lengua Quichua o del Inca*, 328ff.

21 Bertonio, *Vocabulario de la lengua Aymara*, 2.94.

22 Olano, *La medicina en el idioma incaico*: "*Soncco*. It means the center of the organism or perhaps deep organ. *Soncco* is also the central or medular tissue of the stem; *soncco* is the bread crumb (or the soft part of the bread?); *soncco* is a synonym for hidden feeling; *Chaychu sonccoyqui?* Is that what you feel?" (9).

23 Posnansky, "Tiahuanacu, la cuna del hombre de las Américas."

24 Guaman Poma de Ayala, *Nueva crónica y buen gobierno* (*The First New Chronicle and Good Government*), 880.

25 This information was provided by Gabriel Martínez, a Chilean theater director who performed theatrical experiments with natives under the sponsorship of the Universidad Técnica de Oruro.

26 Eliade, *Tratado de historia de las religiones*, 352*ff.*

FOUR KNOWLEDGE

1 *Yatiri* means "witch." Kusch is referring to Apaza Rimachi.—Trans.

2 Jung comments, "While something remains behind in the unconscious, it does not have any cognizable properties, and thus it is part of that which is unknown generally, part of the unconscious which is everywhere and nowhere. . . . But when the unconscious content becomes manifest, that is, when it enters the field of consciousness, then it is divided in four." He points out later that the usual structure of this symbol of totality is 3 + 1, and that when it appears in the form of a triad it adopts the formula 4 − 1 in which "the fourth function is the undifferentiated or inferior function (opposed to the first and fundamental function), which character-izes that aspect of personality which remains in the shadows." *Sobre cosas que se ven en el cielo* (*Flying Saucers: A Modern Myth of Things Seen in the Skies*), 167*ff.*

3 "They made sacrifices to the earth spilling on her coca, chicha, and other things" (Cobo, *Historia del Nuevo Mundo*, 203).

4 Jose Imbelloni mentions the "*Hananpacha*, the 'superimposed plane,' . . . [and] *Urinpacha*, also called *Kaypacha*, or 'this ground,' which coincides with the earth's surface. . . . In the depth of the underworld they placed the plane or 'interior ground,' called *Uk'upacha*. The deep cavities were the seat of powerful entities in the rule of nature, in evidence in Mochica pottery, in which a chthonic divinity appears insistently, often accompanied by or transformed into the tiger. In the syncretism of Christian times these entities transform themselves into 'devils'" ("La Weltanschauung de los Amautas reconstruida," n.p.).

5 "Tenían los ynos antiguos conocimiento de que abia un solo, dios tres personas" (Guaman Poma de Ayala, *Nueva crónica y buen gobierno* [*The First New Chronicle and Good Government*], 55–56).

6 Cobo, *Historia del Nuevo Mundo*: "The eighth and last *guaca* of this *ceque* was a mountain called Chuquipalta, which is next to the fort, in which are placed three stones representing the Pachayachachic, Intullapa, and Punchay: and in this mountain a universal sacrifice of boys and girls and small figures of them made of gold was performed; and clothes and rams were burnt, because this was held as a very solemn place of worship" (171).

7 The combination of *callao*, *pallan*, and *collana* is the most frequent since it is found nine times.

8 The numinous and fascinating aspect of the archetype is due to its issuing from the collective unconscious, and it is considered by the indigenous person to be

revelatory. The archetype functions in turn, according to Jung, as a principle of organization of the psyche. It can overflow the psyche and encompass a social group. That is why there is not much difference between Lévi-Strauss's *structure* and the archetype. The distinction between them is due to the distinct cultural context of each author. The conception of the archetype is characteristic of German Neo-Romanticism, while "structure" is characteristic of the sociological intellectualism of the French.

9 Bertonio, *Vocabulario de la lengua Aymara*: "Knowledge: Yatitha, unanchatha" (1:419).

10 Gonçalez Holguín, *Vocabulario de la lengua general de todo el Perú llamada lengua Quichua o del Inca*, 355.

11 Santacruz Pachacuti Yamqui, *Relación de Antigüedades deste rayno del Pirú*. In a section devoted to Viracocha, the first hymn reads: "Ricuptiy, yachaptiy unanchaptly hamuttaptly ricucanquim vachavanquim" (220). José Maria Arguedas in his "Estudio preliminar a himnos Quechuas católicos cuzqueños," translates this as: "When I can see / when I can know / when I know how to *signal* / when I know how to reflect / you will see me, / you will understand me" (3).

12 Gonçalez Holguín, *Vocabulario de la lengua general de todo el Perú llamada lengua Quichua o del Inca*, 360.

13 Middendorf, *Wörterbuch der Runa Simi oder der Keshua Sprache*, 103.

14 Bertonio, *Vocabulario de la lengua Aymara*: "Yataatha, veï Huacaatha: Hazer o adereçar, o componer alguna cosa, y *criar, que es propio de Dios*" (To make or to dress, or fix something, and *to raise, which is proper to God*) (394).

15 Rowe, *Eleven Inca Prayers from the Zithuwa Ritual*, 88. Also see Domingo de Santo, *Lexicon o vocabulario de la lengua general del Perú*: "To multiply like sown land-yachacuni" (78).

16 Gonçalez Holguín, *Vocabulario de la lengua general de todo el Perú llamada lengua Quichua o del Inca*, 361.

FIVE RITUAL

1 This manner of divining with coca seemed to be the most common in the region. Sometimes, he would alternate with less common procedures. One of these consisted in placing a folded bill and forming a cross atop it with two leaves. (This process will be described more fully later.) Another way of divining I observed in Tiahuanaco consisted in folding a blanket on top of a pile of coca leaves and then lifting it up with both hands in such a way that some of the leaves would be caught in the blanket. Those leaves would then be read once the blanket was unfolded again. A blind witch from Tiahuanaco would shift the leaves from hand to hand, keeping a short distance between the hands.

2 Bertonio translates *amu* as "flower bud" (*Vocabulario de la lengua Aymara*, 2:17).

3 Ellen Ross, *Rudimentos de Gramática Aymara*, 224.

4 Lira, *Diccionario Khechua-Español*: "Pachan and also Pacha, m. Bottom, the low-

est part of something that is hollow. That which is below something. Depth. The bottom a large cavity" (722). Lira also includes the other, more ordinary senses of the same term.

5 Bertonio, *Vocabulario de la lengua Aymara*, 2:173. He also notes that the indigenous women of Oruro also call old coins *illa*. Tschopik translates the same word as "amulets" (*The Aymara of Chicuito, Perú*, 238).

6 Gonçalez Holguín notes, "Çacsa. Dress that is worn out, rags" and "Cacçani. Satiated, to become completely satisfied with food and drink" (*Vocabulario de la lengua general de todo el Perú llamada lengua Quichua o del Inca*, 74).

7 Scheler explains this distinction in *El saber y la cultura* (20*ff*). He also distinguishes between an educated knowing, implicated to a greater degree than the other two with the person. In *Sociología del saber*, he draws a similar distinction: "There is, first, the incessant striving that leads the whole group and, only secondarily, the individual, to 'secure' a 'saving' of one's self, one's fate, and to relate through knowledge to an intuited reality as 'overpowering and sacred' and esteemed as the supreme good and the reason for 'everything.' This is the enduring emotional root of all search for a *religious* knowledge. . . . There is, second, the intentional feeling of *admiration* that is surely related to educated knowledge. And, finally, the third emotion . . . which is the *desire* for *power* and *dominion* over the course of nature, men, and social processes, the course of psychic and organic processes, and, with the techniques of magic, also the attempt to lead to the supernatural 'forces,' or those that appear to us as supernatural, to come to possess them, and, because of *their virtue*, foresee the phenomena" (69*ff*). This also leads to a striving of knowledge of dominion. There is no doubt that this classification belongs to the conception of the European world and does not encompass the problematic of a domain such as ours. But nevertheless it lends us a way of characterizing indigenous knowledge.

8 Bertonio, *Vocabulario de la lengua Aymara*, 2:231. He translates *nayra* as "Eye, or eyes of the face" and also as "First, or first of all." He adds: "*Nayra*; a grain of some seed" (2:232).

9 Eliade: "The access to the 'Center' is equivalent to a consecration or to an initiation. The previous, profane, and illusory existence is followed by a new, real, lasting and efficacious existence" (*Tratado de historia de las religiones*, 358). Even though this refers to more important rituals than those of simple foretelling, it contains the same symbolism.

10 Gonçalez Holguín, *Vocabulario de la lengua general de todo el Perú llamada lengua Quichua o del Inca*.

11 "It has been said that when Viracocha Pachayachi destroyed this earth, he kept with him three men, one of whom was called Taguapácac. He did this so that they would serve him and help him raise the new people he speaks of in the creation of the Second Age, after the flood." Then, the Sun and the Moon were created. Finally, "when Viracocha ordered his servants to do some tasks, Taguapaca was disobedient," so he "ordered the other two to take him, bound hand and foot, and throw him on a

raft into the lake. . . . He was carried from the water by the runoff from that same lake" (Sarmiento de Gamboa, *Historia de los incas*, 105–6).

12 Gonçalez Holguín, *Vocabulario de la lengua general de todo el Perú llamada lengua Quichua o del Inca*, 344.

13 Wiener, *Pérou et Bolivie*, 770ff.

14 Gonçalez Holguín translates: "Huañuni, to die, the last breath, or faint" (*Vocabulario de la lengua general de todo el Perú llamada lengua Quichua o del Inca*, 179). But he adds afterward, "Huañuy, or millay. These are adjectives of adjectives that are always placed before another adjective or a noun that expresses quality, and mean that which is whole, or perfect, even within contraries." One can then form "huañuy allín, huañuy mana allín. Extremely good or extremely evil" (180). *Huañuy* understood in this last sense means a kind of limit. Can it be then that death is also given as the limit of a process? Could it be maturation?

SIX THE THEORY OF THE TURN

1 Bertonio, *Vocabulario de la lengua Aymara*, "Yannca. Adjectival noun, and adverb. Evil" (2:391).

2 Monast, *L'univers religieux des Aymaras de Bolivie*.

3 The *así* can be linked to the *that* (*que*) related to existence by García Bacca. This is opposed to the *what?* (*qué*) which asks about essence. Plotinus's *Absolute* fits the *"that"* as do theology, dialectics, and sensory reality as part of that which is. The *what?* (*qué*) on the other hand corresponds to science. García Bacca, *Introducción general a las Enéadas*. [In Spanish the non-accented *que* marks a relation or qualification, while the accented *qué* marks a question.—Trans.]

4 Bertonio, *Vocabulario de la lengua Aymara*, 2:65ff. Also see Gonçález Holguín, *Vocabulario de la lengua general de todo el Perú llamada lengua Quichua o del Inca*, 57ff. José Imbelloni provides a good summary of the meaning of the term in *Pachakuti 9*, 121ff.

5 Lira, *Diccionario Kkechuwa-Español*, 342.

6 In *Curso de filosofía indígena*, 12–13. [See chapter 3, note 1.—Trans.]

7 Paredes, *Mitos, supersticiones y supervivencias populares de Bolivia*, 129.

8 Montesinos, *Memorias antiguas historiales y políticas del Perú*.

9 Imbelloni, *El 'Génesis' de los pueblos protohistóricos de América*, 251ff.

10 Guaman Poma de Ayala. *Nueva crónica y buen gobierno* (*The First New Chronicle and Good Government*), figs. 49–78.

11 "In effect, Four Ages are counted which are intimately connected with the four cardinal points, and their chronological set fills the great vacuum of passed time; a fifth age, spatially correlated to the conception of the Center, is historical Age, actually lived by its respective people . . . in waiting for the definitive end. . . . This 'ending of Age' is always an annihilation. . . . But with the annihilation, there is a sense of punishment, which implies the admission of a guilt and the respective sanction" (Imbelloni, *Pachakuti 9*, 103).

12 Betanzos, "Suma y narración de los Incas."

13 La Barre, *The Uru-Chipaya*. The version transcribed by this author is similar to the one I gathered in Chipayas, 535.

14 Murúa, *Historia del origen y genealogía real de los Reyes Incas del Perú*. Cobo's account figures among those that mention the construction of Tiahuanaco. He writes: "Others [*sic*], that the large stones which we see here were brought by the air *to the sound of a trumpet* played by a man" (Cobo, *Historia del Nuevo Mundo*, 2:197).

15 Cobo, *Historia del Nuevo Mundo*, 2:172.

16 Jiménez Borja, "Instrumentos musicales peruanos."

17 Cobo, *Historia del Nuevo Mundo*, 2:174.

18 Sarmiento de Gamboa, *Historia de los Incas*: "There were other groups besides these ones . . . and above all one called Humanamean, who lived beside Hindicancha, in a nearby corral, and who lived between Indicancha and Cayocache" (132).

SEVEN   DIVINE TEACHING

1 Cobo, *Historia del Nuevo Mundo*, 2:155.

2 Ibid., 2:169.

3 Ibid., 2:157: "Some relate that these three figures (referring to the sun) were made because once three suns were seen in the sky. Others say of the three figures that the one was for the sun, another the day, and the third the ability to beget. There was also the opinion among them that the main statue represented the sun and the other two were its guards. Each one had a different name: the first one was called Apu-Inti, the second one Churi-Inti and the third one Inti-Gauqui." Cobo adds: "They called thunder by three names: the first and most important was chuquilla, which means the resplendence of gold; the second name was catuilla, and the third intiillapa. For each name they made a statue of the same shape as that of the sun from cloth because they said that thunder had a son and a brother" (2:160).

4 "Even when the sacrifice was aimed at any particular god, they would first speak with Viracocha, who they considered the Creator" (Cobo, *Historia del Nuevo Mundo*, 2:200).

5 The three citations are from Cobo, *Historia del Nuevo Mundo*, 2:173–80. "The seventh guaca was said to be Churuncana: it is a round mountain which is above Carmenga, where the royal path divides the Chinchero path from the Yucay path. The sacrifices to Ticciviracocha were done from this mountain" (2:173). "It was a mountain called Llulpacturo, bordering Angostura, which is deputized to offer to Ticciviracocha" (2:180). "The second guaca is called Turuca: an almost round stone placed next to the temple of the sun, in a window. It was said to be guauque of Ticciviracocha" (2:175).

6 "The first guaca (from Antisuyu) is said to be Chiquinapampa: it was an en-

closure next to the temple of the sun where sacrifice was done on behalf of the universal health of the Indians" (ibid., 2:174–75).

7 It is probable that the link between the sun and the sowing season could be in the other nine shrines. The names of these shrines, Sayba, Tuiro, and Mudca, make reference in Quechua to the idea of the signpost or landmark. These, added to the other three stone landmarks, perhaps constitute the twelve denounced by the Inca Garcilaso and which according to him were used to measure the position of the sun.

8 Rowe, *Eleven Inca Prayers from the Zithuwa Ritual*.

9 Lira translates *wáka* as "Familiar or domestic deity and small idol which represents it, penates" (*Diccionario Kkechuwa-Español*, 1076). Further on he translates *wákka* as "weeping, crying, the action of crying, tears" (1080).

10 Urteaga's observation is in the Peruvian edition of the chronicle of Cristóbal de Molina, *Relación de las fábulas y rituales de los Incas*, 1916.

11 Sarmiento de Gamboa, *Historia de los Incas*, 124.

12 Santacruz Pachacuti Yamqui, *Relación de Antigüedades deste rayno del Pirú*, 215.

13 Lira, *Diccionario Kkechuwa-Español*, 1093. Elsewhere, he adds, *kauli*: "It is said of the one who has nothing, is poor, or empty." According to this, does Guanacauri mean "empty of guilt"?

14 "Kau: hem of the blankets or blankets made of red thread" (Bertonio, *Vocabulario de la lengua Aymara*, 2:48).

15 Valda de Jaimes Freyre, *Costumbres y curiosidades de los Aymaras*, 53. Cobo says that the *Villac-umu* was "the clairvoyant and sorcerer who speaks" and who resides in the Coricancha. He was chosen in this manner: "If a male was born in the fields during a storm with thunder, they acquaint themselves with him, and later when he was old, they would ask him to become skilled in all of this. He would be called from birth the one who was born 'son of thunder' and they believed that any sacrifice made by his hand was more accepted by his guacas than anyone else's" (Cobo, *Historia del Nuevo Mundo*, 2:224). In the same vein Mircea Eliade notes that "one can become a shaman as a consequence of an accident or an event: it happens this way among the Buriatos, the Soyotes, and Eskimos when lightning hits them or they fall from a tree" (*Mitos, sueños y misterios [Myths, Dreams, and Mysteries]*, 96).

16 Cobo, *Historia del Nuevo Mundo*, 2:177–80.

17 Ibid., 179.

18 Asian thought as well as pre-industrial European thought always start from a global concept of life rather than from a theory of understanding.

19 Already in Lao-Tse one can find the link between naming and existence. What is named becomes reality, which must be a reference to its becoming part of one's consciousness. In general, this thought is proper to protohistoric cultures. In almost all the creation myths in the Américas, one finds this act of naming. Leenhardt writes with respect to this: "The word as such is an object. The object

comes from man and man supports himself on it, and without the object man is lost and the group dissolves" (*Do Kamo*, 186).

20 Farfán, *Colección de textos Quechuas del Perú Central*, 16:85–122; 17:120–50; 19–20:191–269.

21 On the use of *estar*, please see the "Translators' Introduction."—Trans.

22 Gonçalez Holguín, *Vocabulario de la lengua general de todo el Perú llamada lengua Quichua o del Inca*, 340.

23 See note 4, chapter 1.—Trans.

24 See note 8, chapter 5.—Trans.

25 Guaman Poma de Ayala, *Nueva crónica y buen Gobierno* (*The First New Chronicle and Good Government*), 54.

26 Murúa, *Historia del origen y genealogía real de los Reyes Incas del Perú*, 43. There are also references to these personages in the Jesuita Anónimo ("Relación de las costumbres antiguas de los naturales del Perú," 165*ff*).

EIGHT   INDIGENOUS LOGIC

1 Father Lira translates *chiuchi* as "chick, chicken, newborn or a bird a few weeks old" (*Diccionario Kkechuwa-Español*, 133).

2 See Kusch's description of *tios* below.—Trans.

3 According to Oblitas Poblete the Callawayas make *chiuchirecados*, "combining some figures with others" (*Cultura Callawaya*, 233).

4 According to Cobo, in each of these shrines offerings were made "often of silver and gold, and sometimes small pieces in different shapes and sizes, small and large images of men and animals made of these metals" (*Historia del Nuevo Mundo* 2:203).

5 Bandelier, *The Islands of Titicaca and Koati*, 271–72.

6 Domingo de Santo, *Lexicon o vocabulario de la lengua general del Perú*, 102.

7 Lira, *Diccionario Kkechuwa-Español*, 148.

8 Lara, *La cultura de los Incas*, 2:247.

9 Cobo, *Historia del Nuevo Mundo* 2:162.

10 Gonçalez Holguín, *Vocabulario de la lengua general de todo el Perú llamada lengua Quichua o del Inca*, 190.

11 Santacruz Pachacuti Yamqui, *Relación de Antigüedades deste rayno del Pirú*, 213.

12 Cited by François Bourricaud, "El mito de Inkarrí," 178*ff*.

13 Bertonio, *Vocabulario de la lengua Aymara*, 2:124.

14 Dick Edgar Ibarra Grasso writes of the Quechua: "*Huiñay* is 'eternity' but not an immovable eternity as we understand it, rather one in movement toward increase, growth and multiplicity from which comes the future" (*Argentina indígena y prehistoria Americana*, 473). The indigenous prayers to which I referred are in another book by Ibarra Grasso, *La escritura indígena andina* (178–90). These concepts are not far from Renou's discussion of tantric philosophy, which uses, according to him, "more or less arbitrary syllables called *bija* or germs because they contain the germ of the physical form of god" (*El Hinduísmo*, 33).

15 This information was provided by Marcelino Alconz Mendoza.

16 Ibarra Grasso correlates it with *tucuy*, in Quechua, which "means 'everything,' but in the sense of 'everything is already here,' within which there is automatically a past" (*Argentina indígena y prehistoria Americana*, 473).

17 Bandelier remarks on the religious and political importance of the Chamacanis. Bandelier, *The Islands of Titicaca and Koati*.

NINE SYMMETRY AND TRUTH

1 Santacruz Pachacuti Yamqui, *Relación de Antigüedades deste rayno del Pirú*. See my work on this topic in *América profunda*.

2 Posnansky, *Tihuanacu*.

3 Frankfort, Groenewegen-Frankfort, Wilson et al., *El pensamiento prefilosófico* (*Before Philosophy*), 82*ff*.

4 I point out a similar opposition in my book *América profunda*, when I analyze the story told by Cristóbal de Molina that refers to Imaymana Viracocha and Tocapo Viracocha. Imaymana is related to the idea of the abundance of all things, and Tocapo to austerity or scarcity. Renou characterizes Vishnu as the one who preserves the world and Siva as destructive, as associated with death, time, the one who takes away, and fright (*El Hinduísmo*, 20).

TEN SALVATION AND ECONOMY

1 Garcí Diez de San Miguel, *Visita hecha a la Provincia de Chucuito por Garcí Diez de San Miguel en el año 1567*. This volume also includes other works, including one by John Murra entitled *Una apreciación etnológica de la visita*.

2 Garcí Diez de San Miguel, *Visita hecha a la Provincia de Chuchito por Garcí Diez de San Miguel en el año 1567*, 438.

3 Ibid., 216–17.

4 Ibid., 217.

5 Guaman Poma de Ayala, *Nueva crónica y buen obierno* (*The First New Chronicle and Good Government*), 898.

6 Lara, *La cultura de los Incas*, 1:285*ff*.

7 Ibid., 1:284–85.

8 Bertonio, *Vocabulario de las lengua Aymara*, 2:29.

9 Ibid., 2:220. It is interesting that he notes above, "Mayni: One, of rational things, like man, Angel, God, etc." There is no doubt that reciprocity belonged to the indigenous rational order, because, according to Jung, what is rational is simply what is traditional.

10 Garcí Diez de San Miguel, *Visita hecha a la Provincia de Chuchito por Garcí Diez de San Miguel en el año 1567*, 430.

11 Ibid., 435.

12 Ibid., 438.

13 Weber, *Historia de la cultura*.

14 Hamilton. *El florecimiento del capitalismo y otros ensayos de historia económica*, 51ff, "La inflación monetaria en Castilla/The Monetary Inflation in Castile."

15 Morote Best, "La vivienda campesina de Sallaq con un panorama de la cultura total."

16 I have already discussed this in my book *América profunda*. The androgynous character of the divinity is a common concept, especially in Jung and Eliade.

17 "The most real actions are actions without contact and without waste of energy." There is also a principle according to which "the activities, passions, and sensations use being and diminish its substance and potency." Granet, *El pensamiento Chino*, 269ff.

18 Gonçalez Holguín, *Vocabulario de la lengua general de todo el Perú llamada lengua Quichua o del Inca*: "Cauçay, the sustenance necessary for life" (51); "Cauçay, life" (52).

19 Garcí Diez de San Miguel, *Visita hecha a la Provincia de Chuchito por Garcí Diez de San Miguel en el año 1567*, 435.

20 Ibid.: "Before 1532 the *tupu* expressed the equivalencies in a reciprocal agriculture which contemplated the minimal needs as culturally accepted of each domestic unit, understanding variable criteria of foresight with respect to agriculture and productivity" (432–33).

21 Gonçalez Holguín, *Vocabulario de la lengua general de todo el Perú llamada lengua Quichua o del Inca*, 247.

22 Condarco Morales, *Zarate, el "temible" Willka*. He writes that Zárate Willka "affirmed that he had respected 'other people's property,' but this was questioned by Francisco Catari . . . who affirmed that the Indian leader . . . ordered his people to move . . . 3,000 heads of cattle belonging to the hacienda of Pongo" (388). The accusation stated that the indigenous chief raised "the flag of extermination and destruction against the owners."

ELEVEN SALVATION AND SOLUTION

1 Ponces Sangines, "*Importancia de la cuenca paceña en el período precolombino*," 210.

2 Jung, *Tipos psicológicos* (Psychological Types), 2:212.

3 This follows from his conception of races. He classifies them in two groups, H and F, each of which has eight divisions. The eighth is a "new renaissance" of the first type, though surpassed. Ibarra Grasso, *Argentina indígena y prehistoria Americana*, 69.

4 Lévi-Strauss said in an interview that "human thought does not ever show itself absolutely, but rather, always in relation to a certain number of restrictions which are in the first place external restrictions." Levi-Strauss et al., *Problemas del estructuralismo*, 189.

5 Jung et al., *L'homme et ses symboles* (Man and His Symbols), 114.

6 He notes that in Western man there is an unconscious pre-concept, and that the

primitive lacks both differentiation and integration. Radin, *El hombre primitivo como filósofo* (*Primitive Man as Philosopher*), 88–89.

7 *Lunfardo* is the slang of the marginal classes of Buenos Aires.—Trans.

8 Imbelloni, *Pachakuti 9*, 267.

9 Guaman Poma, *Nueva crónica y buen gobierno* (*The First New Chronicle and Good Government*), 910.

10 Ibid., 2.

11 Ibid., 1157.

12 Condarco Morales, *Protohistoria Andina*, 297.

13 Jung, *Tipos psicológicos*.

TWELVE POPULAR THINKING

1 See Rosenblat, *La población indígena y el mestizaje en América*.

2 See Mignolo's introduction for a gloss on the use of *Criollo/a* in Argentina.—Trans.

3 Lewis, *Los hijos de Sánchez* (*The Children of Sánchez*).

4 Graciarena, *Poder y clases sociales en el desarrollo de América Latina*, 107ff.

5 Germani, *Política y sociedad en una época de transición*, 154ff.

6 Ibid., 312.

7 Graciarena, *Poder y clases sociales en el desarrollo de América Latina*, 146, 192.

8 Germani, *Política y sociedad en una época de transición*, 291–92.

9 In my prior work, *América profunda*, I devote a chapter to showing the close connection between Western civilization, the middle class, and the production of objects (112 –56).

10 Stern, *Psicología general desde el punto de vista personalistico* (*General Psychology from the Personalistic Standpoint*), 2:55.

THIRTEEN SEMINAL THINKING

1 Stern, *Psicología general desde el punto de vista personalístico* (*General Psychology from the Personalistic Standpoint*), 2:54.

2 Ibid.

3 See chapter 9.—Trans.

4 Jung, *Tipos psicológicos* (*Psychological Types*), 2:269.

5 Heidegger, *El ser y el tiempo* (*Being and Time*), 98ff. He says of utensils that "one conforms-oneself-to it (the utensil) *into* something." With this he takes notice of the relation of utility and purpose of the utensil and the existential conformity it offers. Then he points out that "on the basis of the no-more-than-being-before-the-eyes of this entities, their mathematical *properties* can be determined in *functional concepts*."

6 "God, no longer sought in a dissolving identification of Things, nor a dehumanizing evasion outside of Things, but a God accomplished (and thus infinitely more

inspiring and enabling of communion) through access to the center (in formation) of the total Sphere of Things" (Teilhard De Chardin, *La activación de la energía* [*Activation of Energy*], 329).

7 See "Translators' Introduction" for Kusch's use of *connotation*.—Trans.

8 Heidegger writes that life "is neither pure *being-before-the-eyes*, nor *being-there*" and he reaches this conclusion because "the ontology of life develops through the path of a selective exegesis: it determines what it must be, so what is called 'just-living' can be" (*El ser y el tiempo*, 59).

9 Heidegger, *Introducción a la metafísica* (*Introduction to Metaphysics*).

10 Read, *Imágen e Idea* (*Icon and Idea*), 137. The concept is taken from Collingwood, *Los principios del arte* (*Principles of Art*), 263.

11 I have already discussed this in *América profunda*. It is the natural conclusion one reaches after reviewing N. Hartmann's *Metafísica del conocimiento*.

FIFTEEN INFANTILE SEMINALITY

1 Kusch, *De la mala vida porteña*.

2 "What Argentina needs is the great collective quixotic act. And that task can only be accomplished by a group; it will be the function of a whole generation" (Imaz, *Los que mandan*, 238).

SIXTEEN THINKING THE "ASÍ"

1 Kusch is referring to his discussion of *uk'u* in chapter 3.—Trans.

2 Levene, *Historia de la Nación Argentina*, vol. 5, 139.

3 Mitre, *Historia de Belgrano y de la Independencia Argentina*, vol. 7, 31.

4 Levene, *Historia de la Nación Argentina*, vol. 1, 81.

5 Otero, *Historia del Libertador D. Jose de San Martin*, vol. 1, 692–93.

6 Levene, *Historia de la Nación Argentina*, vol. 6, 28.

7 Mitre, *Historia de Belgrano y de la Independencia Argentina*, vol. 1, 11.

8 Levene, *Historia de la Nación Argentina*, vol. 7, 363.

9 Ibid., vol. 6, 667.

SEVENTEEN THE CROSSROADS OF MERE *ESTAR*

1 Much of the subsequent discussion hinges on the distinction in Spanish between *ser* and *estar*. See the "Translators' Introduction."—Trans.

2 For a discussion of Kusch's use of *connotation*, please see the "Translators' Introduction."—Trans.

3 "*Estar en el ser*," or temporarily being within and disrupting the permanent state of being.—Trans.

4 Lévi-Strauss et al., *Problemas del estructuralismo*: "Savage thought thinks the very foundation of its thinking of the world: it does not change it. The Caduveo or the

Bororo are the metaphysicians of the existential development of society but they suffer from *the temptations toward Nothingness: 'they do not want to be'*" (110).

EIGHTEEN RECOVERING THE ABSOLUTE

1 Lévi-Strauss, *Anthropologie structurale* (*Structural Anthropology*), 133*ff.*
2 On savage thinking, see also Lévi-Strauss, *The Savage Mind.*—Trans.
3 In my earlier book *De la mala vida porteña*, I develop this theme.
4 See Oscar Lewis, *Children of Sánchez.*—Trans.

BIBLIOGRAPHY

We have compiled the editions that Kusch references (which include texts in Spanish, French, German, and English). In order to assist the English-language reader, we have included references to English-language editions whenever possible. Where Kusch relies on a translation of an English text, our reference is to the original English edition; in other cases, the reference is to an English translation.—Trans.

Abu-Lughod, Janet L. *Before European Hegemony: The World System A.D. 1250–1350*. New York: Oxford University Press, 1989.

Altamirano, Carlos. *Bajo el signo de las masas (1943–1973)*. Buenos Aires: Emecé, 2007.

Anzaldúa, Gloria. *Borderlands/La Frontera: The New Mestiza*. 1987. Reprint, San Francisco: Aunt Lute Books, 1999.

Arguedas, José Maria. "Estudio preliminar a himnos Quechuas católicos cuzqueños." *Folklore Americano* 3.3 (1955): 121–66.

Armstrong, Karen. *Islam: A Short History*. New York: Modern Library, 2000.

Bambach, Charles. *Heidegger's Roots: Nietzsche, National Socialism and the Greeks*. Ithaca, N.Y.: Cornell University Press, 2004.

Bandelier, Adolph Francis Alphonse. *The Islands of Titicaca and Koati*. New York: Hispanic Society of America, 1910.

Bertonio, Ludovico P. *Vocabulario de la lengua Aymara*. 1612. A facsimile of the first edition. Leipzig: B. G. Teubner, 1879.

Betanzos, Juan de. "Suma y narración de los Incas." In *Historia de los Incas y conquista del Perú*, 8:73–208. 2d ed. Lima: Sanmarti y Ca., 1924.

Bourricaud, François. "El mito de Inkarri." *Folkore Americano* (Lima) 4 (1956): 178–87.

Celine, Loius-Ferdinand. *Voyage au bout de la nuit*. Paris: Denoel et Steeke, 1932.

Celms, Teodore. *El idealismo fenomenológico de Husserl*. Madrid: Revista de Occidente, 1931.

Cobo, Bernabe. *Historia del Nuevo Mundo*. Vol. 2 of *Obras*. Madrid: Atlas, 1956.

Collingwood, R. G. *Los principios del arte*. Mexico City: Fondo de Cultura Económica, 1960.

———. *Principles of Art*. Oxford: Oxford University Press, 1958.

Condarco Morales, Ramiro. *Protohistoria Andina, Propedeutica*. Oruro: Universidad Técnica de Oruro, 1967.

———. *Zarate, el "temible" Willka: Historia de la Rebelión Indígena de 1899*. La Paz: Talleres Gráficos Bolivamos, 1965.

Crahay, Franz, and Victor A. Velen. "El 'despegue' conceptual: Condiciones de una filosofía bantú." *Revista Diógenes* 13.52 (October–December 1965): 55–78.

Domingo de Santo, Tomas. *Lexicon o vocabulario de la lengua general del Perú*. 1560. Reprint, Lima: Instituto de Historia, 1951.

Domingo Faustino Sarmiento. *Facundo: Civilación y barbarie*. 1845. *Facundo: Civilization and Barbarism*. Trans. Katherine Ross. Berkeley: University of California Press, 2004.

Drever, James. *Diccionario de psicología*. Buenos Aires: Escuela, 1967.

———. *Dictionary of Psychology*. New York: Penguin, 1956.

Du Bois, W. E. B. *The Souls of Black Folk*. 1903. Reprint, New York: Signet Classic, 1995.

Dussel, Enrique. "Europe, Modernity, and Eurocentrism." *Nepantla* 20.3 (2000): 465–78.

Eliade, Mircea. *Mitos, sueños y misterios*. Buenos Aires: Compañía General Fabril Editora, 1961.

———. *Myths, Dreams, and Mysteries: The Encounter between Contemporary Faiths and Archaic Realities*. New York: HarperCollins, 1960.

———. *Tratado de historia de las religiones*. Translated by A. Mainavenita. Madrid: Instituto de Estudios Políticos, 1954.

Fanon, Frantz. *Black Skin, White Masks*. 1952. Translated by Charles L. Markmann. Reprint, New York: Grove Press, 1967.

Farfán A., J. M. B. *Colección de textos Quechuas del Perú Central*, 16:85–122. Revista del Museo Nacional, Lima, 1947.

Frankfort, Henri, H. A. Groenewegen-Frankfort, John Albert Wilson, Thorkid Jacobsen, and William Andrew Irwin. *Before Philosophy: The Intellectual Adventure of Ancient Man: An Essay on Speculative Thought in the Ancient Near East*. New York: Penguin Books, 1949.

———. *El pensamiento prefilosofico: Egipto y Mesopotámica*. Mexico City: Fondo de Cultura Económica, 1958.

García Bacca, Juan David. *Introducción general a las Eneadas*. Buenos Aires: Losada, 1948.

Garcí Diez de San Miguel. *Visita hecha a la Provincia de Chucuito por Garcí Diez de San Miguel en el año 1567.* Lima: Casa de la Cultura del Perú, 1964.

Germani, Gino. *Política y sociedad en una época de transición.* Buenos Aires: Paidos, 1968.

Gonçalez Holguín, Diego. *Vocabulario de la lengua general de todo el Perú llamada lengua Quichua o del Inca.* Lima: Instituto de Historia de la Universidad de San Marco, 1952.

Gordon, Lewis. *Existentia Africana: Understanding Africana Existential Thought.* London: Routledge, 2000.

Graciarena, Jorge. *Poder y clases en el desarrollo de América Latina.* Buenos Aires: Paidos, 1967.

Granet, Marcel. *El pensamiento Chino.* Mexico City: Unión Tipográfica Editorial Hispano Americano, 1959.

Guaman Poma de Ayala, Felipe. *The First New Chronicle and Good Government.* Translated by David L. Frye. Indiana: Hackett Publishing, 2006.

——. *Nueva crónica y buen gobierno.* Paris: Institut d'Ethnologie, 1936.

Guerrero, Patricio. "Posicionamientos críticos giros de-coloniales." Paper presented at "Encuentro internacional: Insurgencias políticas epistémicas y giros de-coloniales." Universidad Andina Simon Bolivar, Quito, Ecuador, 17–19 July 2006.

Gurvitch, Georges. *Las tendencias actuales de la filosofía alemana: E. Husserl, M. Scheler, E. Lask, N. Hartmann, M. Heidegger.* Buenos Aires: Losada, 1944.

Halperin Dongui, Tulio. *Proyecto y construcción de una nación (1846–1880).* Buenos Aires: Emecé, 1995.

——. *La república imposible (1930–1945).* Buenos Aires: Emecé, 1997.

——. *Vida y muerte de la república verdadera (1910–1930).* Buenos Aires: Emecé, 1996.

Hamilton, Earl J. *El florecimiento del capitalismo y otros ensayos de historia económica.* Madrid: Revista de Occidente, 1948.

Hartmann, Nikolai. *Metafísica del conocimiento.* Buenos Aires: Editorial Losada, 1957.

Heidegger, Martin. *Being and Time.* Translated by John Macquarrie and Edward Robinson. New York: HarperCollins, 1962.

——. *Imperialismo y cultura.* Buenos Aires: Editorial Hachea, 1957.

——. *Introducción a la metafísica.* Buenos Aires: Nova, 1959.

——. *Introduction to Metaphysics.* Translated by Gregory Fried and Richard Polt. New Haven, Conn.: Yale University Press, 2000.

——. *Nacionalismo y liberación.* 1973. Reprint, Buenos Aires: Peña Lillo, 2004.

——. *Qué es el ser nacional?* Buenos Aires: Editorial Hachea, 1964.

——. *El ser y el tiempo.* Mexico City: Fondo de Cultura Económica, 1951.

Hernández Arregui, Juan José. *La formación de la conciencia nacional.* 1957. Reprint, Buenos Aires: Plus Ultra, 1973.

Horswell, Michael J. *Decolonizing the Sodomite: Queer Tropes of Sexuality in Colonial Andean Culture.* Texas: University of Texas Press, 2006.

Ibarra Grasso, Dick Edgar. *Argentina indígena y prehistoria Americana.* Buenos Aires: Tipográfica Editorial Argentina, 1967.

——. *La escritura indígena andina*. La Paz: Alcadía Municipal, 1953.

Imaz, José Luís de. *Los que mandan*. Buenos Aires: Eudeba, 1968.

Imbelloni, José. "El 'Génesis' de los pueblos protohistóricos de América: Segunda sección, las fuentes de México." *Boletín de la Academia de Letras* 9.34:235–311 and 9.36:33–772.

——. *El medio pelo en la sociedad argentina (Apuntes para una sociología nacional*. Buenos Aires: Plus Ultra, 1973.

——. *Pachakuti 9 (El inkario crítico)*. Buenos Aires: Nova, 1946.

——. *Los profetas del odio y la yapa: La colonización pedagógica*. 1957. Reprint, Buenos Aires: Peña Lillo, 1964.

——. "La Weltanschauung de los Amautas reconstruida." In *Actas y trabajos científicos del 27th Congreso Internacional de Americanistas*, 245–71. Lima: 1943.

Jauretche, Arturo. *El plan Prebisch: Retorno al coloniaje*. Buenos Aires: Ediciones "45," 1955.

Jesuita Anónimo. "Relación de las costumbres antiguas de los naturals del Perú." In *Tres relaciones de Antiguedades Peruanas*, 133–203. Ed. Marco Jiménez de Espada. Buenos Aires: Editorial Guarania, 1950.

Jiménez Borja, Arturo. "Instrumentos musicales peruanos." *Revista del Museo Nacional* (Lima) 19–20 (1950): 37–80.

Jung, C. G. *Flying Saucers: A Modern Myth of Things Seen in the Skies*, Princeton: Princeton University Press, 1979.

——. *Man and His Symbols*. New York: Dell, 1964.

—— *Psychological Types, or the Psychology of Individuation*. Translated by H. Godwin Baynes. New York: Pantheon Books, 1962.

——. *El Secreto de la flor de oro: Un libro de la vida Chino*. Buenos Aires: Paidos, 1955.

——. *The Secret of the Golden Flower: A Chinese Book of Life. Translated and explained by Richard Wilhelm. Foreword and commentary by C. G. Jung.* Translated by Cary F. Baynes. London: Routledge and Kegan Paul, 1979.

——. *Sobre cosas que se ven en el cielo*. Buenos Aires: Editorial Sur, 1961.

——. *Tipos psicológicos*. Buenos Aires: Sudamericana, 1965.

Jung, C. G., Jospeh L. Henderson, Aniela Jaffé, Jolande Jacobi, and Marie-Luise von Franz. *L'homme et ses symboles*. Paris: Pont Royal, 1964.

Kusch, Rodolfo. *América profunda*. 1962. Reprint, in *Obras Completas*, 2:1–254. Córdoba: Editorial Fundación Ross, 2000.

——. *Esbozo de una antropología filosófica americana*. Buenos Aires: Castañedad, 1978.

——. *De la mala vida porteña*. Buenos Aires: Peña Lillo, 1966.

——. *La negación en el pensamiento popular*. 1975.

——. *La seducción de la barbarie. Análisis herético de un continente meztiso*. Buenos Aires: Raigal, 1953.

La Barre, Weston. "The Uru-Chipaya." In *Handbook of the South American Indians*, ed. Julian H. Steward. Vol. 2, *The Andean Civilizations Bureau of American Ethnology Bulletin* 143:575–85. Washington, D.C.: Smithsonian Institution.

Laclau, Ernesto. *On Populist Reason*. London: Verso, 2005.

Lara, Jesús. *La cultura de los Incas*. La Paz: Los Amigos del Libro, 1966.

Leenhardt, Maurice. *Do kamo*. Buenos Aires: Eudeba, 1961.

———. *Do kamo: Person and Myth in the Melanesian World*. Translated by Basia Miller Gulati. Chicago: University of Chicago Press, 1979.

Levene, Ricardo. *Historia de la Nación Argentina: Desde los orígenes hasta la organización definitiva en 1862*. Buenos Aires: El Ateneo, 1939.

Lévi-Strauss, Claude. *Anthropologie structurale*. Paris: Plon, 1958.

———. *El pensamiento salvaje*. Mexico City: Fondo de Cultura Económica, 1964.

———. *The Savage Mind*. Chicago: University of Chicago Press, 1968.

———. *Structural Anthropology*. Translated by Claire Jacobson and Brooke Schoepf. New York: Basic Books, 2000.

Lévi-Strauss, Claude, Paul Ricoeur, Enzo Paci, Pierre Verstraten. *Problemas del estructuralismo*. Editorial Universitaria de Córdoba, 1967.

Lewis, Oscar. *The Children of Sánchez: Autobiography of a Mexican Family*. New York: Random House, 1961.

———. *Los hijos de Sánchez: Autobiografía de una familia Mexicana*. Mexico City: Joaquin Moritz, 1968.

Lira, Jorge A. *Diccionario Kkechuwa-Español*. Tucumán, Argentina: Universidad Nacional de Tucumán, 1944.

Lugones, María. "Heterosexualism and the Colonial/Modern Gender System." *Hypatia* 22.1 (2007): 186–209.

Makreel, Rudolf A. *Dilthy. Philosopher of the Human Studies*. Princeton: Princeton University Press, 1992.

Maldonado-Torres, Nelson. 2007. "On the Coloniality of Being: Contributions to the Development of a Concept." Special issue, *Cultural Studies* 21.2–3 (2007): 240–70.

Mesa, Teresa Gisbert de. "Commentaire to 'La colonization des langages.'" Proceedings of the international conference, *Le nouveaus monde/Monde nouveau: La experience américaine*. Ed. Serge Gruzinski and Nathan Wachtel. Paris: Ecole des hautes études en sciences sociales, 1996.

Middendorf, E. W. *Wörterbuch des Runa Simi oder der Keshua Sprache*. Leipzig: F. A. Brockhaus, 1890.

Mignolo, Walter D. *The Darker Side of the Renaissance: Literacy, Territoriality and Colonization*. Ann Arbor: University of Michigan Press, 1995.

———. "Delinking: Don Quixote, Globalization and the Colonies." In *Quixotic Offspring: The Global Legacy of Don Quixote*, 3–39. Macalester International: Macelester College, 2006.

———. "Delinking: The Rhetoric of Modernity, the Logic of Coloniality and the Grammar of De-coloniality." Special issue, *Cultural Studies* 21.2–3 (2007): 449–514.

Mitre, Bartolomé. *Historia de Belgrano y de la Independencia Argentina*. Editorial Juventud Argentina, 1945.

Molina, Cristóbal de. *Relación de la fábulas y ritos de los Incas por el párroco Cristóbal de Molina* [ca.1573]. Ed. Horacio H. Urteaga and Carlos A. Romero. Lima: San Martin and Compañia, 1916.

Monast, Jacques Emile. *L'univers religieux des Aymaras de Bolivie: Observations recueillies dans les Carangas, Jalins de Pastorale.* Ottawa: Institut de Missiologie de l'Universite d'Ottawa, 1965.

Montenegro, Carlos. *Nacionalismo y coloniaje: su expresión histórica en la prensa de Bolivia.* La Paz: H. Alcaldía Municipal, Ediciones Autonomía, 1943.

Montesinos, Fernando. *Memorias antiguas historiales y politicas del Perú.* Edited by Marcos Jimenez de la Espada. Madrid: Impreza De M. Ginesta, 1882.

Moraga, Cherríe. *The Hungry Woman: The Hungry Woman: A Mexican Medea and Heart of the Earth: A Popul Vuh Story.* New Mexico: University of New Mexico Press, 2001.

Morote Best, Efraín. "La vivienda campesina de Sallaq con un panorama de la cultura total." *Revista Tradición* 2.3 (August 1951): 7–10.

Murúa, Martin de. *Historia del origen y genealogía real de los Reyes Incas del Perú.* Madrid: Consejo Superior de Investigaciones Cientificas, Instituto Santo Toribio de Mogrovejo, 1946.

Oblitas Poblete, Enrique. *Cultura Callawaya.* La Paz: Ediciones Populares Carmarlinghi, 1963.

Olano, Guillermo. *La medicina en el idioma incaico.* Lima: Tipografía La Voce d'Italia, 1913.

Otero, J. P. *Historia del Libertador D. Jose de San Martin.* Editorial Sopena Argentina SRL, 1949.

Palermo, Zulma. "Inscripción de la crítica de género en procesos de descolonización." In *Cuerpo(s) de mujer: Representación simbólica y crítica cultural,* edited by Zulma Palermo, 237–65. Córdoba, Argentina: Ferreyra Editor (Universidad de Salta), 2006.

Paredes, Manuel Rigoberto. *La Paz y la Provincia El Cercado.* La Paz: Editorial Centenario, 1955.

———. *Mitos, supersticiones y supervivencias populares de Bolivia.* La Paz: Arno Hermanos, 1920.

Pérez, Laura Elisa. "El Desorden, Nationalism, and Chicana/o Aesthetics." In *Between Woman and Nation: Nationalisms, Transnational Feminisms, and the State,* edited by Caren Kaplan, Norma Alarcón, and Minoo Moallem, 19–46. Durham, N.C.: Duke University Press, 1999.

Ponce Sangínes, Carlos. "Importancia de la cuenca paceña en el periodo precolombino." *Revista Khana* (La Paz) 11 (1967): 207–16.

Portilla, Miguel León. *Aztec Thought and Culture: A Study of the Ancient Nahuatl Mind.* Translated from the Spanish by Jack Emory Davis. Oklahoma: University of Oklahoma Press, 1963.

———. *La filosofía Náhuatl estudiada en sus fuentes.* Mexico: Instituto Indigenista Interamericano, 1956.

Posnansky, Arthur. "Tihuanacu, la cuna del hombre Americano." In *Sociedad Geográfica de la Paz y Sociedad Arqueológica de Bolivia*, 28. La Paz: Ministerio de Educación 1943.

———. *Tihuanacu: The Cradle of American Man*. New York: J. J. Augustin, 1945.

Quijano, Aníbal. "Coloniality and Modernity/Rationality." 1990. Translated by Sonia Therborn. Reprint, special issue, *Cultural Studies* 21.2–3 (2007): 168–78.

Quobna Ottobah Cugoano. *Thoughts and Sentiments on the Evil of Slavery and Commerce of the Human Species*. 1787. Ed. Vincent Carreta. New York: Penguin, 1999.

Radin, Paul. *El hombre primitivo como filósofo*. Buenos Aires: Eudeba, 1960.

Ramos, Jorge Abelardo. *El Marxismo de Indias*. Barcelona: Editorial Planeta, 1973.

———. *Revolución y contrarevolución en Argentina. La era del bonapartismo: 1943–1972*. Buenos Aires: Ediciones del Mar Dulce, 1972.

Read, Herbert. *Icon and Idea: The Function of Art in the Development of Human Consciousness*. New York: Schocken Books,1965.

———. *Imágen e idea*. Mexico City: Fondo de Cultura Económica, 1960.

Renou, Luis. *El Hinduísmo: Los textos, las doctrinas, la historia*. Buenos Aires: Eudeba, 1962.

Rosenblat, Angel. *La poblacíon indígena y el mestizaje en América*. Vol. 2. Buenos Aires: 1954.

Ross, Ellen. *Rudimentos de gramática Aymara*. La Paz: Canadian Baptist Mission, 1963.

Rowe, John Howland. *Eleven Inca Prayers from the Zithuwa Ritual*. Reprinted from the Kroeber Anthropological Society Papers, nos. 8–9, 82–99. Berkley, 1953.

Santacruz Pachacuti Yamqui, Joan. *Relación de Antigüedades deste reyno del Perú*. In *Tres relaciones de Antigüedades Peruanas de Marco Jiménez de Espada*, 207–81. Buenos Aires: Editorial Guarania, 1950.

Sarlo, Beatriz. *La batalla de las ideas (1943–1973)*. Buenos Aires: Emecé, 2007.

Sarmiento de Gamboa, Pedro. *Historia de los Incas*. Buenos Aires: Emecé, 1947.

Sartre, Jean-Paul. *The Emotions: Outline of a Theory*. New York: Citadel Press, 1993.

———. *Esquisse d'une théorie des émotions*. Paris: Hermann, 1948.

Sayres, William C. "Status Transition and Magical Fright." *América Indígena* 15.4 (October 1955): 292–300.

Scheler, Max. *El saber y la cultura*. Madrid: Di J. Gomez, 1926, 1934.

———. "Sociología del saber." Trans. Jos *Revista del Occidente* (1949).

Scheler, Max, and Hilario Rodriguez Sanz. *Ética: Nuevo ensayo de fundamentacion de un personalismo ético*. Buenos Aires: Revista de Occidente Argentina, 1948.

Schwartzmann, Felix. *El sentimiento de lo humano en América: Ensayo de antropología filosófica*. Vol. 2. Santiago de Chile: Universidad de Chile, 1952–53.

Silverblatt, Irene M. *Moon, Sun, and Witches: Gender Ideologies and Class in Inca and Colonial Peru*. Princeton, N.J.: Princeton University Press, 1987.

Stern, William. *General Psychology from the Personalistic Standpoint*. Translated by Howard Davis Spoerl. New York: Macmillan, 1938.

———. *Psicología general desde el punto de vista personalístico*. Buenos Aires: Paidos, 1951.

Teilhard de Chardin, Pierre. *La activación de la energía*. Madrid: Taurus, 1965.

———. *Activation of Energy: Enlightening Reflections on Spiritual Energy*. Fort Washington, Pa.: Harvest Books, 2002.

Tschopik, Harry. *The Aymara of Chucuito, Peru*. Vol. 44 of *Anthropological Papers of the American Museum of Natural History*. New York: American Musuem of Natural History, 1951.

Valda de Jaimes Freyre, Maria Luisa. *Costumbres y curiosidades de los Aymaras*. La Paz: Express Editors "Universo," 1964.

Weber, Alfred. *Historia de la cultura*. Mexico City: Fondo de Cultura Económica, 1960.

Whorf, Benjamin L. "The Relation of Habitual Thought and Behavior to Language." In *Language, Culture and Personality: Essays in Memory of Edward Sapir*. Menasha, Wisc.: Sapir Memorial Publication Fund, 1941.

Wiener, Carlos. *Perou et Bolivie: Recit de voyage suivie d'études archéologiques et ethnographiques et de notes sur l'écriture el les langues de populations indiennes*. Paris: Librairie Hachette, 1880.

Wolff, Werner. *Introducción a la psicología*. Mexico City: Fondo de Cultura Económica, 1962.

Wynter, Sylvia. "Towards the Sociogenic Principle: Fanon, the Puzzle of Conscious Experience, of 'Identity' and What It's Like to Be Black." In *National Identity and Socio-Political Change: Latin America Between Marginalisation and Integration*, edited by Mercedes Duran-Cogan and Antonio Gomez-Moriana. New York: Garland, 2000.

Zavaleta Mercado, René. *Bolivia: El desarrollo de la conosciencia nacional*. Cochabamaba and La Paz: Editorial Amigos del Libro, 1990.

———. *El poder dual: Problemas de la teoría del estado en América Latina—*2 ed corr. y aum. Mexico City: Siglo 21, 1977.

———. *La revolución Boliviana y la cuestión del poder*. La Paz: Dirección Nacional de Informaciones, 1964.

GUNTER RODOLFO KUSCH (1922–1979) was born and died in Buenos Aires. He studied philosophy at the Universidad de Buenos Aires and taught for many years at the Universidad de Salta, until 1976. After being forced to leave his teaching post during the military dictatorship, he lived in Maimará, Jujuy. He is the author of *La seducción de la barbarie* (1953), *América profunda* (1962), *Geocultura del Hombre Americano* (1976), *Esbozo de una antropología filosófica Americana* (1978), *Pensamiento indígena y pensamiento popular en América* (1976), *De la mala vida porteña* (1966), *La negación en el pensamiento popular* (1975), and *Esbozo de una antropología filosófica Americana* (1979).

MARÍA LUGONES is a philosopher and popular educator. She teaches at the Escuela Popular Norteña and at Binghamton University, where she directs the Center for Interdisciplinary Research in Philosophy, Interpretation, and Culture. She is the author of *Pilgrimages/Peregrinajes: Theorizing Coalition Again Multiple Oppressions* (2003) and is currently working on *Decolonial Feminisms*, an elaboration of her essay "Heterosexualism and the Modern, Colonial Gender System" (2003).

WALTER D. MIGNOLO is the William H. Wannamaker Professor of Romance Studies and Literature and Director of the Center for Global Studies and the Humanities at Duke University. He has authored *The Darker Side of the Renaissance: Literacy, Territoriality, and Colonization* (1995), which won the MLA's Catherine Singers Kovacs Prize in 1996; *Local Histories/Global Designs: Coloniality, Subaltern Knowledges, and Border Thinking* (2000), later translated into Spanish and Portuguese;

The Idea of Latin America (2005), which received the Frantz Fanon Award from the Philosophical Caribbean Association in 2006. He has a forthcoming book with Duke University Press, *I Am Where I Do: Decolonial Thoughts for a World to Come*.

JOSHUA M. PRICE directs the Program in Philosophy, Interpretation, and Culture at Binghamton University. He writes on translation, social-science knowledge, and domination.

Library of Congress Cataloging-in-Publication Data

Kusch, Rodolfo.
[Pensamiento indígena y popular en América. English]
Indigenous and popular thinking in América / Rodolfo Kusch ; introduction by Walter D. Mignolo ; translated by María Lugones and Joshua M. Price.
p. cm.—(Latin America otherwise)
Includes bibliographical references and index.
ISBN 978-0-8223-4629-6 (cloth : alk. paper)
ISBN 978-0-8223-4641-8 (pbk. : alk. paper)
1. Indian philosophy—South America.
2. Indians of South America—Religion.
3. Indian mythology—South America.
4. Philosophical anthropology.
I. Mignolo, Walter. II. Lugones, Maria, 1944–
III. Price, Joshua M. IV. Title. V. Series: Latin America otherwise.
F2230.1.P53K8713 2010
299.8—dc22
2009037307